MW00576970

THE QUIET ONE

General Roscoe Robinson, Jr.

A Biography

Leon L. Haley

Published in the United States of America

www.Fortis-Publishing.com

The Quiet One | General Roscoe Robinson, Jr.

By Leon L. Haley

ISBN 978-0-9777884-7-7 (hardcover edition)
Library of Congress Control Number: 2010926935

Published by Adducent, Inc. – Fortis Publishing
Jacksonville, Florida—Herndon, Virginia
www.Fortis-Publishing.com

Manufactured in the United States of America

CONTENTS

FOREWORD

Since the early days of the American Republic, African Americans have been active participants in the military history of the nation. However, until the late 1940s, their experiences in the military, for the most part, occurred during the period of racial segregation, which often resulted in their being assigned to non-combat duties. Nevertheless, in spite of their status, they continued to exhibit loyalty to their country and have served honorably.

Students of American history are familiar with great military leaders whose heroic deeds during the military conflicts of the 19th and 20th centuries have become a part of our historical legacy. Much has been written about them as highly visible symbols of courage and leadership. Yet some have not received the same visibility in terms of public recognition and are unknown among the public. When I became aware of the life and career of General Roscoe Robinson, Jr., the first United States Army African American four-star general, I was surprised how few people even among my generation of African Americans had heard of him. Even in one of the most comprehensive history books about African Americans – *From Slavery to Freedom*, written by the well-known scholar, John Hope Franklin, Roscoe Robinson is not mentioned.

In authoring this biography, the writer has sought to fill this gap in our knowledge of a remarkable man who from humble beginnings rose to the pinnacle of military success through perseverance, discipline, and commitment to duty and country. To this end, perhaps the most important insights into Robinson's life and military career were extracted from two primary sources - his personal papers at the Library of Congress compiled and catalogued by Cyril Jones of Washington, D.C, and his Oral History written by Lieutenant Colonel Duane E.

Hardesty, USA, (Ret'd), in 1988, as part of the Senior Officer Oral History Program at the United States Army War College. This history was compiled based on interviews with Robinson, and, therefore his own words add a measure of authenticity to this biography.

Whenever I write something of a historical nature pertaining to the life and times of African Americans, I am always reminded of the admonition of one of America's most distinguished men of color – William E. B. Du Bois. It was he who - in a presentation in 1898 before the American Academy of Political and Social Science - advanced the notion that understanding black life in America required a systematic assessment of the influence of broad historical, cultural, social, economic, and political forces that shaped the times. There is no way of denying the subject of race in the military. It was an inescapable phenomenon that riveted American social, cultural, and political systems before and during Robinson's time in the military. I have tried to convey that circumstance as accurately as possible. Indeed, in many respects, from his early childhood through his retirement years, Robinson lived through one of the most historic periods in race relations in this country – both within and outside the military.

Today, men and women of all races make immense sacrifices to serve their country, defend our liberties, and protect our interests around the world; often without the gratitude and recognition, they deserve. It is my firm hope that this book will not only serve as an inspiration to all who read it, especially to the current generation of young African Americans about whom General Robinson cared deeply, like my children and grandchildren, but that it will enable the readers to develop a greater appreciation for those who serve in the military.

General Roscoe Robinson, Jr.

ACKNOWLEDGMENTS

I am indebted to several individuals who helped to both inspire this book and to several individuals and organizations that provided me with information about Roscoe Robinson. I first became interested in General Robinson through talks with John Keeler, Dean of the Graduate School of Public and International Affairs at the University of Pittsburgh, who first brought to my attention his life and career. I owe him a debt of gratitude. My colleague, Harvey White, was especially supportive and helpful during the writing of this book.

I want to express my appreciation to my good friend, Eric Springer, who collaborated with me in writing a short monograph on Robinson, which helped to inspire this book.

I want to acknowledge and am thankful for the time given by General Robinson's widow during the several interviews I had with her and for granting me permission to access to his papers at the Library of Congress, without which this book could not have been written. With her enthusiastic support and encouragement, the book became a labor of love.

To his sister Janet, I acknowledge, with appreciation the information shared about his early life in St. Louis. The same is true for his daughter and son, Carol and Bruce, who shared many of their experiences with their father during their childhood and early adult years.

I want to express my appreciation to the U.S. Military Academy at West Point, whose archives helped us to chronicle his military career. I acknowledge also, with appreciation, the information received from the men who knew Robinson and or served with him. These include Julius Becton, who enthusiastically responded to my offer to him to write the introduction to this book, and Edward Atkeson, William Matney, Joseph Clemons, James G. Boatner, Seldon B.

Graham, Jr., John Leffler, Richard Wells, Charles Walker, Arthur Brown, Jr. and John Vessey, Jr.

With special gratitude, I want to acknowledge the warm and insightful comments about Robinson that Frederick Black provided. A neighbor of mine, Joseph Thomas, is a native of St. Louis. I appreciate his help with understanding the racial dynamics of that city during the early years.

To Frank Hamilton who was a classmate of Robinson, I am indebted not only for providing names of some individuals who were his company mates, for information on Robinson's West Point years, and for his careful editing of the manuscript. I extend the same gratitude to Yuliana Kim-Grant who also reviewed the first draft and provided some useful suggestions.

Finally, but importantly, I am indebted to my wife, Ann and my son, Loren, who also reviewed and edited various drafts of the manuscript. My two other children, Leon, Jr. and Lisa were also always encouraging and supportive during the writing period. My wife deserves special "thanks" for her patience and support throughout the writing period, especially when I was away from home conducting research at the Library of Congress and while I spent hours away from her companionship during the writing of this book.

The author always assumes responsibility for the accuracy of his work. In this respect, I have tried to report and record events as accurately as possible. Therefore, I assume for responsibility for any errors or omissions in the book.

Leon L. Haley
Pittsburgh, Pennsylvania

INTRODUCTION

Although African Americans participated in every war that the United States fought from the Revolutionary War to the present, Roscoe Robinson, Jr. was born at a time when there were very few role models to follow in the business of soldiering, particularly as officers. From *Crispus Attucks,* a patriot of the pre-Revolutionary War era, to the Buffalo Soldiers of the six regiments of Cavalry and Infantry during the Indian Wars, to the "Harlem Hellfighters" of the 93rd Division who fought under the French Flag in World War I because the American Expeditionary Force commander did not trust that many armed Black Soldiers, to Colonel Charles Young, USMA class of 1889, who rode horseback 500 miles from Wilberforce, Ohio to Washington to petition the Secretary of War as to his fitness to command a combat unit in Europe. Finally to the Tuskegee Airmen and the award winning (Presidential Unit Citation) tankers of 761st Tank Battalion. None of which reached the heights Roscoe Robinson, Jr. achieved.

Roscoe Robinson Jr., soldier, scholar, diplomat as well as a courageous decision maker was truly a role model for any youngster to use as standard. The author has (most appropriately, I believe) entitled this biography as THE QUIET ONE because this is the perfect description of General Roscoe Robinson, Jr., who I considered a peer and friend. I first met Roscoe and Millie (his wife) in 1964 when we were both assigned to personnel activities in Washington, D.C. in the Department of the Army - Roscoe to Office of Personnel Operations, Officer Personnel Directorate, and I to Office of Deputy Chief Staff for Personnel

THE QUIET ONE provides an excellent detailed historical accounting of the post WWII era and how the Army dealt with segregation before and after President Harry Truman's Executive Order 9981 in July 1948, establishing the President's Committee on Equality of Treatment and Opportunity in the Armed Services.

While General Robinson may have had very few role models of color, he was quite fortunate having West Point classmates, senior officers like Gen George Blanchard, Gen Fritz Kroesen, and others, and a very supportive spouse – Millie, and family to always come through during those difficult times with the right course of action,

His performance of duty was always *mission oriented,* thereby letting his professionalism demonstrate his support of the societal mood of the country, in other words it wasn't necessary for him to demonstrate in the streets his support of the civil rights movement. Additionally, he was willing to take on those tough issues, e.g., on one extreme was the subject of women in the military and more specifically in his division, and on the other end was the issue of headgear (Robinson's 82d Airborne Division wore maroon berets and my 1st Cavalry Division wore black berets) - the only two divisions in the 70s wearing berets; and of course today the entire Army wears the *black beret.*

Assignment patterns of staff, schooling both military and graduate school, and commanding were almost right out of the career development manual and he performed them so well that it was almost impossible to overlook his clear demonstrated potential for more demanding and challenging assignments- all the way to the top, General i.e., that is four stars. Along the way, he collected a long list of supporters, loyalist and friends at all levels, from his early tour in Liberia, not too unlike Colonel Charles Young some 50 years earlier, to Okinawa, Japan, and Belgium in the 70s and 80s, where he represented our government at the highest level. Even in post-army retirement after a few setbacks and rejections, he was able to break the glass ceiling precluding Black Americans from corporate boards.

Throughout General Robinson's years as a senior officer, he was never the "black" general, but the general who happened to be black. While keenly sensitive to the myths of pre-World War I and even to the start of the Korean War that blacks were incapable of command, he was content to let his performance challenge such irresponsible comments. At every level, he enjoyed the confidence of his superiors, to include even in post-army retirement being requested by the Secretary of the Army to make an evaluation about the performance in the Korean War of one of the oldest black regiments. To quote the author, "Thus for Robinson, resolving and putting to rest the legacy of racism in the U. S. Military was long overdue."

General Roscoe Robinson, Jr. was the right man to be the first African American to wear the four stars of an Army general officer. This view is shared by his USMA classmates, who have made a Herculean effort to convince the U.S. Postal Service to create a stamp honoring that fact, by General Jack Vessey, Chairman, Joint Chief of Staff and his last uniformed boss, and General Jack Merritt, his replacement in NATO, who lauds with high praise the final posting of Roscoe and Millie Robinson.

THE QUIET ONE is a story that every young American would enjoy and from which learn about the life of a true patriot.

***J W Becton Jr.**

*Authors Note: Lieutenant General, U.S. Army, (Retired)

CHAPTER ONE

EARLY ST. LOUIS AND THE FORMATIVE YEARS

I

Over the course of human history, cities have played a significant role in shaping the lives of those who live in them. It was not surprising that - like many others of his and antecedent African American generations - Roscoe Robinson's experiences during his formative years were the product of the cumulative historical events that occurred in the city and state of his birth - St. Louis, Missouri, as well as the roles certain individuals played in influencing that city's social, economic, and political environment.

In the 1920s, St. Louis was emerging as one of the leading commercial and industrial cities of mid-America with a growing population, which placed it as the nation's sixth largest. It would take on many of the same characteristics of other growing metropolitan cities. Working class neighborhoods were developed around factories, and, as was the practice at the time, the neighborhoods were segregated by race and ethnicity of the early urban arrivals – the Irish, German, Polish, Italian, and African Americans. While the former four groups of arrivals were mainly foreign born, the African Americans (or Negroes as they were then called) were primarily migrants from the American southern countryside who came to northern or Midwestern cities in pursuit of a new vision of social and economic opportunity.

As was the case of all cities faced with large population growth in the early decades of the 20th century, the arrival of the newcomers to St. Louis accelerated the demand for housing. To meet that demand, both the ethnic immigrants and the Negro migrants gravitated to cheap apartment or tenements housing in city neighborhoods. The neighborhoods inhabited by African Americans – frequently characterized by dilapidated and overcrowded buildings - were concentrated to the west and north of downtown St. Louis. As a growing metropolis, the city's cultural influence had also grown, with the hosting of the International World's Fair in 1904 and the Summer Olympics during that year, marking the first Olympics games held in the United States. Aviation history would be associated with the city in 1927 when Charles Lindbergh piloted non-stop a single engine plane *The Spirit of St. Louis* – named after his St. Louis financial backers - from New York to Paris.

It was also a city influenced by the dawning in the 1920s of the Harlem Renaissance – a period that unleashed one of the most profound cultural revolutions in the black experience in America. Also called the "Negro Movement," it would produce a generation of gifted writers such as Zora Neil Hurston, James Weldon Johnson, Langston Hughes, and Alain Locke. Though centered in New York, the impact of the Harlem Renaissance would reverberate in black communities across the United States, and St. Louis would become one of the cities where it would take roots. While expressions of artistic, dramatic, and poetic talents of black Americans would emerge across the cultural spectrum, the Renaissance would create a greater social consciousness among African Americans. It became a channel in which to vent African American resistance to segregated conditions and discrimination in employment, public accommodations, and housing. All of these conditions were embedded in the established social and political order of St. Louis before and during the first decades of the 20th century and beyond.

Once called the "Gateway to the West," it was in St. Louis years before the Civil War where slaves were sold on the steps of the Court House, and by 1850, the city would become one of the leading slave auctioning centers - serving slave traders and buyers from the lower Mississippi River delta region. While not a part of the plantation and agrarian economy which characterized the southern tier of the United States in the 18th century, slavery was permitted in the state as a result of the Missouri Compromise of 1820 under which the U.S. Congress allowed Missouri – the first state west of the Mississippi River – to be admitted as a slave state in exchange for the prohibition of slavery in the remaining territory acquired under the Louisiana Purchase. However, when the Civil War began, St. Louis was where almost half of Missouri's free black population lived, estimated at approximately 1,400.

It was from this group of free blacks that emerged what was called "the Colored Aristocracy;" a term based on the title of a book written in 1858 by Cyprian Clamorgan to describe free people of color in St. Louis who had considerable wealth - either inherited or earned - which they controlled in the form of real and personal property. It was this aristocracy that would shape much of the vibrant black culture, which emerged in that city.

One of the best known of that early "aristocracy" was John Berry Meachum, a former slave, who in 1815 as a freedman came to St. Louis. He became an ordained Baptist preacher and founded the First African Baptist Church, which is regarded as the first black Protestant congregation west of the Mississippi River. He was also an entrepreneur who owned a barrel factory where he employed slaves he purchased from their white owners until they earned enough money to purchase their own freedom. While owning slaves would have disqualified Meachum for membership in the "colored aristocracy" as defined by Clamorgan, his wealth did not.

Among Meachum's distinguishing and relevant characteristics was his passion for the education of African American children – free and slave – which he regarded as the key to their success. His educational ideology embraced the ideas of both economic and educational empowerment, which led him to encourage the establishment of manual labor schools for young black children through which they could acquire marketable skills. Meachum built a steamboat, known as the "Floating Freedom School," and anchored it in the Mississippi River to begin teaching young black children in a disciplined school-like setting. For those who admired Meachum and respected his willingness to challenge the social norms of that time, he would leave a legacy and a vision for the education of black children that would become an undisputable part of the history of St. Louis.

In 1857, a few years after Meachum's death, another African American - then living in St. Louis – cemented the City's place in U.S. Constitutional history because of one of the most controversial slavery issues of that time. For it was here in the Old Courthouse where Dred Scott, a domestic slave in St. Louis, would unsuccessfully sue for his freedom on the grounds of having lived for five years with his owner, John Emerson, in the free state of Illinois and the Wisconsin Territory. When Dred Scott's petition was appealed to the United States Supreme Court, it was rejected under the equal protection clause of the Constitution, with the Court's majority taking the position "That the Negro – whether emancipated or not – was not a citizen and had no rights and privileges but such as those who held the power and the government choose to grant them." The bitterness surrounding the Dred Scott decision only deepened the pro-slavery- anti-slavery fracture that had been developing and threatening the future of the Union. That bitterness was also felt in Missouri.

Although slavery in Missouri ended on January 11, 1865, by the action of a state convention convened for this purpose, the institution of slavery "died hard" and the slave code mentality lived on for many years after the Civil War. Over 8,000 black Missourians fought and died for the Union during the Civil War, yet there was little change after the War, and efforts to advance recognition of freedmen's constitutional rights were resisted. From the end of the Reconstruction Period through the 1930s, racial segregation in Missouri remained the norm in education, housing, as well as in other areas. While Missouri state laws did not specifically mandate racial segregation (though in the late 1890s there were failed attempts to do so) because it was a matter of "custom," integrated facilities such as hotels, restaurants, theaters, and hospitals did not exist. In St. Louis, surrounded by seas of ethnic and racial hostility, blacks were thrust together in overcrowded neighborhoods, where appalling and unsanitary health conditions prevailed, and vice and crime were all too common.

Despite residential segregation, vibrant black communities emerged in St. Louis. This was most evident in *The Ville*, a neighborhood in North St. Louis where young Robinson would spend his early childhood and where his personality would be shaped. He was the product of an urban experience, which one of America's early and well-known social philosophers saw "as an integral component in the development of human culture and human personality." Originally settled by German and Irish immigrants along with a small community of African Americans, *The Ville* would, by 1920, be transformed from being 8 percent African American to 86 percent African American. In time, it would become the economic, social, and cultural center for the early twentieth-century black residents of St. Louis and the pre-eminent middle-class neighborhood where many of the black professionals – lawyers, physicians, entrepreneurs, social workers and teachers – resided and made their living.

With support and encouragement from the Negro Business League, which was founded in 1900 by Booker T. Washington, the great black educator, to promote the commercial and financial development of the Negro, *The Ville* would also become the home for some of the most successful black-owned businesses, which by 1930 numbered over 300. Among the most successful enterprises was the Poro College of Beauty Culture, which was housed in a million dollar building built by Annie Pope Malone – a millionaire who had built a fortune on beauty products.

Nowhere were the strength, vitality, and persistence of the black community and its leaders more evident than when, after years of struggle against white resistance, the famed Homer G. Phillips Hospital was finally built in *The Ville* to serve blacks not allowed at the segregated City Hospital. Opened in February 1937 and named after a local attorney who had fought courageously to gain a modern facility for blacks, the hospital was staffed by blacks and served as a training facility for black doctors from around the country unable to complete their residency or gain staff privileges at white hospitals. Homer G. Phillips would become one of the nation's finest African American hospitals and source of pride to black St. Louisans.

This pride would be matched by the political astuteness of blacks in St. Louis who, under the leadership of the Citizens Liberty League, were successful in helping to win the election of Walthall Moore in 1920 to the Missouri General Assembly, the first black person to serve in the Missouri State Legislature.

II

It was in this paradoxical, hopeful, and yet racially charged social, political and culturally segregated environment in north St. Louis that Roscoe Robinson, Jr. - in some respects a "child of the Renaissance" - would spend his childhood and formative years. It was here on October 11, 1928 at 4:30 in the afternoon, in the segregated maternity ward of Barnes Hospital, that Roscoe Robinson, Jr., was born to Lillie Robinson, a homemaker, and Roscoe Robinson, Sr., a steel mill laborer who was born on March 7, 1895 in Tennessee, and who, as part of the great migration from the rural South that occurred in the early 1900s, moved to St. Louis in search of employment in the growing industrial sector.

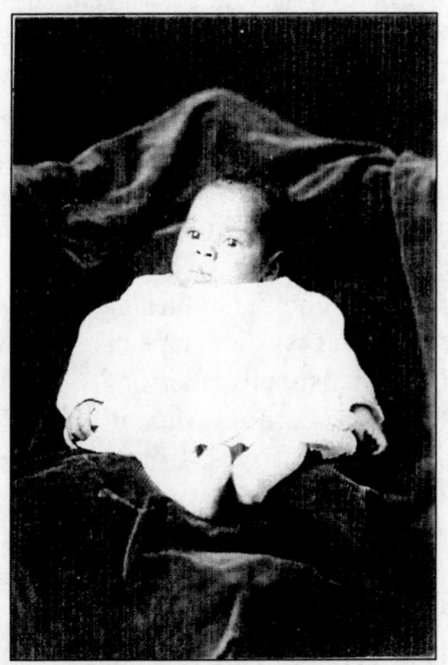

Roscoe at 2-months old

Roscoe's father had served in World War I from the beginning of the conflict. He was among those between the ages 21 and 32 who were required to register under the Selective Service Act of 1917, and who had little hope of avoiding being conscripted – short of any mental and physical handicap. It is most likely that his assignment followed the existing pattern, which was typical of most Missouri African Americans, and if so, he was probably assigned to either the 92nd or the 93rd infantry division. Both of these were segregated units as racial separation was the official policy of the U.S. War Department then and even after the end of World War I.

The senior Robinson's military records indicate that he served overseas from June 19, 1918 to February 24, 1919. Since most U.S. troops deployed overseas were sent to France, it is there, most likely, that Robinson, Sr. served. He was assigned to an Ambulance Company where the work was heavily involved with transporting the sick, and with the gruesome task of carrying out burial details. Except for the few who were involved in combat operations against the Germans, most enlisted "colored" soldiers (as they were then called) in the infantry carried out service work as unloading ship cargo, working as bakers, drivers or laborers; it was not that these specialties were their choice; rather it was what they were considered "fit" to do. It was a perspective that viewed colored people as "servile and distinctly inferior."

Lillie Robinson, born on March 30, 1897, was a native of Missouri, as were her parents. In the early years of the 20th century, African American women, unless they were professionally trained or were willing to take a job as a domestic, had few employment options. So they, like Lillie, often stayed at home to care for their children. When Roscoe was born, the Robinsons were living on Finney Avenue, but in the following year, they found it necessary to move in with Mrs.

Robinson's parents, Henry and Ida Crews. Multiple families – sometimes biologically related and sometimes not – living together in the same house where household expenses could be shared was common at that time in newly industrializing cities like St. Louis. While this form of living arrangement was clearly dictated by low wages and unemployment, it was often the only means of survival during periods of hardship.

At the time of Roscoe's birth, the Robinsons had one other child, a fourteen-year old daughter named Dorothy. But a year after Roscoe was born, a second sibling, a sister named Janet, was born in 1929. Close in age, they forged a tight sibling bond that would characterize their growing-up years together.

Young Roscoe had a normal childhood. Other than the usual childhood illnesses, he was healthy. In many respects, having the presence of both a mother and a father in the household, supported by a close extended family, provided him with a measure of stability and parental direction that would be instrumental in his development. Early on, his parents – in the spirit of Meachum - put a high premium on education. To them, it was a means for acquiring the knowledge and skills their children needed to succeed in life. So when young Robinson and his sister Janet were of school age, they would always walk several blocks to school together, further strengthening the bond between them. Like most children, after school – once any homework was finished, they would join their friends to play games on neighborhood streets, but never too far away from home to escape the always-protective eyes of their parents.

Roscoe and his sister Janet

Roscoe would also receive early exposure to the Black Church, which has played a significant role in the life of African Americans. Even during slavery, proselytizing among Negroes was carried out and many were brought into the Christian faith largely through the work of the Methodists and Baptists who, during the Great Awakening of the mid 19th century, conducted revivals in the South. Large masses of the Negro population were attracted to the fiery preaching style of the Methodists and Baptists and joined these churches, even though they were relegated to the balconies where they were physically segregated from the other worshippers. When confronted with the reality that their common faith did not bring with it equality, they formed their own churches where they could be "shielded from the contempt and discrimination of the white world and find the opportunity for self-expression and status."

The urban migration of African Americans weakened the social cohesion that had characterized their communities in the South, most noticeably the absence of the church. That physical absence would be short lived, as the centrality of church in the life of African American communities like *The Ville* would be reestablished with the formation of new houses of worship. For those who faithfully worshipped in them, these sacred sites and the prophetic words spoken in them would serve as an anchor to hold on to during the midst of life's inevitable struggles, disappointments, heartaches and pain. It was their "rock in a weary land."

It was not unexpected that on Sunday mornings, Mrs. Robinson, a woman of deep religious faith - as part of her determination to instill the same religious values in her children - could be seen walking Roscoe and Janet to the Good Samaritan Methodist Church (later renamed the Samaritan United Methodist Church) which they regularly attended. The routine of taking Roscoe and Janet to church was not simply done to "give them something to do," it was done, on the part of their mother, as a matter of responsibility for nurturing her children in matters of faith so that they might grow into mature, caring, and spiritually empowered adults.

The church of Robinson's childhood years had an interesting history. Originally, the nucleus of the congregation of Samaritan were residents of East St. Louis, a separate municipal entity, yet still a part of greater St. Louis. But in pursuit of new economic justice and educational opportunities and to escape the violence brought on by the East St. Louis race riot in 1917, the church moved across the river to St. Louis. It was at this church, located on West Belle Place, where, under the watchful eyes of the elders, Roscoe and Janet would join with other children in learning bible stories taught by their Sunday School teachers. Afterwards, they would join their mother in the same pew – as was the custom - for the main service, the central feature of which was the preacher's sermon, which was usually full of biblical imagery and practical application.

To lift the spirits of the congregation, there was always music, particularly the singing of Negro spirituals that had been passed down from earlier generations. The regularity of religious worship became the norm for Robinson and his sister, and it was through this weekly exposure that the basic tenets of the Christian faith would be learned and practiced throughout the course of their lives. Robinson's mother's dedication and faithful membership in that same church would last throughout her lifetime.

By the time Roscoe was in his early teen years, family circumstances, however, began to change. His father became ill and was unable to continue working at the Southern Car Wheel Foundry where he had been employed for many years. Soon after that period of unemployment, he was offered a job managing an apartment on St. Ferdinand Avenue in *The Ville* and the Robinson family moved into one of the modest apartments in the building.

Within a few years after moving to *The Ville,* the worst depression in U.S. history would make life especially difficult for the Robinson family. As in many other cities, a general deterioration of economic conditions - accompanied by large-scale unemployment - characterized St. Louis. Though economic hardships, irrespective of race, reverberated throughout the city, the impact of the depression was more severe for African Americans. By 1930, an estimated 43 percent of the city's black population was unemployed, with over half of the families becoming incapable of self-support and were forced to rely on public welfare. This situation, notwithstanding, the black community in St. Louis did not stand idle; rather, it took action by starting the *Jobs-for-Negroes Movement*, which was prompted by the refusal of a white chain store to hire blacks, even though their clientele was heavily black. From St. Louis, the movement would spread to other large cities throughout the country.

Even in the midst of the hard times that the city's black families were experiencing, a distinctive African American culture continued to thrive in St. Louis, typified by the strong traditions of jazz music on the one hand, and baseball on the other. The latter had developed around the black community's Negro National League team known as the St. Louis Stars. It was, at the time, a popular professional sport for talented and gifted black men. And since participation in the other national leagues was off-limits to men of color, the Negro National League provided the outlet for their talents. On the St. Louis Stars, one of the greatest players of the twentieth century – James "Cool Papa" Bell – would play.

It was also in St. Louis where Scott Joplin, one of America's most famous "ragtime" musicians, composed some of his best-known works, including *The Entertainer*, and where Josephine Baker, who would later become a world-renowned singer and dancer, would get her start performing on street corners of the city's slums. The achievements of these celebrated people of color would become a part of Robinson's growing up experiences in St. Louis.

When Robinson was of age to attend school, the patterns of racial segregation, long since institutionalized due to the Missouri Constitution of 1875, required Roscoe to attend racially separate educational facilities. This practice continued during Robinson's elementary and secondary school years. When the Robinson family lived on Cook Avenue, Roscoe attended West Bell Elementary School, but when the family moved to *The Ville*, he transferred to Simmons School. Previously called Elleardsville Colored School No. 8, it was the neighborhood's first black institution when it opened in 1873. Roscoe's exceptional academic talents and intellect would soon become evident and having achieved academic distinction at West Bell, he was promoted to one grade higher when he entered Simmons – a common practice at that time for students who excelled beyond what was expected at a given grade level. Roscoe's academic talents were further demonstrated when he graduated first in his class from Simmons as senior class president.

In the fall of 1942, Roscoe entered Sumner High School - an elegant and architecturally beautiful building located in *The Ville*, just a few blocks from his home on St. Ferdinand Street. For most high school students, the time spent during those years are among the most memorable; it was no less so for Robinson, as it was at Sumner where his adult life would begin to take shape. Given his intellect, he was "one of the big wheels" at Sumner, which is how one alumnus of the school described the bright students, athletes and the "rich" kids who attended the school at that time. And like all high school students, he had a group with whom he would hang out. Along with other brother and sister sibling duos - like he and Janet, Roscoe's group included two close friends and classmates, Daniel Estes and Virgil McKissick. Their friendship provided an important bond during Robinson's early teenager years.

When Robinson attended Sumner, it was one of only two high schools in St. Louis open to black students; the other being Vashon High School which opened in 1927. Originally called the "High School for Colored Students" when it opened in 1875, Sumner was the first high school for blacks west of the Mississippi, and many regarded it as a venerable and historic institution. The school was named for Charles Sumner, a U.S Senator from Massachusetts who, because of his passionate opposition to slavery, suffered a brutal cane beating while seated at his desk at the hands of an irate Southern Congressman in 1856.

The school would become known for its academic excellence and for producing graduates who would excel in many different endeavors. Among Sumner's illustrative alumni is opera singer Grace Bumbry, pop singer Tina Turner, social activist and comedian Dick Gregory, and actor Robert Guillaume, who was a student at Sumner during the years Robinson also attended. With its strong athletic program, a star athlete who graduated from Sumner was Elston Howard, Yankee catcher and outfielder, who became the American League's first black Most Valuable Player.

Sumner's academic reputation was a result of having teachers who nurtured and encouraged excellence and who understood that education was a means through which barriers of race could be overcome. As a consequence of school segregation and the non-existence of opportunities elsewhere in the school system, the teachers at Sumner were highly educated and represented the "cream of the crop" when hired to teach. Following in the tradition of John Meachum of the 19th century, these men and women – products of 20th century experiences in a segregated society, which often had low expectations of African Americans – conversely, had high expectations for their students. Having experienced hard times themselves while growing up, they were demanding, nurturing, and insisted upon high performance from their students. In the process, they became powerful influences in the lives of their students and highly visible role models.

Robinson loved school and had great respect for his teachers. He would later recall several who had an influence on him. One was Julia Davis, his eighth grade teacher, who would say to him (and other students) "You are going to segregated schools today, but you won't always go to segregated schools. When you go to other schools, you want to be prepared as you possibly can so you don't embarrass yourself; don't embarrass me as your teacher and don't embarrass your family." Knowing his academic potential, Ms. Davis also would say to Robinson as he approached graduation that "he ought to go to one of those eastern colleges." It was a thought that Robinson's other teachers would reinforce, and one that was probably motivated by the belief that those schools offered stronger academic programs than those in Missouri. Another teacher who greatly influenced him was Preston Ingram from whom he took a class while in high school, but who was also his Sunday School teacher and a good role model.

During Roscoe's childhood years, not only were the schools and neighborhoods segregated by race, but also were most of the swimming pools, playgrounds, and other public accommodations. For young blacks like Roscoe, it was the Tandy Community Center, which opened in *The Ville* in 1938 that served to meet their recreational needs, offering such activities as boxing, basketball, swimming, crafts and dramatics. Named after Charleton Tandy – a social activist who moved from Kentucky to St. Louis in 1857 to organize the Underground Railroad and who later led a protest that broke the city's streetcar segregation system - the Center flourished as a gathering place for the city's black youth. It was on the tennis courts adjacent to the Community Center where tennis great Arthur Ashe would, under the tutelage of his trainer, hone his talents to become one of the best of all times, winning the U.S. Open and winning twenty-seven Davis Cup matches. He would eventually become the Captain of the U.S. Davis Cup team. Although he was a native of Richmond, Virginia, Ashe spent his senior year at Sumner after moving to St. Louis at the invitation of a tennis official who had witnessed his potential.

Apart from his passionate interest in things academic, when he was a young boy, one of Roscoe's other consuming interest was the Boy Scouts, which he joined at an early age. Undoubtedly, the discipline and the service orientation of the Boy Scouts was something his parents wanted to encourage, but Roscoe, like many other boys, was probably equally attracted to the wearing of uniforms and badges which sets it apart from other youth organizations. Given the existing practice of racial segregation within the Boy Scouts, his was an all black troop that had been formed at Antioch Baptist Church not far from his home.

Although many of his friends who joined Troop 145 at the same time as he did would drop out after a few years in the scouting movement, Roscoe did not. Exhibiting early signs of being his own man, he stayed and diligently applied himself to mastering the many requirements for advancement and achieved the rank of Life Scout. In the Boy Scout rank hierarchy, Life Scout is second only to Eagle Scout. For Roscoe, this rank required, among other things, taking on leadership roles in his troop, giving service to his community, being actively involved in weekend and summer camps, and serving as a role model. On occasions, the priority Robinson gave to scouting sometimes interfered with his job of delivering newspapers, and when it did, he would have his sister Janet delivery the papers for him. And with each badge he earned, he would make a point of informing his sister of its significance, even though she was not always that interested.

As a Boy Scout during the early years of World War II, Roscoe developed a clear sense of patriotism and the responsibilities of citizenship by readily participating in home-front efforts such as collecting tin cans for recycling to be processed into material for airplane instrument panels, aircraft bearings, and – as the only metal that wasn't harmed by salt water - for shipping food overseas. At such a young age, Robinson probably didn't realize how important this little task was to ensuring America's readiness to wage war. Most importantly, however, Robinson's involvement in scouting, with its values-based emphasis on character-building, personal fitness, and responsible leadership, would help lay the foundation for his life and subsequent military career.

Growing up in a family of very modest circumstances and during the depression when his father was frequently unemployed meant that Roscoe had to work to earn some money - indeed; it seemed he was never without some kind of job. In many respects, however, having to work typified how one historian characterized black families in the early years, noting, "Black family patterns encouraged greater self reliance among progeny and black children were raised to meet the demands of survival on their own." So when he was twelve, Roscoe - like so many young boys who were willing to brave the sometimes adverse weather conditions - started selling newspapers, first the *St. Louis Argus* – an African American-oriented weekly founded in 1912, and then *The Call*, the Kansas City version of the *Argus.* In those days, an African American newspaper was often the only regular source of information to and from the black community of St. Louis about the social, political and economic issues of concern to them. This made it easier for Robinson to find enough willing and interested customers to enable him to earn a dollar or two a week.

Later, at age 13, Roscoe started working after school and on weekends as a grocery clerk in Joe's New Cottage Market around the corner from the family home on St. Ferdinand Street. It was a job he enjoyed, as it gave him an opportunity to socialize with customers – most of whom were his neighbors. During the summer of his junior year in high school when he was able to work more hours and earn slightly more money than the grocery clerk position paid, Robinson found employment as a jigger for Jackes-Evans Manufacturing Company- a metal fabricating firm. He had wanted to go to work in the foundry where his father had worked, but was discouraged from doing so as it was hard and dirty work. As Roscoe recalls, his father said, "*I want you to get an education. I don't want you working in a foundry. I want you doing something that I was not able to do.*"

Although both of his parents were "uneducated" in the formal sense, the importance of getting an education was something that was drilled into Roscoe by both his father and mother throughout his young life. Parents are luck of the draw, Robinson was lucky, and indeed, he owed much to parents. They instilled in him and his younger sister the values of responsibility, academic discipline, hard work, and preparedness. They knew that it was not where you came from that mattered, but which path you were taking and where you were going that did. For like so many of his parents' generation, formal educational opportunities – beyond elementary school - were limited due to race or economic circumstances. But, Roscoe's parents wanted more for their children, so as much schooling they could get was a necessity, and they were prepared to make whatever sacrifices necessary to see that happen.

If there were any sibling rivalries in the Robinson household, they were not evident. Robinson cared deeply about his sister, and took steps to demonstrate his caring. So whenever he was working, he often used some of his earnings – after always putting some money away for savings, which he was always encouraged by his parents to do - to take his younger sister to the Douglas Theater to see a movie. During his high school years, when neither work nor the Boy Scouts claimed his time, he participated in the YMCA's Hi-Y youth group; a high school club program for boys which stressed leadership development and giving service to one's community. At one point in his Hi-Y experience, Robinson served as the group's vice president.

With his strong interest in athletics and sports, one of Robinson's great ambitions during his high school days was to play football for Sumner with the hope of helping continue the school's reputation of fielding great football teams and playing in the annual Thanksgiving Day game against its bitter rival, Vashon High School. The game was then (and still is) a valued tradition in St. Louis and attracted considerable interest among the city's African American residents. It was high school football at its best. For Robinson, his ambition to play in the game was thwarted when he came down with pneumonia in 1943, and on doctor's orders, he was advised not to take the risk of playing. He was 15 years old then and, for all practical purposes, his aspiring football days were over and he would have to give up winning the "little brown jug" trophy that goes to the victor.

During Roscoe's senior year at Sumner, his father experienced yet another bout with illness. In the past, it had been a worry to the family, but this time his condition was more serious and it troubled Roscoe. Times became increasingly more difficult for the family, as his father was unable to work and, as a last resort, the family had to go on welfare. The immediate economic burden of providing for the family fell on Roscoe's mother who took on odd jobs. As primary support of the family, his mother eventually secured a job as a cook at Lindell Trust Company where she prepared meals for the management staff. She had a small savings account at Lindell and since they knew her, she got the job. As a woman with considerable thrift habits, she had acquired a reputation of "being able to stretch a penny" further than anyone. It was an important attribute to possess during those difficult and lean years.

While the family situation was anything but normal during his father's prolonged illness, Roscoe remained resolute and determined to move forward in his academic career. And with the continuing support and encouragement from mother and extended family, he graduated on January 21, 1946 at age 17 from Sumner as Salutatorian – second highest academic ranked student in his class. With that ranking, along with his leadership, service, and character, also came his induction into the National Honor Society. With early leadership qualities so evident, he was also elected President of both his Senior Class and the Student Council (Senior Yearbook photo below). Whatever intrinsic motivation drove Robinson's early years, he somehow always managed to assume a leadership role in the organizations in which he was involved.

As he prepared to move forward with his academic career, his high school teachers had high expectations for him. In keeping with a Sumner graduating class tradition of having words written about you in your high school autograph book, Lucile Williams, his science teacher, wrote in his book *"My very best wishes to you, Robinson! You have all the qualities that will make for a successful life I am wishing you."* Another teacher, Nellie Benson, wrote, "*I'm proud to have taught you. There is*

something very splendid and fine about you. I'm expecting great things from a boy of your ability." He was determined not to disappoint them.

III

To fill the intervening six months between high school and being admitted to the college to which he had applied, Roscoe took advantage of the time to enroll for one semester in the all-black Stowe Teachers College, which had been established in 1890 to prepare future African American teachers for St. Louis city elementary schools. Even though a teaching career was not what Robinson had in mind, he achieved, nevertheless, one of the highest grade point average ever recorded at that institution. But regardless of his career preference, Roscoe simply performed as he had conditioned himself – to excel at whatever endeavor in which he was involved.

When the semester at Stowe College was over and looking forward to college and yet another academic challenge, Roscoe took a concessionaire job at Sportsman's Park, the home of the St. Louis Cardinals and the then St. Louis Browns. The job provided him with the opportunity to earn money toward his tuition at St. Louis University where he had been accepted after being denied admission to the University of Iowa, his first choice school because of its engineering program and because of its reputation for openness to people of color. But like many other institutions, Iowa was giving first preference to the large number of returning World War II veterans who – aided by the 1944 G.I. Bill of Rights that provided educational support - were seeking admission.

From Roscoe's perspective, the concessionaire job at Sportsman's Park was, however, more than just a job; it provided him the opportunity to watch the game of baseball -

one of his other great passions. In fact, Robinson harbored such love for the game of baseball that he could easily have seen himself playing the game as a professional. But the time arrived when he had to give up the concessionaire job and begin the academic road toward a degree. His acceptance by St. Louis University, which was founded by Jesuits, must be viewed in the context of the times. It had only been two years since the institution was racially integrated. In becoming so, it was the first school on any level in St. Louis to admit black students.

With racial integration at St. Louis University still in its infancy, Roscoe entered the institution in September 1946 as an undergraduate with the intent of pursuing a degree in Industrial Engineering, and not unexpectedly, he was the only black student in his classes. He was socially isolated, so he sought and found camaraderie with other black college students outside of the University. Sometime between the end of the semester at Stowe College and his first year at St. Louis, at the urging of an old friend, he joined the Omega Psi Phi fraternity. Founded in 1911 at Howard University in Washington, D.C. to provide a socializing outlet for college men of color, it is the second oldest of the Greek Letter African American fraternities, with a long history of having some of America's most prominent African Americans leaders among its brotherhood.

However, before he had fully settled into the routine of college life at St. Louis University, events began to unfold that would be a major turning point in his life. It was in his second semester at St. Louis University when Roscoe received an unexpected telephone call from Goldie Cruther, a French teacher and assistant to George Dennis Brantley, the Principal of Sumner High School. The call conveyed the message that Brantley planned to put up his name for possible nomination to the U.S. Military Academy at West Point. Being a prominent civic and academic leader and well connected, the possibility of such an appointment had come to Brantley's attention.

In reality, the opportunity for the nomination of black St. Louisans to both West Point and the Naval Academy had been advanced as a distinct possibility to the black community by Claude Bakewell, the Republican candidate for the Eleventh District of Missouri seat in the U.S. House of Representatives, if they would get out the vote for him in the 1946 election. It was a calculated promise inasmuch as the Eleventh District contained most of the city's African American population, but which was also a solidly Democratic and pro-labor district since the New Deal. Although he was well recognized in St. Louis, having served as a member of the board of aldermen and as Postmaster for the city, Bakewell, bucking the Democratic machine, won the seat with the help of blacks in his district. His election was a fortuitous event in the life of Robinson, as after taking office, Bakewell set about making good on his promise of African American appointments to the two service academies; one to West Point in the Congressman's first year and in his second year, an appointment to Annapolis. Unfortunately, for Bakewell, whether it was his attachment to the black community or the particular convergence of bitter partisan politics, he was an unsuccessful candidate for reelection to Eighty-first Congress in 1948, losing to the Democratic Party backed candidate, John B. Sullivan.

Having watched Roscoe's development as a young man when the Robinson and Brantley families were neighbors, his polite and respectful character, and having observed his outstanding performance as a scholar and leader at Sumner, Brantley was confident that Roscoe had the discipline and requisite character to be successful at the Academy. Brantley called to inquire further about his interest in attending West Point. Convinced that he did not have anything to lose by competing for the appointment, it didn't take long for Roscoe to make his decision - personal and family circumstances helped dictate the outcome. Faced with the uncertainties of how he would finance his undergraduate years at St. Louis University, Roscoe, who neither knew - at the time- anything about West Point, nor aspired to a military career, nevertheless welcomed the opportunity to get an all-paid for education by attending West Point. With encouragement from his family, he allowed his name to be advanced for the highly competitive appointment.

The West Point nomination and arduous acceptance process was now underway. On March 8, 1947, Robinson, now eighteen years of age, traveled to Station Hospital at Fort Leavenworth, Kansas to take the rigorous physical examination required for admission. Equally, rigorous academic tests to determine the likelihood of academic success were required as well. But the importance of the results would become a secondary worry, when while awaiting the outcome of the tests and the nomination process, his father died in the spring of May 1947 at the age of 52.

His father had been a solid supporter of the West Point opportunity and Roscoe felt a void in his life now that his dad was gone. But he persisted, as he knew his father would have wanted him to do. While still awaiting the results of the West Point qualifying examinations, Roscoe took a job in June 1947 – which he hoped would be short-lived – as a warehouse worker for the giant Monsanto Chemical Company. When the letter came letting him know that he had passed the tests, Roscoe was informed, however, that he was appointed as the First Alternate candidate. It was the first major disappointment in his early life, as he had always been successful in whatever he set out to do, but there was always the option of returning to St. Louis University and resuming his studies.

That option would not be necessary. As if by "divine intervention," the disappointment was short-lived when the principal candidate for the Academy appointment failed to meet the qualifying physical requirements and was not accepted. This left Roscoe up for the nomination, which he readily accepted. The gloom that had cast a cloud of sadness over the family by his father's death just one month before was now replaced with rays of joys and anticipation. His one great disappointment was that his father had died without knowledge of his being accepted to the venerable military academy. The unforeseen and unexpected event that brought Roscoe to this stage of his young life as a future cadet would shape his life forever. It would be matched by the yet unforeseen events that would follow.

CHAPTER TWO

THE WEST POINT YEARS

I

From the crowded, urban and cosmopolitan environment of St. Louis where he spent his early years to the military academy at West Point, Robinson would travel a distance of approximately one thousand miles by train; but the cultural and social distance would be considerably greater. It would be initially and visibly evident from where on a high plateau on the western bank of the scenic Hudson River in upstate New York – forty miles north of New York City – sits the beautiful grounds of West Point Academy, with its fortress-like granite stone buildings and awe-inspiring monuments to military heroes. The great natural beauty of the river's valley, which can be seen from its various overlooking promontories, and its scenic vistas and rustic landscapes, were so loved that they gave birth, in the early 19th century, to the Hudson River School that is regarded as America's first art movement. This group of naturalist painters would, through their breathtaking masterpieces of the valley's majestic landscape, carve an enduring place in American art history.

Unlike the city of St. Louis, which came into being as a convenient resupply location for travelers migrating westward, the Academy came into being to fill a young country's need for a trained military. Like the landscape that surrounds it, the Academy has played a major role in the nation's history, producing some of America's well-known military leaders and some lesser known as well. In the process, the Academy earned the reputation as the nation's premier training ground for military aristocracy and among its graduates are such illustrious figures as Ulysses S. Grant, William T. Sherman, John J. Pershing, Douglas MacArthur, Dwight D. Eisenhower, and Omar Bradley.

It was just two years after the end of World War II when, in the summer of 1947, Robinson – along with four other African American young men – Norman Brown from Philadelphia; Douglas Wainer, Norwalk; Connecticut, William Woodson, Washington, D.C, and James R. Young, St. Albans, New York - entered the United States Military Academy at West Point. They were part of a contingent of over 600 other young men who entered the Academy that summer. Coincidentally, the Superintendent of the Academy at that time was General Maxwell D. Taylor – a native Missourian like Robinson. Described as a brilliant man, he would later become Army Chief of Staff under President Dwight Eisenhower. Taylor played a role in the civil rights movement when, in September, 1958, he was ordered by Eisenhower to dispatch – as quickly as possible - riot-trained paratroopers of the 101st Airborne Division to Little Rock, Arkansas to quell the resistance to the court-ordered integration of Central High School.

The post-war period during which Robinson entered West Point would usher in changes at home and abroad. On the international front, tensions between the United States and Russia were intensifying, signaling the beginning of the Cold War era. Discussed at the same time, were plans on how to assist the post World War II economic recovery of Western Europe. These discussions would lead to the creation of the Marshall Plan that would transform much of Europe from post-war physical and economic devastation to a diverse, progressive continent. In the domestic political arena, change – fueled by the anger and resentment of returning black veterans regarding their post-war treatment as second-class citizens – was also occurring. Given that recognition was not always bestowed upon them at home for their sacrifices in the defense of freedom, this was a justifiable resentment. The intensity of the feelings of many soon-to-be returning African American World War II veterans was expressed in the words of a black army corporal from Alabama who was about to be discharged: *"I spent four years in the army to free a bunch of Dutchmen and Frenchmen, and I'm hanged if I'm going to let the Alabama versions of the Germans kick me around when I get home. No siree-bob! I went into the Army a nigger; I'm coming home a man."*

* * *

Considered from a historical perspective, and while Robinson may not have fully realized the significance of it when he entered the Academy, the year 1947 would become a watershed time in the United States. It was in that year that President Harry Truman, recognizing the growing post-war political influence of African Americans and sensing the need to respond to their pressure, took the bold step to create the first Civil Rights Commission. In its report *"To Secure These Rights,"* The Commission called for – among other recommendations – the end to segregation in the U.S. armed forces. On April 15, in that same year, another African American named Robinson would make history. For on that day, Jackie Robinson, who had in 1943 been commissioned as a Second Lieutenant in the U.S. Army, but whose military career had been derailed on "trumped-up" charges of resisting arrest for refusing to take a seat at the back of a bus in Texas, became the first African American to play in the major leagues. In making his debut with the Brooklyn Dodgers, he would break the baseball color line.

In time, Robinson's entry into major league baseball and the other black baseball players who would follow would speed the end of the Negro Baseball League and Negro teams that played in St. Louis during Robinson's childhood years. Many African Americans would lament the end of "Negro Baseball," but others saw it as a major breakthrough; not only in baseball, but something that would increase the participation of African Americans in all professional sports, as well as other aspects of American life, including the military.

* * *

When Robinson was admitted to West Point, he was one of a small number of African Americans since an Act of Congress originally founded the Academy in 1802. And until the latter half of the twentieth century, he would become one of an even smaller number who completed the four years and graduated. The historical reality was that men of color who attended West Point in the early days mirrored the pattern of the treatment of black people in America, in general. Denial of opportunity and discrimination were the norms in those days. Realizing that racism hostility and discrimination to African American still prevailed and that her son might experience some hostile treatment, Robinson's mother, who was apprehensive anyway about her son's new venture, first said: "You can do as well any of the other young men." Then she followed with these cautionary words: "If they don't treat you right, just come on back home."

Before Robinson's time at West Point, the treatment of black cadets was – for the most part - different from what he encountered and about which his mother had concerns. To appreciate that difference, one needs to understand that earlier history, beginning with the first man of color admitted to the

Academy. He was James Webster Smith, who entered in 1870. From his first days to his last, Smith was harassed and treated to scorn and ridicule. He was given the silent treatment meaning that other cadets would have nothing to do with him except on official business, and he was required to room and eat by himself. He suffered racist slurs and taunts. His own description of the treatment he received is captured in the following excerpt from a letter, dated July 14, 1870, he wrote to *The New Era* just a few days after his arrival at West Point.

> *"Your kind letter should have been answered long ere this, but really I have been too harassed with examinations and insults and ill treatment by these cadets that I could not write or do anything else scarcely...We went into camp yesterday, and not a moment had passed since then but some of them has been cursing and abusing me...It is just the same at the table, and what I get to eat I must snatch for like a dog. I don't wish to resign if I can get along at all; but I don't think it will be best for me to stay and take all the abuses and insults that are heaped upon me..."*

According to an Army review of his tenure at West Point, Smith was court-martialed twice and had to repeat a year. Despite these severe hardships, Smith persevered for four years at the Academy, but did not receive a commission. He was expelled under suspicious circumstances in 1874 for failing an examination at the end of his junior year. As an act of redemption for Smith, in September, 1996, one hundred and twenty-two years later, a posthumous commissioning ceremony which was approved by President William Clinton at the request of South Carolina Representatives John Spratt and Jim Clyburn and Senator Strom Thurmond.

From 1870 to 1898, twenty-three other black men were appointed to West Point. Twelve actually attended; six stayed longer than one semester, and three graduated. The first to graduate was Henry Ossian Flipper in the class of June 1877. He endured with strength and determination the social ostracism and silent treatment inflicted by some of the cadets. The one exception he himself subsequently recalled was the respect and kindness shown to him by Butler Ames who he regarded as a friend during their Academy years. Ames was the grandson of Benjamin Butler, a decorated Union General during the Civil War and later a member of the House of Representatives from Massachusetts where, with Charles Summer, he co-authored the Civil Rights Bill of 1875.

As graduation was nearing, Flipper, who began his own autobiography while a cadet, wrote, "*My four years were drawing to a close. They had been years of patient endurance and hard and persistent work, interspersed with oases of happiness and gladness and joy, as well as weary barren wastes of loneliness, isolation, unhappiness, and melancholy.*"

Upon Flipper's graduation, he was commissioned as Second Lieutenant in the 10th U.S. Cavalry. Unfortunately, Flipper's experience with racial hostility did not end with his graduation as evidenced by the social isolation he received from his fellow white officers from 1878 to 1882. The experience reached its ignominious climax when in 1881 he was charged with and tried for embezzling Army funds while serving as post quartermaster and commissary officer at Fort Davis and for conduct unbecoming an officer. The so-called conduct charge was related to his friendship with a Miss Mollie Dwyer, a young white woman who was the sister-in-law of his troop commander. Flipper had been seen on several occasions out riding with Miss Dwyer. Clearly, in those years, public interracial social contact – even if the relationship was platonic – was an unwritten taboo.

During his trial the embezzlement charge was dropped for lack of evidence, but he was found guilty of the "unbecoming an officer" charge and was dismissed from the U.S. Army on June 30, 1882. Sadly, Flipper – a man of great intelligence and ability – spent the rest of his life, without success, seeking to have the action overturned and his commission restored. Notwithstanding Flipper's treatment, he never harbored hostility toward the Academy; indeed, in his autobiography, he insisted that the officers (administration) of the Academy were gentlemen who were fair and objective about him.

> *"At the hands of the officers of the institution my treatment didn't differ from that of the other cadets at all, and at the hands of the cadets themselves it differed solely "in the matter of personal public association." I was never persecuted, or abused, or called by opprobrious epithets in my hearing after the first year. I am told it has been done, but in my presence there has never been anything but proper respect for me."*

West Point's fourth black graduate, Benjamin O. Davis, Jr. (Class of 1936), was the son of the first man of color to achieve the rank of Brigadier General. Davis' treatment at the Academy was quite similar to that of the three who preceded him. He never had a roommate and he ate, studied, and spent most of his free time by himself. Shunned by his classmates; few spoke to him outside the line of duty, Davis described himself in his autobiography as "an invisible man."

> *"Except for the recognition ceremony at the end of the plebe yea, I was silenced for the entire four years of my stay at the Academy. Even though West Point officialdom could maintain that this silence had no official basis, they knew precisely how I was being treated and that I was the only cadet in the corps treated in this manner....This situation was ridiculous, but in way was it funny. To this day I cannot understand how the officials of West Point and the individual cadets, with their continually and vociferously stated belief in "Duty, Honor, Country" as a way of life, could rationalize their treatment of me."*

That treatment, designed to make him buckle and give up, did not deter Davis; rather, it spurred his resolve to complete what he started. My father, he said, "*taught me to be strong; he had endured adversity, and so could I.*" Davis completed what he started, and graduated 35th in a class of 276. Subsequently, he commanded the famous Tuskegee Airmen and became the first African American General in the United States Air Force.

While the racial experiences of those African Americans who preceded Roscoe Robinson reflected the realities of race relations in America in the late 19th and early twentieth centuries, their treatment by their fellow cadets was not solely a matter of dislike of African Americans by all the cadets. In many instances, those who did not harbor dislike of people of color were simply victims of not wanting to go against the norms of treatment out of fear of being ostracized by other white cadets, if seen fraternizing with cadets of color.

II

By the time Robinson entered West Point, the experiences of black cadets, their relationships with white cadets had begun to change, and a period of transition was dawning. The ostracism, shunning, and marginality that many of his predecessors at the Academy had experienced had virtually disappeared. As Robinson noted: "I didn't go through that (the shunning). When I went in, the only thing that would be of a nature of segregation at all is that I had black roommates. I don't know what would have happened if I had been the only black in class…..I would never want to say that I was singled out because I was black." Yet, one of Robinson's white classmates who later became a good friend saw it differently, saying, "*In our cadet days, I had sensed that there was an invisible internal barrier, even between classmates. Aside from classes and drill formations, we lived different lives.*"

Robinson's reference to segregation he experienced was because he was assigned a room in Company G-1 with two other African American cadets – Douglas Wainer and Norman Brown. Since it was the practice to assign cadets to companies based upon their height, Robinson's assignment to Company G-1 indicated that he was close to average height of all cadets. The other two African Americans roomed together in a different cadet company.

The course at West Point is four years long and the life of a cadet is rigorous and demanding. Every cadet—especially so in the first year at the Academy when they are called plebes—goes through a hard time since the intense academic curriculum is the same for all. In Robinson's words, *"it wasn't a picnic for anybody."* Plebes were required to be in ranks at first call for any formation, to march to class, to eat while sitting at "attention" on the forward edge of dining hall chairs, to recite plebe knowledge when required, and to stand at attention in an upperclassman's room for any violation of "Plebe System." To accomplish all that was required, many plebes were forced to study or shine shoes after Taps (Lights Out) risking being caught by a Tactical Officer.

During the first two months of a cadet's plebe year, they undergo what is called at the Academy–"Beast Barracks." An old West Point tradition, Beast Barracks is ostensibly when upperclassmen are teaching plebes instant obedience and inculcating the foundations of military discipline. They learn how to march, field strip weapons, shine shoes, shower in two minutes, and recite required plebe knowledge. In Robinson's plebe year, the culmination of Beast Barracks was a five-day tactical hike in eastern New York State where the plebes made camp each night, ate field rations, and sometimes dug foxholes in preparation for threatened attacks by upperclassmen.

In his own account of hard times and the resilience required to cope, Robinson recalled an incident during Beast Barracks, which to others, including the leadership of the Academy was just another form of hazing. The following is how Robinson saw the incident:

> *"I think I was one first classman's favorite cadet, because he really gave me a hard time. I don't think he was giving me a hard time because I was black. There was another first classman giving the guy right next to me equally as hard a time. I remember this guy well. I was his personal project. I also knew for a fact that he was not going to run me of out of the Corps of Cadets. He could be as hard as he wanted to be on me, but he wasn't going to make me quit.....I could take whatever he gave."*

In reality, during his years at West Point despite the segregated rooming patterns, some personal relationships based upon mutual respect did develop between blacks and whites. Major General Edward Atkeson, Retired, who was a classmate of Robinson, recalled an experience he had with him, and whom, on later reflection, he would label the "Brave" one.

> *"I came to know a man I will call "Brave" early in our military careers...During our second summer of training, I was fortunate enough to be paired with him (Robinson) on the small arms range. We were hefting rifles, squad automatic weapons and machine guns. I was the coach while he fired, and he coached me when it was my turn to squeeze the trigger. He was a better coach than I was, so I probably benefited more from the relationship than he did."*

Robinson would also later recall how a white cadet from Maine – one of obvious inclination to open association with blacks - would come to his room after study hours and say that he didn't like his fellow white cadet roommate and wondered if he could somehow room with the three African Americans. The change, for obvious reasons, could not occur because of the segregation rule. But the cadet from Maine still wanted to pal around with Robinson and the other black cadets, which, when they would go to New York City on off weekends, was not a problem since racial mingling in that city was not a substantive issue.

Following plebe year, the cadets are allowed about four weeks home leave, and upon their return, they undergo combat arms training at Camp Buckner about 10 miles west of the main campus of West Point. In July, 1948 while Robinson's class was at Camp Buckner, General of the Armies John J. Pershing, a graduate of West Point (Class of 1886), died. Pershing once commanded the 10th Cavalry (one of the original 'Buffalo Soldier' regiments) and was one of the early and outspoken advocates of the value of African American soldiers in the U.S. military. Having achieved distinction for bravery in the Spanish and Philippine-American Wars, Pershing went on to be the nation's highest-ranking military officer.

Because Robinson's class was the only intact one that summer with parade experience (the new plebe class had been in Beast Barracks only a few weeks), it was formed into a battalion of two companies each led by members of the Class of 1949 who were conducting the training at Camp Buckner. This battalion represented the United States Military Academy in the state funeral of General Pershing. Starting at Union Station, the battalion marched to the U.S. Capitol where General Pershing's body had lain in state. Then with the general's body on a caisson, the march continued down Independence Avenue to Memorial Bridge, ending at the general's gravesite in Arlington National Cemetery.

His wife of later years recounts the story about the Pershing funeral that he told her. After the service for Pershing, Robinson, his roommates, and the white cadet from Maine agreed to meet at a pre-determined site for some sight-seeing and fun. When the appointed time for their getting together arrived, Robinson and his roommates were hesitant – and even perhaps afraid – to be seen in the then segregated Washington, D.C with a white cadet and they decided not meet him; after that episode, the "palling around" ended.

After combat arms training at Camp Buckner, Robinson's class returned to West Point and with the entire Corps of Cadets reassembled, the academic year began. Like all others, Robinson was faced with getting through his course work, which included mathematics, military topography and map making, physics, chemistry, foreign language and English. In January after the return from Christmas leave, Robinson and the rest of the Corps participated in the inauguration parade for President Harry S. Truman. It was as cold that day as it was hot for Pershing's funeral the summer before. The USMA band led the parade but as one of Robinson's classmates recalls, their battalion was "next to the last and could not hear our band." However, behind them was another marching unit with a band, so – in true military fashion - their battalion got in step with its beat.

III

It was the summer of 1949, after his second year at West Point, that Robinson's class took their Air Force trip to give cadets direct exposure to life and activities on an air force base. Robinson's visit to MacDill AFB near Tampa, Florida would become a significant and defining experience in his life. It was customary for the Academy, in cooperation with local hosts, to arrange for the cadets to meet some of the young local women for purposes of dancing and socializing. It was a welcomed diversion from the daily routine of cadet life. Most important, it was an opportunity to meet and interact with the opposite sex on neutral grounds.

When the time arrived for the social gathering, the white cadets in Robinson's class were invited to an event at the exclusive and very private Tampa Yacht and Country Club. Black cadets had been forewarned – even before leaving the Academy – that they were not to show up at the dances and social events that were going to be held for white cadets when they traveled to the various posts. For the black cadets a separate event would be scheduled. To facilitate this, the Air Force Chaplain at MacDill Field in Tampa was asked if he knew any one in town who could arrange a social event for Robinson and two other black cadets in his class who were on the trip. The Chaplain got in touch with a Miss Anderson, a black schoolteacher and the owner of small building that she had turned over to the military to be used as an USO for black military personnel. She was asked if the building could be used as the site for the social event for the African American cadets. Miss Anderson not only approved the request, but also agreed to help in arranging the event.

The segregation of cadets for off-duty socializing reflected a long-standing practice found on military bases located in, though not exclusively, Southern communities where "Jim Crow" laws and traditions in the 1940s tended to frown on the mingling of African Americans and whites. Although the social event for the cadets did not involve base-community relations in the traditional sense, nor was it a military affair, it was expected that existing community racial segregation practices would be respected. In doing so, it would prevent any possibility of mixed racial dancing and avoid any potential problems that might arise, real or imagined.

For the black cadets, the local black hostesses – all of whom were teachers recruited by Miss Anderson - invited a group of young African American ladies to meet, dance, and socialize with the cadets. From among the large group of young ladies in attendance, Robinson was immediately drawn to a very attractive young high school senior by the name of Mildred Simms. A native of Tampa, she first read her name in the newspaper, along with a couple of other young ladies, as being invited to the affair at the Tampa Yacht and Country Club. Given the racially segregated environment of Tampa, she knew that this had been a mistake and attended the event being held for the black cadets.

As the social event unfolded, Robinson and Millie (as she was known to her friends), danced, talked and got to know each other. When asked her first impressions of Robinson, she said, "*Well, he had finished high school, was in college, and was a nice young man.*" Tall and resplendently dressed in his cadet white uniform, she could not but be impressed with Robinson. But Millie shared the same personal ambitions as Robinson. She wanted to finish high school and attend college, which she did by enrolling at Fisk University in Nashville, Tennessee – one of the oldest historically black universities in the U.S. Little did Millie realize that this chance encounter with Robinson would begin a lifetime relationship.

Robinson returned to West Point, and though he and Millie were separated by a considerable distance, their relationship continued to flourish over the next few years through phone calls and letters. But life at academy continued at its normal hectic pace. During the early spring of 1950 following the Christmas break, Robinson participated in an exchange program with his corresponding class at Annapolis. A group of approximately fifty cadets would travel to Annapolis and stay for a week in the room of one of the same number of midshipmen visiting West Point. One of the roommates would act as the sponsor of the visitor. Cadets and midshipmen went to class with their sponsor, stand formations with him, and, of course, took meals with him in the dining hall. For Robinson, it was an instructive, memorable, and enjoyable experience. The exchange trips spawned many lasting friendships.

June of 1950 and graduation marked the final 'dry run' for the Class of 1951. After the graduation ceremony in the field house, Robinson and his classmates were now First Classmen, or in more common academic language, they were seniors. On the same day the Class of 1950 graduated, Robinson's class began a Combined Arms trip that would take them to military bases in four southern states. The Academy had begun by then to make some strides toward breaking down the segregated living arrangements among cadets, and the Combined Arms trip provided an opportunity to test these new arrangements outside of the Academy. Sheldon Graham, Jr., a white classmate of Robinson and who was the Head Cheerleader, tells of being told that he had been selected by the tactical officers to be asked by the Academy Superintendent if he would be willing to room with a black cadet during the Combined Arms trip. The decision to room with a black cadet had to be voluntary on the part of the white cadet. On his own volition, Graham, a native Texan whose grandfather had been a noncommissioned officer in the Confederate Army, was not only amazed that the Academy would ask a Southern cadet, but he was delighted and consented to room with an African American cadet.

After an initial stop-over at Wright-Patterson Air Force Base in Ohio, the combined arms trip would take Robinson's class to Fort Bliss, Texas, the home of Air Defense Artillery, Fort Sill, Oklahoma, home of the Field Artillery ,Fort Knox, Kentucky, home of the Armored Corps, and Fort Benning in Georgia, home of the Infantry. At each installation, the class received an orientation to the mission and the equipment of each branch. It was while at Fort Benning that Graham roomed with Robinson. However, to broaden white and black cadet experiences with each other, at each base, the roommates changed. This was a disappointment to Graham as he hoped to room with Robinson at all the posts, as he enjoyed their, albeit short, time together. But the time they did spent together was, according to Graham, a "wonderful opportunity to get to know his quiet classmate better."

Apparently, overall, the "experiment" went off without a hitch, and to the Academy's credit, the integrated rooming arrangements were a step forward. Moreover, it was an important gesture of concern about making sure that the black cadets were "taken care of" in the event they might encounter some race-related difficulties while traveling and residing in the segregated south. During another occasion when the cadets were on a summer trip in the South, a group of Robinson's classmates suggested that they go to a restaurant together, but Robinson knowing that the management would not welcome him there said:. "You know I can't do that." When the group realized the racial implications of Robinson's comment - rather than go their separate ways, they decided to go somewhere else where they would be accommodated. For his fair-minded colleagues, experiences such, as these were often painful, but eye openers as well. But such experiences were not limited to Robinson's time at the Academy. Charles Walker, who graduated with Robinson and then were together after graduation when they were in the Infantry Officer basic course at Ft. Benning, recalled how hurt and sad he was when Robinson, whom he described as one of the nicest guys he knew, turned down his invitation to go off post to have a beer because he feared being denied service on the basis of his color.

Outside of the occasional "socializing" that occurred during Academy sponsored trips, the other opportunity for blacks to fully participate at West Point was through varsity sports. It was one of the few on-campus activities then open to blacks in many predominantly white academic institutions during the late 1940s. Robinson's roommate, Douglas Wainer, was on the varsity track and cross-country teams for all four years, while Brown- the other roommate - was on the track team. Together they constituted half of the Academy's mile relay team during Robinson's plebe year.

Not to be outdone by his roommates, Robinson also went out for the varsity track team, but after the first winter track season, he concluded that he wasn't good enough to continue. He decided instead to switch to the intramural program, which cadets not members of an athletic department team sport were required to participate. Depending upon the season, you had the choice of football, boxing, softball, soccer and others. The program better suited Robinson's talents, and throughout his four years, he enjoyed the program very much and did well in it. It was during his participation in the intramural program where Robinson learned and honed his skills as a handball player, enabling him later to boast that he was the best in the Army at that sport.

Robinson playing handball, NATO 1982-83

Though always conscious of the segregated environment of West Point, Robinson's memories of his days at "The Point" were, overall, positive. He knew that he stood on the shoulders of the men of color who had preceded him, and was determined to make the best of his experiences at the Academy. "I wanted to learn as much as I could. I wanted to be the best officer that I could be when I graduated." He was also excited by the challenges he faced and the various – sometimes-amusing – encounters he experienced.

Later, with the years at West Point behind him, he shared some of his Academy memories, especially those during his Plebe year. One of those plebe experiences he remembered was spending his first Christmas away from home. As the upperclassmen departed for home, Robinson's class assumed the command position of the Corps from acting brigade commander to squad leader in each company. Because cadets represented every state in the Union, travel to a home state on the west coast might require one-half the Christmas break and the return the other half. Therefore, the policy at the time was that Plebes stayed at West Point during Christmas. He had plenty of company to spend the holidays with, but without the company of family, it was quite a different kind of Christmas than he had ever experienced

But the Academy made sure the Christmas break was as enjoyable for plebes as possible with a full range of activities including a dance (or "hop" as cadets called them) each night; choral, band, and organ concerts; skiing and ice skating; and the "Southern Sweepstakes", a hockey game whose players had never before been on ice skates. Old Man Winter made sure everyone had a white Christmas that year; he dumped 24 inches of snow on West Point on Christmas Eve. The heavy accumulation was more snow than Robinson had ever witnessed at one time in St. Louis. It created a picturesque canvas of the Academy grounds, but it limited the cadets' travel across the campus.

One of his other favorite Plebe memories was being "chewed out" vehemently by an upperclassman for "gazing around" while in formation during a dress parade. So fascinated by the whole military atmosphere around him – the pageantry, the disciplined formations, the colorful uniforms - he couldn't keep his eyes forward. He recovered from this early experience. He had to, since during some months, a cadet might have three parades a week.

The Academy had one requirement that reminded him of home when his mother made him attend church every Sunday. At the Academy, mandatory chapel attendance was also a requirement during Robinson's cadet years. For those of the Protestant faith, like him, services were held in the spectacularly sited Gothic style Cadet Chapel overlooking the main campus. Catholic cadets attended services in the beautiful Catholic Chapel and Jewish cadets attended services in the Old Cadet Chapel.

It would take Hollywood, however, to provide Robinson with a memorable experience unlike any other. During his plebe year the Academy was transformed into a virtual movie set for the filming in September of the movie, *Beyond Glory*, starring Alan Ladd in the role of a somewhat tormented by guilt older soldier who enters West Point and becomes a model cadet until he encounters problems with a jealous plebe. Many times as Robinson marched to class, he would see film crews shooting scenes, and the film crews were often at work during brigade parades. The movie was released in the summer of 1948 and shown at Camp Buckner where the class was undergoing training.

He also told the story about one of his most laughable experiences. It occurred during an inspection when one of the white officers said to him – "*I'm going to show you how to shine your shoes.*" Amused by the words, Robinson kept thinking to himself that you don't need to tell a black man how to shine shoes (an oblique reference to the "boot-black" occupation in which a number of African American men, in the early days, made their livelihood).

But, it was in 1951 - Robinson's last year at the Academy - when what has been referred to as "a defining moment" in the history of the Academy occupied center stage, drawing national attention. Regrettably, Robinson remembered the occasion all too well. A cheating scandal, involving mostly the football team – the pre-season choice for the number one football team in the country - took place and after a review by the Investigating Board headed by General Collins, ninety cadets, mainly in the second and third class, were dismissed. An episode that would reshape West Point and its mission for years to come.

Robinson knew personally some of those involved in the scandal, but he regarded the dismissal decision - while unfortunate - as appropriate and in accordance with the Honor Code by which cadets are expected to live. To him, respect for the Code and what it implied for those expected to lead in combat was what distinguished the Academy from other collegiate institutions. In a bit of irony, some thirty-five years later, Robinson would be asked to participate in a review of the Academy's Honor Code and Honor System and to make recommendations about it.

I V

After successfully completing his four years at the Academy, Robinson graduated from the Academy in June 1951 with a Bachelor of Science in Engineering. It was a memorable day as the Commencement Speaker was the Secretary of Defense, General George C. Marshall whose leadership of the Allied victory in World War II was legendary. So influential in the postwar recovery period that it was after him the Marshall Plan was named, and who would – because of his sponsorship of the European Recovery Program, become two years later a recipient of the Nobel Peace Prize. Attentive as you would expect Robinson and his classmates to be about military matters, undoubtedly, they were aware that the address by this statesman was coming only three months after Marshall had, albeit reluctantly, participated in the dismissal of a distinguished West Point graduate – General Douglas MacArthur – as Commander of the U.N. Forces in Korea over policy differences with President Truman regarding how the war should be pursued.

Also, in the commencement audiences – beaming with immense pride in Robinson's accomplishments – were his mother, Lillie Robinson and his sister, Dorothy. Sadly, the woman to whom he had fallen in love and to whom he would become engaged, Mildred Simms, could not afford to attend. His graduating class also included the four other African Americans who entered the Academy with him, which - up to that time - was the largest number of African Americans cadets to graduate from the academy.

Graduating cadets are given the option of choosing their post-graduation assignments, and requests are approved as much as possible. Robinson asked to be assigned to Fort Campbell, Kentucky, and his request was approved. He made that choice with a specific purpose in mind; Fort Campbell would put him closer to Nashville and Fisk University where Millie was now enrolled. Robinson took advantage of Fort Campbell's proximity to Nashville and frequently visited to be with Millie. She would later remark that he visited so often that "it was almost like he was a student at Fisk."

Despite Robinson's own assessment that his West Point career was "very undistinguished and that he just survived," the years he spent there were, nevertheless, a testament in perseverance and determination to survive in a tough and demanding environment. Though the cadet years were challenging, he would later acknowledge that he never seriously gave his mother's words much thought. For if he left, it would cause him to abandon the principles that he had been brought up with as a young man, and more importantly, these principles fitted well with the West Point motto: *Duty, Honor, Country*.

Cadet Roscoe Robinson, Jr., Class of 1951 USMA LIBRARY

Upon graduation, Robinson was now a member of the "*Long Gray Line*" of thousands of others who lived and studied at the Academy. His years at the Academy provided him with a first-rate education, leadership skills, and a love for athletics, particularly handball at which he excelled. He left with a deep respect for the Academy and the life-long camaraderie of his classmates, even though the latter came later, as he notes:

> *"I think about the friendships that I made that have lasted over the years....There is just a closeness among classmates. I am good friends of many of my classmates today even though I may not have been close to them at West Point. When I was at West Point, the guys I was close to were the guys who were in my company, because we lived together, we had classes together, sports and so forth. I was very close to those guys. Some*

of the other folks I became close friends with in later years."

One of the "guys" in his company was Edwin E. "Buzz" Aldrin who Robinson described as being quite bright and always an impressive person in the company. Later Aldrin would join the NASA space exploration program and become the second man – after Neil Armstrong - to walk on the moon when the Apollo 11 spacecraft, piloted by Aldrin, was launched on July 20, 1969. Another classmate of Robinson who would also have a distinguished military career was Edward C. "Shy" Meyer. Described by Robinson as one who stood out among his classmates, Meyer would become a four-star general and the Chief of Staff of the Army in the 1970s.

But among those in his class who would become one of his best friends in the Army was Joseph C. Clemons. They would later work together as lieutenants in the Airborne Division at Fort Benning. Clemons, who Robinson described as one of the best combat leaders he ever knew, would later distinguish himself, in April 1953, as a courageous and outstanding commander while leading an infantry company against a larger Communist Chinese army force to recapture Pork Chop Hill during the Korean War. The heroics of Lieutenant Clemons and those who fought along him would later be documented in a 1959 movie entitled *Pork Chop Hill* in which the legendary actor Gregory Peck played the role of Clemons. Robinson knew firsthand the heroics of Clemons and his men since his unit was stationed on the next hill over from Pork Chop watching the battle as it was taking place.

When Robinson walked off the historic grounds of West Point in 1951, he, of course, had no idea of what the future would hold, but he was prepared to become a leader in the Army. He would not return to West Point until 1981 – his 30th class reunion. Even though he had wanted to return for other reunions, overseas duty responsibilities made the trip difficult to schedule. To Robinson and others at the reunion, it was evident that the strong intellectual, tactical and leadership foundations which were laid during his years at West Point had – career wise - paid off for him. He was now a Lieutenant General.

CHAPTER THREE

A MILITARY CAREER BEGINS

I

Upon Robinson's graduation from West Point in late spring of 1951, he was commissioned a 2nd Lieutenant of the Infantry, the branch upon which he had decided long before graduation. The reason for his preference is uncertain, but perhaps it was because the Infantry is more physically demanding than other branches of the army and places a greater emphasis on fitness, a quality that would characterize much of his later career. In addition, the branch offers more opportunities for leadership and promotion. Robinson was equally enamored with airborne officers at West Point who were frequently seen impressively dressed in their "pinks and green" uniforms and jump boots. Excited and ready to launch his active military career, Robinson chose the 11th Airborne Division as his first assignment. He wanted to earn his jump wings, so much so that the first uniform item he bought was a pair of jump boots.

However, when he made known his preference for Airborne, he was informed by his company tactical officer (T) that assignment would not be possible because there were no black officers assigned to the 11th Airborne. The T suggested instead that Robinson go to the 3rd Battalion, 505th Airborne Regiment, 82nd Airborne Division at Fort Bragg, North Carolina because the 3rd was an all black battalion. Robinson, having done his homework, knew the 11th Airborne Division had recently begun to accept the assignments of black officers, and so he persisted. It paid off, as on December 7, 1951, after attending a three-month basic training course at Fort Benning,

Georgia, followed by training at the jump school, Robinson was assigned to the 3rd Battalion, 188th Airborne Infantry Regiment, 11th Airborne Division at Fort Campbell, Kentucky. His first official assignment was as communications platoon leader, but later served as rifle platoon leader in L. Company.

The assignment to Fort Campbell – a large, sprawling military reservation straddling parts of southwestern Kentucky and northern Tennessee - turned out to be a different, but not a totally unexpected experience for Robinson. He would quickly learn that despite the fact the Executive Order signed by President Harry Truman in 1948 stating that the Armed Forces would be integrated, it had not been fully implemented, nor had the order changed the operations of the 11th Airborne Division. The 3rd Battalion was, like the 3rd in the 82nd, also all black, except for the Battalion Commander, Lieutenant Colonel George Malezewski. It was a situation that was reminiscent of early and mid 20th century American military history during which the command of black units was always under white officers. But having Malezewski in command had other downsides. On one hand, Robinson respected his toughness and his rigid adherence to time scheduling, but he thought he lacked important interpersonal skills in handling men.

During Robinson's time in the 3rd Battalion, not only were black officers confined to segregated Bachelor Officers Quarters, but also the entire all-black unit was confined to separate barracks. It was an unsettling reality, but they had no choice but to live with it. It was in the context of these segregated living arrangements where Robinson would first experience the full depth of the impact of race and the inequality in the military. It occurred during an upcoming Inspector General inspection of barracks when the process of getting ready for the inspection was imminent. Robinson recalled the following event:

> *"A platoon sergeant came to me telling me that the platoon had taken up some money and wanted me to go into Clarksville and get some paint so we could paint the barracks. I told him, "No, we are not going to do that. We don't have to take up a collection. I have everything covered on a work order and we'll get our barracks painted when the post engineers get down to it." He said, "Lieutenant, I would like to say again that we have taken up some money and we really want to get our barracks painted. Would you please go into town and get some paint for us?" I repeated myself and said, "No, I have a work order." He straightened up and said, "Sir, they may paint the barracks for the 1st Battalion. They may paint the barracks for the 2nd Battalion, but I assure you that they will run out of paint before they get to the 3rd Battalion. Now, would you please take this money and go into town and buy us some paint." I did. I brought the paint back. We painted the barracks. The barracks looked great, but he was right. The post engineers never showed up in the 3rd Battalion to the paint the barracks."*

That experience of being a soldier in a segregated unit was an eye-opener for Robinson and it left its imprint on him in several ways. First, he learned that you need to listen to your men; they might know something you don't know. He was impressed with the willingness of the men in the 3rd Battalion to make a personal and monetary sacrifice to assure that they would not be viewed as "second-class" on inspection day. He was proud of their character and their commitment to military service. Rather than opting for a state of disillusionment, they expressed, by their actions what they were willing to endure while serving their country. He said:

"I gained a great amount of respect for those soldiers in that battalion, because they really wanted to soldier. They wanted to prove that they were as good as anybody else. Whether it was on the parade ground, jumping out of airplanes, or in the field, they really wanted to show that they could do a good job....They were good soldiers. They were airborne soldiers so to me that automatically put them in a special place, "Hard charging."

As a still newly minted second lieutenant, Robinson regarded the time he spent at Fort Campbell as an opportunity to obtain knowledge for anticipated future combat duties. He was able to observe several things that would serve him well throughout his career, whether it was the role of the non-commissioned officer in the development of soldiers, how others exercised discipline and were still able to build rapport among those in the company, how to get along with others, and most importantly, how to get done what needed to be done. From officers returning from Korea, Robinson learned how to apply his newfound knowledge to possible situations he might encounter when his time came to serve in a combat zone. It was also at Fort Campbell where Robinson honed his skills as a paratrooper when he attended through the jump master school - the mission of which is to train paratroopers to lead other paratroopers in actual jumps and mastering the release of combat-related equipment as well. Robinson's mastery of "jumping" would become a combat activity that he would not only enjoy, but one in which he would sometimes boast about being "one of the best."

In the final analysis however, Robinson's assignment to the 3rd Battalion positioned him to make an observation about the dysfunctional aspects of segregated units. Notwithstanding his high regard of the excellent quality of the black soldiers under his command, Robinson viewed segregation as imposing limitations on opportunities for their advancement. Speaking about this, he noted, "*Before (integration) they (referring to black soldiers) were going nowhere. They knew they were going nowhere. They weren't going to be selected to go to school; they weren't going to be selected to command companies or anything like that.*" For someone so early in his career, the consequences of segregation were a sobering reality for Robinson.

Robinson would remember Fort Campbell, however, for other reasons. It was during this assignment that he received his first promotion to the rank of 1st Lieutenant. In his recommendation for the promotion, his commanding officer called Robinson an "*efficient, intelligent, and an aggressive officer who performs his duty in a commendable manner. He commands the respect of his fellow officers and enlisted personnel.*"

Fort Campbell would also be etched in his memory, as it was the culmination of the courtship of Millie Robinson whom he had met during his senior year. As part of the courtship, he wanted to show her what it was like to live on a base, and to do so, when there were special dinner parties on Fort Campbell, he would invite her as his guest. In the ensuing time, the relationship became more serious and during Christmas of 1951, Robinson proposed marriage and gave Millie – whom he had chosen to be his "soul mate"- an engagement ring. Given the low salary of lieutenants, it cost a tidy sum. But Millie was still young and in college, and to avoid the possibility of being dissuaded by her mother from getting married because of her age, Robinson and Millie agreed to set the marriage date as soon as possible.

In a simple service held six months later, they were married on June 1, 1952 in the 188th Airborne Infantry Regiment Chapel at Fort Campbell. The marriage was the beginning of a love affair and a partnership that would endure throughout his lifetime.

Marriage Reception

As expected, many of the guests were Robinson's friends in the 11th Airborne Division, a few of Millie's friends from Fisk, their mothers, and other close family relatives. The wedding was followed by a reception at the 188th Air Officers' club. The next day, Millie - now Mrs. Robinson - graduated from Fisk University with a Bachelors Degree. Once they made sure that their mothers were safely on a train headed back to their respective homes, it was off on a honeymoon in a car that was loaned to Robinson by his company commander, Captain Randal P. Stevens who suggested to Robinson that his own car – a Chevrolet in not the best of condition – might not make it. It was a nice gesture on the part of Stevens (who happened to be the only black company commander in the 11th Airborne Division) and Robinson took him up on the offer.

Looking forward to spending some time alone, the Robinsons began a half-day's drive to Springfield, Illinois, which was their immediate honeymoon destination, and chosen because of its historical significance. Springfield was the site of the only home owned by President Abraham Lincoln, which the Robinsons visited, along with other tourist attractions. As a National Historic Landmark, the elegant Lincoln home is often considered the place where his social and political beliefs were formed, most notably his opposition to the expansion of slavery. It was also where – because of his success in the debates with Stephen Douglas – that his bid for presidency would be launched in 1860. For the Robinsons, the particular attraction of Lincoln's home, aside from its aesthetic qualities, had another motivation. It was an opportunity to pay respect to Lincoln who stood before Congress and pleaded for freedom for the slave, and then on January 1, 1863, issued the Emancipation Proclamation freeing the slaves. An event that would become a defining moment in American history. Even though there was considerable reluctance on his part to arming blacks, following the Proclamation, Lincoln also opened up service – albeit in segregated combat units – in the Federal Army to black volunteers. From Springfield, the honeymooners' car trip took them to Robinson's hometown where his mother – wanting to make sure that all her friends could extend their congratulations to the newly married couple - had planned a second reception.

It was then back to Fort Campbell to finish an assignment that would be of short duration. Robinson's anxiousness and youthful exuberance about getting into combat would soon come to end when he received overseas orders for Korea and was reassigned in October 1952 to the 31st Infantry Regiment, 7th Infantry Division. That assignment would be the beginning of Robinson's involvement in two of the most important and highly controversial United States military involvement of the last half of the 20th century. The other was Vietnam. Located in Asia, jutting out from the Asian continental land mass, Korea, once labeled the "The Hermit Kingdom," and about the same size as the state of Minnesota, was not a familiar country to most Americans, certainly not as well known as it nearby neighbors as China and Japan –both of whom were major global actors by the time the Korean Conflict emerged. Like his American contemporaries, Robinson also probably had little knowledge of the place, which had become an ideological battleground and where he would serve.

The assignment to Korea would mean an early marital separation. The normal and expected "extended" honeymoon period of early-married life was over, and leaving his new bride was painful. It would require a difficult adjustment on both his part and that of Millie's. But Millie was a strong and determined woman of incomparable charm. She would meet the exacting demands of a military wife, especially given Robinson's military assignments, which often took him outside the country. She was well prepared for the challenges since her own family life was often difficult. For example, she had to drop out of Fisk in order to earn money so that she could return and finish her degree. Now with Robinson gone, Millie moved to St. Louis to live with Robinson's mother and sister Janet, and, with the help of Robinson's oldest sister Dorothy, she secured an office job working in the Missouri State Employment Office. She kept herself busy writing to Robinson and with each letter she received from him, he would remind her that it was "cold" in Korea and would she please send him some tea bags since he was not a coffee drinker. Millie would not only send the tea bags, but also include some homemade cookies, which, of course, Robinson had to share with the other men in his company.

II

In June, 1950 – the year before Robinson's graduation - global attention would be focused on Korea, "The Land of the Morning Calm," (an English nickname for the country) when the Soviet backed Democratic People's Republic of Korea (DPRK) in the north crossed the 38th parallel which divided the peninsula following World War II and invaded the American supported Republic of Korea which occupied the southern half of the peninsula. On June 25th of that year, the United Nations Security Council, after considering the American position that the North Korean invasion constituted a danger to all the free nations of the world, passed a resolution denouncing the invasion as "a breach of peace." It called for withdrawal of the invading DPRK forces. A few days later, the Security Council passed a second resolution that this time called for "urgent military measures to repel the armed attack." The Council's resolution further authorized the establishment of a UN command to control all forces in Korea. This action would signal the beginning of the formal Korean War – properly referred to as the "Korean Conflict" since it was never officially declared a war by the U.S. Congress. Regardless of the appropriate nomenclature, for the next three years, "The Land of the Morning Calm" would be transformed into a bitter and costly battleground.

The Security Council's action would be followed by President Truman's authorization of American ground forces on June 30, 1950. This action was something he apparently committed to taking even before the Council's resolution. Five days earlier, he had said, "*The attack upon Korea makes it plain beyond all doubt that Communism has passed beyond the use of subversion to conquer independent nations and will now use armed invasion and war. It has defied the orders of the Security Council of the United Nations issued to preserve international peace and security."*

The common political justification about America's decision to enter the Korean Conflict was based upon the threat posed by the Soviet Union expansionist ambitions following World War II and the need to "contain" potential Soviet aggression, particularly in Western Europe. To Truman, his foreign policy advisors, and U.S. allies in the West, North Korea's invasion of South Korea was seen as a "proxy" for the Soviet Union. While there was no official or formal acknowledgement of any direct Soviet involvement in the war, there was considerable evidence of Soviet air personnel participation in Northern Korea, including the flying of MiG-15 fighter aircraft. Later uncovered documents also indicated that the actions of North Korea were aided and abetted by the Soviet Union and China. The latter, however, would assume a greater combat role in the Korean Conflict when it put large numbers of what were called "Chinese People's Volunteers" into the conflict, an action that prompted a UN Resolution in December 1951 condemning the People's Republic of China for its aggression in Korea.

Since the Korean War was in progress during his senior year, Robinson had actually expected to have his class' graduation date moved up earlier like what happened for four West Point classes during World War II. However, because the Department of the Army had dropped the "directly to active duty units" policy, that did not happen. Robinson later expressed that not seeing immediate combat in the Korean War was somewhat of a disappointment to him and his classmates:

"I think we wanted to be a part of it; we wanted to get over there; we wanted to get to it. We thought we had missed the war. We thought World War II was going to be the last one. I think there was an attitude that, "Well, what are we going to do for the next 30 years? There isn't going to be a war." That kind of stuff. We were anxious to go. I think we were very anxious to get to Korea. Maybe more so than we had sense enough to know."

III

From a historical point of view, the Korean Conflict would also signal that it was time to re-examine the practices of the Army, which up to that time had kept African Americans in segregated combat units. From the black soldiers' perspective, the unfair cloud of combat inferiority continued to hover over them and to say the least, and rightly, so, it was a source of anger on their part. Undoubtedly, there was an unflattering history regarding black soldiers and their treatment both during and after wars in which they had served. These were stories that they either could recall or was told to them. They knew that racial separation in the military found its rationale in white Americans' thoughts about Negroes, including negative perceptions about their aptitude for combat, including the belief that blacks were cowardly, and the residual fear of arming and training large numbers of Negroes.

The concern about arming blacks had its roots as far back as the Revolutionary War and in 19th century fears of slave uprisings such as those led by Denmark Vesey in South Carolina and Nat Turner in Virginia in the mid 1800s. In the more immediate pre-World War I period, the fear was a carryover from the Houston, Texas riot in August 1917 involving armed black soldiers of the 3rd battalion, 24th Infantry stemming – initially – from a racial incident involving a Houston policeman, but was followed by goading and inflammatory insults from white citizens. Seventeen white citizens were killed and during the controversial trial of the black soldiers that followed, thirteen were hanged for murder and forty-one were imprisoned for life.

The depth of racial feelings toward blacks in the military during World War I went, of course, beyond segregated units. It extended to leadership roles and promotions since it was then the accepted policy to discourage the promotion of blacks beyond the grade of captain. A practice that had existed even during the Civil War when black regiments were first organized. During the World War I era, not only were the black segregated units generally under the command of white officers, but white enlistees refused to serve under the command of the few black commissioned officers.

Despite white command, however, Negro combat troops in the 92nd Infantry Division which consisted of four regiments – the 365th, 366th, 367th and 368th - performed well during the fighting in France. The Commanding Officer of the 367th was Colonel James Alfred Moss, a white southerner who graduated from the U.S. Military Academy in 1894. The all-black 369th Infantry Regiment from New York, known as the "Harlem Hellfighters," was also commanded by a white officer named Colonel William Hayward. Their performance during the war was legendary, and even though the Regiment suffered heavy casualties, they succeeded in taking over several German-controlled French cities. The bravery and heroism of African Americans who fought alongside the French against the Germans resulted in 171 African American veterans receiving the French Legion of Honor medal. Dating back to the French Revolution, it is France's oldest and highest honor, but unfortunately, such formal recognition was not given to those same African Americans by their government. However, in some cities as New York, Chicago, Washington and Cleveland parades, which included both white and black onlookers, honoring African American soldiers who had served during World War I were held.

The reality was that returning black service men expected more in terms of their day-to-day status, especially in terms of fair and equal treatment. That did not happen; indeed the status of blacks in the military, and their treatment during and after World War I is best summed up in these words:

> *"Black America had gone to war in the hope of earning equality, but not even 750 and some 5,000 wounded could abolish a system of institutionalized injustice based solely on race. Failure to buy full citizenship with blood and suffering brought disillusion and alienation."*

Tragically, that disillusion and alienation were precipitating factors that led to deadly race riots in several American cities following World War I, the effects of which would linger for many years. In the years after World War II, however, black disillusionment with the military would turn to optimism. On the urging of black civil rights leaders who had been successful in bringing a number of court challenges to the separate but equal principle, pressures to desegregate the military began to mount.

But there was little, if any, support for desegregation among the military branches and their leaders. Racial stereotypes held by many white military leaders about the lack of intellectual ability of African Americans and their inherent "cowardliness" was still deeply entrenched. However, despite the opposition and views many in the military still held toward

African Americans of which he was fully cognizant, on July 26, 1948, President Harry Truman, having won the election with black support, signed Executive Order 9981 calling for equal treatment in the Armed Forces.

> *"It is the declared policy of the President that there shall be equality of treatment and opportunity for all persons in the armed services, without regard to race, color or national origin. This policy shall be put into effect as rapidly as possible, having due regard to the time required to effectuate any necessary changes without impaired efficiency or morale."*

In many respects, President Truman's Executive Order was a "watershed" action in the history of the U.S. military, in importance, ranking high alongside the broader anti-discrimination legislation as the Civil Rights and Voting Rights Acts that would come later. It would take some time, however, before the ultimate goal, i.e., desegregation of all of the Armed Forces, of Executive Order 9981, would take place. Progress in the implementation of integration varied among the service branches. The Air Force took the lead, and in February, 1950 in its first report on the racial integration program announced, among other changes, that personnel at the Lockbourne Air Force, which was the home of the all-Negro 332 Fighter Wing, would be reassigned to other commands.

The Navy, saddled with a personnel practice which had historically limited Negro service to the stewards' branch, moved considerably slower in integration, and as late as 1952, the steward branch was still 65 percent black. Although, on October 1, 1949, the Army announced that it was opening all service positions, regardless of race, to all personnel, acceptance of an integrated Army remained difficult to achieve. It was evidenced by the 1950 *Report of the Board of Officers on Utilization of Negro Manpower in the Army.* It said:

> "*The fundamental decision as between amalgamated and the Negro unit must be based on the combat effectiveness of the Army as a whole, and not on the exploitation of all Negro manpower. The best evidence as to how maximum effectiveness can be achieved is found in the opinions of war-test combat leaders who testified before this Board. Almost without exception, they vigorously opposed amalgamation and strongly urged the retention of the Negro unit. This Board concurs.*

A year later the position of the Army on integration would change when, during the Korean Conflict, the immediate issue of black soldiers' readiness for combat surfaced during the first months of the war when the adequacy of U.S. front-line troop strength became a matter of concern. The resistance to integration in the Army would exhaust its last breath and the "mother of necessity" began to take over. In the summer of 1951, General Matthew Ridgway, now in command of U.S. Forces in the Far East, having replaced General Douglas McArthur, and recognizing that the Eighth Army did not have enough combat units deployed in Korea, asked the Army for permission to assign black riflemen to white infantry units. Ridgway, a graduate of West Point, who had previously served as commander of the 82nd Airborne Division and had fought courageously in the Battle of the Bulge during World War II, had - by now - become recognized as a powerful and influential military leader having taken over command of the 8th Army after it had suffered several reversals at the hands of the North Koreans.

Demonstrating remarkable courage and wisdom during a period still rife with skepticism about the fighting ability of Negroes, General Ridgway, who earlier had said in a speech to a military audience, "*Human courage is universally distributed. It is daily display by the yellow, the brown, and the black as well as those of lighter pigments. It needs no battlefield stage to show its actors. It knows neither race, nor sex, nor age,*" now took an even stronger moral position on the issue of desegregation. In a cable sent to Washington, one month after replacing McArthur, he said: *"It had always seemed to me that segregation was both un-American and un-Christian for free citizens to be taught to downgrade themselves in this way, as if they were unfit to associate with their fellow or to accept leadership themselves."*

The Army heeded his message about the need to bolster and strengthen America's capacity to wage war. Ridgway's plan for the utilization of Negro personnel in integrated units was approved by the Department of the Army; an action confirmed in a July 19, 1951 memorandum from the Assistant Secretary of the Army to the Assistant Secretary of Defense that, in part, read:

> *"The proposed plan for the utilization of Negro personnel in the Far East Command has been approved by the Department of the Army and discussed with the Commander-in-Chief, Far East Command.........The Far East Command is to proceed with general integration throughout the Eight Army in Korea and in units other than the 40th and 45th Infantry Division in Japan on a basis of not to exceed 12% Negroes in all types of combat units. This integration is to be phased over a three months period."*

Though some at the top-level of the Army bureaucracy continued to oppose integration or urged gradualism, the Korean War would herald the dawning of a new era in racial deployment and assignment patterns in the military. Full integration of military units, however, would not come until 1954, the year in which the Department of Defense officially announced the end of segregation in the armed forces. In the intervening years, however, with continued support from some military leaders, racial segregation of some units at home and in the European theater continued for a number of years until it was no longer defensible. Even though full integration did eventually come to the entire Army, it did not mean that the issue of race would be fade away; it would simply take on a different character. Indeed, the Army, as well as the other service branches, would continue to encounter racial problems between black and white soldiers, particularly in communities where military bases were located when it came to equal access to public accommodations. Fortunately, the latter problems receded when the Civil Rights Act of 1964 was signed into law by President Johnson outlawing segregation in public accommodations throughout the country.

Throughout the long controversy over desegregation of the military, the influence of prominent black leaders, civil rights organizations, and the black media in moving forward the integration agenda cannot be ignored. A. Philip Randolph, the passionate advocate of desegregation, organized in 1947 the League for Nonviolent Civil Disobedience Against Military Segregation, and led protests calling for desegregation of the U.S. military. The repercussions of these protests and the fear of widespread social unrest in the black community have been cited as being factor leading to President's Truman decision to sign the 1948 Executive Order.

In a December 13, 1950 letter from Clarence Mitchell, Director of the Washington Bureau of the National Association for the Advancement of Colored People, to the Secretary of the Navy, the organization called for the elimination of racial designations in the induction, processing and other records of Armed Services personnel. Further, the letter suggested that use of racial designations "Served to give unnecessary humiliation to those who are being inducted into the service."

The voice of the black press was also heard. During the period following the Order, *The Pittsburgh Courier*, an influential Negro newspaper with a large national circulation, wrote editorials on the subject of racial policies in the military, which were often cited in Defense Department internal communication on the progress, or lack thereof, in desegregation.

IV

Despite the race issue and the political questions that surfaced on the domestic front about the merits of the war, Robinson and the more than a million Americans who fought alongside their UN allies in the Korean War, served as a matter of duty. In Robinson's case, service meant carrying out his duties, over the course of the Korean deployment with the 1st Battalion, 31st Infantry Regiment, as a platoon leader, rifle company commander and battalion
S-2 (Intelligence Officer).

When Robinson arrived in Korea and was being interviewed by his superior officers as to where he would be assigned, his zeal for getting into combat surfaced again. But one of the officers said to him: "*Oh, I know you. I know where you are going. You are going to the 1st Battalion, because you are going to be the commo (*communications) *officer because* *you have commo experience."* Robinson replied, *"Well, I don't think I came to Korea to be a commo officer.*" As important as communications officers were in a combat setting, Robinson had no interest in setting behind a desk – even though it would have been a safer assignment. Fortunately, when the interviews continued with other officers, he was told that he was actually scheduled to go into a rifle company for the first sixty days or so and then become a communications officer. Even that response did not satisfy Robinson and so he persisted in asking to be considered as a replacement officer to a rifle company. Militarily speaking, he wanted to serve his country in the most direct way possible, and that meant being where the action was – on the front line as an infantry soldier.

Despite the difficulties in getting his preferred initial assignment in Korea, he knew his association with the 31st Infantry Regiment brought with it considerable history. Originally formed in 1916, it was a unit known by the nickname "*America's Foreign Legion*" since it had spent almost its entire history outside of the United States. Throughout the Korean Conflict, the unit engaged in combat with the Chinese and the North Koreans under the most difficult conditions in the bitter cold of winter or in blazing hot summer conditions. And they were often outnumbered by the enemy. The 31st was also involved in some of the war's most famous battles as Old Baldy, Pork Chop Hill, and Triangle Hill, and, in the process, it suffered high casualties.

Arriving in Korea after the battalion had fought several fierce battles (one of which was Triangle Hill), Robinson - after only a month in the 1st battalion - was designated a company commander by 1st Battalion commander, Major George Wear. Two other lieutenants were also rushed into company command positions. All three had been called together by Wear one day who said, *"I've got to have some company commanders who can hump the hills"* – a reference to the mountainous and difficult terrain that dominated much of the central Korean landscape. In normal situations, company command position is generally held by someone of captain's rank who had more experience combat. But with the heavy turnover due to Triangle Hill and the King Company outpost battles, the need to replenish the company command positions was imperative.

Lt. Robinson, Commanding Officer of Co. "C" 31st Infantry Regiment at Camp Bak, North Korea

With assurance from Major Wear that he would give the young lieutenants all the help he could in commanding their companies, Robinson was now in a position he had not expected so soon. His company, consisting of between 175-240 soldiers, was frequently assigned to be either in reserve in case of the need to reinforce or counterattack the enemies' position. In the combat sector in which his company was deployed, the enemy combatants were the Chinese whom he described as masters of psychological warfare even to the point of using loud speakers to tell his men what they were having for meals. Robinson and those under his command would need all the help Wear could provide, as the "enemy" was not only those in North Korean or Chinese uniforms, but also the weather. As Halberstam notes:

> *"It was a war fought on strikingly harsh terrain and often in ghastly weather, most particularly a numbing winter cold that often seemed to American troops an even greater enemy than the North Koreans or Chinese. ....The Americans and their United Nations allied faced terrible, mountainous terrain, which worked against their advantage in hardware, most notably their armored vehicles, and offered caves and other forms of shelter to the enemy."*

The severity of the weather, particularly during the bitterly cold Korean winter months, took a huge toll on military personnel, with some later reports indicating that as many as 90 percent of them suffered from frostbite of their feet, hands, ears, or noses. In the most severe cases, frostbite symptoms sometimes resulted in the need to amputate body extremities. Subsequent research on the incidents of frostbite indicated that African Americans – most likely for genetic reasons - were disproportionately overrepresented in the known cases of frostbite.

Climatic conditions notwithstanding, one day while on-line, Robinson received a call to come back to the battalion headquarters as there was going to be a change of command. The new battalion commander was to his surprise, Lieutenant Colonel George Malezewski who had been his battalion commander at Fort Campbell during his time there in 1951. Upon assuming command, Malezewski made it clear that he didn't like the way the battalion had been operating, nor was he satisfied with the way company commanders were performing and he constantly threatened to relieve them of their command. According to Robinson, Malezewski wanted more contact with the enemy and wanted more company attacks – even it might involve placing troops at greater risk. Again, as Robinson would observe, Malezewski's style of leadership was destabilizing and negative. To Robinson, it was a style of leadership not to be emulated.

In one of the six battles for Old Baldy, a strategic site for both sides, Robinson's company provided the first patrols. When it fell, he was in a reserve position, but eventually his company was responsible for counterattacks should the Chinese attempt to regain the position previously held by the Columbian Battalion. It was one of two United Nations battalions assigned to the 31st Division - the other being the Ethiopian Battalion called by the name Kagnew. Each of these battalions consisted of approximately 700 to 850 soldiers. The participation of Ethiopia in the UN command was especially notable because, other than South Africa, it was the only African country to contribute to the United Nations Forces.

The presence of Columbia and Ethiopia – along with seventeen other countries – was in response to the July 7, 1950 United Nations Security Council Resolution 84 which called upon member nations to "render such assistance to the Republic of Korea as may be necessary to repel the armed attack and restore international peace and security to the area, and to make such forces and other assistance available to a unified command under the United States of America." Over the course of the war, fifteen UN member states contributed fighting units to the effort, some more overrepresented than others in relation to their population size. Other UN member states not inclined to contribute combat units provided other forms of assistance such as medical personnel, supplies, and equipment. This combined effort would constitute the reason why the Korean Conflict was called the United Nations' first real and substantive conflict in which all member states were called upon for assistance.

The fighting capacity of the various UN units, however, would vary, and it would be something significant to Robinson as a commander facing a formidable enemy. Upon reflection, Robinson (not one reluctant to express his opinion) would note, for example, that the Columbians were not very good soldiers and attributed the loss of Old Baldy during that attempt to take and hold it to their poor fighting capacity. Despite this somewhat "uncharitable" view of the Columbians, the country was the only South American nation to provide ground troops (and air support) to the Korean Conflict effort and, as noted by one scholar, it was that nation's "first time fighting on foreign soil in 127 years."

The problem with the Columbians – from Robinson's perspective - was a misunderstanding on their part as to what role his battalion was to play in the attack on one of the outposts near Old Baldy, which the Chinese held. Robinson understood his orders to counterattack; the Columbian saw his role as reinforcing their command. By the time his orders were clarified, it was too late, as the Chinese had already gained a foothold. Some of the miss-communication between the Columbians and Robinson's unit, however, could be attributed to language differences among the UN units. As one authority notes, these differences remained throughout the war as one of the "greatest single obstacle to military efficiency."

In contrast to his assessment of the Columbians, Robinson regarded the Ethiopians as excellent soldiers and he felt good about their willingness to fight – with considerable bravery - alongside the Americans. But, for some reason, the Ethiopians would not take a prisoner, which was a source of frustration for Robinson. Notwithstanding this reluctance, his assessment of them was an accurate one, given the long history of the Ethiopian Army of being repeatedly tested to defend their country against foreign invasion, including several attempts by Italy to colonize the country in the late 1890s and the 1930s. Ethiopia's success in repelling these two attempts, with the help of the British in 1941, accounts for the fact that throughout the period of European colonization of Africa, Ethiopia remained the only African country never totally under foreign domination.

In reality, though, the qualitative defining characteristic of the Ethiopian infantry battalion during the Korean War was probably because they were drawn from the elite and well-trained bodyguard of the emperor Haile Selassie. Another was the fact that since 1952, the Ethiopian army had been heavily subsidized by the United States in exchange for use of an electronic communications base called the Kagnew Station. Strategically located on the Red Sea, the station was, during and after the Cold War, an important listening station for Soviet communications. But Robinson was not alone in his favorable assessment of the Ethiopian battalion - it was corroborated by Stanley Sandler who noted:

> *"The Ethiopian battalion was highly motivated and claimed that they did not lose a prisoner or leave a single man unaccounted for on the battlefield, a record even better than that of the fearsome Turks. The U.S. Army Chief of Staff at the time wrote, "They returned as they went out – all together – whether they were living or wounded or dead."*

Despite these assessments of the Ethiopians, for reasons perhaps only understood by the Chinese, they were rarely ever fired upon by the Chinese. It was as though they were saying, "we have no issues with you Ethiopians." It was a classic example of psychological warfare that the Viet Cong would also later apply, on occasions, toward black soldiers in the Vietnam War. But it came as a surprise to Robinson when the Chinese changed the script one night and started firing at every unit, including the Ethiopians. He concluded that when they did, it was because there were several battalions on the front line that evening, and the Chinese, unable to distinguish among them, simply decided to fire at all in their sight.

After six months in a command position where he led his company in patrolling, counter-attacking enemy positions, and taking cover from mortar attacks, Robinson was reassigned to the battalion headquarters as its Intelligence Officer during which time talks about a truce to end the fighting began in earnest.

When the actual time spent in combat fighting is calculated, the Korean War was of relatively short duration, but it was a costly conflict, the third bloodiest in U.S. history, American fatalities numbered over 36,000, with over 92,000 wounded. Robinson, reflecting on one of the times he might have become one of those casualties, recalls being with his radio operator and moving from one exposed position to another while being fired upon with small arms and mortars. In describing the situation, he said, "*We hugged the dirt. We got behind some of the smallest rocks you'd ever want to get behind. The shooting becomes very personal out there when you are by yourself.*"

As a commander, however, when there is the loss of life of those under your command, the experience is painful, especially when so many were young men who would never see their 25th birthday. At the time, he himself was only twenty-five. Robinson knew that no amount of psychological preparation, whether you are a combat veteran or a young commander like him, could immune oneself to battlefield casualties. You learn to cope, and Robinson was no different from others military leaders in having to confront these difficulties. When asked about the first combat deaths of men in his command, he said:

> "*I think the first soldiers that you lose are always very difficult; or anytime you lose a soldier, it is difficult. I do recall quite vividly, the first guys that we lost. In fact, the first guy I lost was an attached engineer. He was probing for mines. I didn't really know him. Then I lost two guys on one of those deep patrols. We were always concerned about leaving somebody. That is what we emphasized we don't leave anybody. If we leave somebody, we are going back to get them. That was very traumatic. I knew both of those kids. I guess it does get very personal when you know them. We took our losses, but were very fortunate in not having lost whole companies. We saw a lot of things that took place right out in front of us on our flanks that you always got a little apprehensive about. I guess it is just something that goes with the responsibility.*"

As his first combat assignment, the harsh realities of this grueling war sunk deeply into Robinson's consciousness, testing his moral fiber and pointing out the need to draw upon coping mechanisms. In doing so, he attributes the availability of an Army chaplain named Tagert who was always ready to lend moral support and counseling to him and other commanders, because he knew that the officers needed it as well as enlisted men. Periodically, Tagert would come to fortified bunker positions where he conducted services, and then talked with the men about what they were experiencing.

The agony of war, of witnessing the death of friends, soldiers, and even the enemy, is trauma of the highest order. Although chaplains are themselves not trauma free, support counseling is a role that U.S. military chaplains have played during war and peace since World War I. Knowing that "War is never easy especially when you are losing young soldiers," Robinson highly valued having chaplains around to provide that critically needed spiritual and pastoral support. He had no hesitancy in drawing upon it. But, like the many around him, the greatest source of comfort was those personal and uplifting letters of care and concern from home and, in particular, those from Millie. She was so dutiful and thoughtful in this regard that she wrote him a letter every night, which sometimes included amusing tidbits about her job and how it was going.

Robinson's time as a platoon leader and rifle company commander during the Korean Conflict made a lasting impact on him and proved to be a valuable learning experience. Moreover, it provided him with the opportunity to observe the different leadership styles of the battalion commanders under which he served, and how each style can affect morale and performance. In particular, he learned the role battalion commanders must play in the development of their company commanders and the importance of prioritizing work efforts. One of the valuable lessons Robinson learned was the importance of ensuring that your men got their proper rest in order to be ready when something happens. Robinson also became aware of his dual responsibilities as a commander: first, accomplish one's mission – even when you are not permitted to do certain things - and second, to take care of the troops under him, and at the same time avoid getting too close to them. From that time on, knowledge of these responsibilities would mark the rest of his military career.

The Korean Conflict was shrouded in considerable political controversy, beginning with the question as to whether Korea even fell within the United States defensive perimeter. It was followed later with questions about American military strategy on what courses of action should be pursued to end the war. As the strategic analysis unfolded, the question became whether the U.S. should halt fighting at the 38th parallel and negotiate a settlement, or end the war by advancing beyond and clear all of North Korea. If the latter choice was made, some feared it would mean widening the conflict and bring China or the Soviet Union even more directly into the war.

These different perspectives on the Korean Conflict policy would spill out into a historic debate involving General Douglas MacArthur on the side of promoting a more aggressive pursuit of the Chinese Communist forces and President Harry Truman and the Defense Department on the other side who wanted to contain the conflict at the 38th parallel. In the end, the issue – at least temporarily - resulted in MacArthur's removal on April 11, 1951 from his position as Commander of United Nations forces in Korea for making public statements regarding foreign policy without first clearing those statements with the Commander-in-Chief. McArthur's position would be assumed by General Matthew Ridgway who had earlier replaced General Walton Walker as Eighth Army Commander when the latter was killed in a collision with an army vehicle in the early stages of the Korean conflict.

General MacArthur's removal from his command position by President Truman would become a major political issue in the U.S. with highly partisan voices both denouncing and supporting the President's decision. However, by the time Robinson arrived in Korea, the strategic position of the United

States (as the lead nation of the UN Command) relative to the war was clear. Certainly as an officer, he was aware of this controversial issue. He heard the volatile and sometimes heated discussions – even among his colleagues - about going or not going across the Yalu River – the border between North Korea and the Peoples Republic of China - and about whether the U.S. is considering the possible use of the atomic bomb to end the fighting; a question which was put directly to President Truman by a reporter for the Chicago Daily News. Truman reply was, "*There has always been active consideration of its use. Always has been. It is one of our weapons.*" Even in the face of such a controversial issue, Robinson he did not concern himself about the politics or the particular tactical options about how the war should be waged. He saw being there as having a job to do, accomplishing his mission, taking care of the troops and getting them back home.

After long and protracted negotiations, that process would begin to happen with the cessation of hostilities upon the signing of armistice terms on July 27, 1953 in Panmunjom. Ironically, even after the armistice and the enormous sacrifice of lives on both sides, the Korean peninsula remained geographically the same as it was when the first invasion of the south took place in 1950 - it was two separate countries who shared a common historical culture, but who were again separated by their particular political and governmental ideology. That reality, notwithstanding, peace had come to the Land of the Morning Calm. In a leaflet written in Chinese and Korean by General Mark Clark, who had replaced Ridgway as Commander of the United Nations forces and who signed the cease-fire agreement, he expressed his and his country's hopes for their adversaries' future. The words were particularly uplifting:

> *With the signing of the armistice, peace and quiet returns to the hills and valleys of Korea. ...We are happy to know that the days of fear, hunger, cold, and exhaustion are over for you. ...With good fortune, you may now turn from the bloody waste of war to the achievement of man's traditional right to rebuild his shattered homeland, till his fields, rear his sons,- and given this good fortune, you may now do this. May you be permitted to return to your homes speedily, may you soon be reunited with your families, may we never meet again on the field of battle."*

Soon after the armistice took effect, Robinson would be headed home after receiving recognition of his Korean service by being awarded the Combat Infantryman's badge and the Bronze Star. Despite the harshness and the futility of a war in which there were no victors, Robinson considered the time he spent in Korea as a learning experience, especially for himself as a young officer. But while he and other returning veterans of the Korean Conflict had done what their leaders asked of them, unlike other wars in which Americans fought and died, there would be no celebration of the armistice, no dancing in the streets or "victory" parades; only a sigh of relief that the brutal conflict was now over.

CHAPTER FOUR

THE AIRBORNE DIVISION AND LIBERIA

I

After a year of combat in Korea, Roscoe Robinson returned to the United States in 1953 and was reassigned to Company A, 503rd Airborne Infantry Regiment, 11th Airborne Division at Fort Campbell, the post where his active military career started. It was also, where he was married, and being in the states meant having the opportunity to enjoy his wife's companionship, which he missed. For Millie, regardless of when the next assignment would mean Robinson's leaving again, it would be the first time she had to really to think about setting up housekeeping and the both of them were looking forward to it. Most important, they could begin to think about starting a family.

Fort Campbell had taken on a new look when Robinson returned to the Division. The 3rd Battalion in which he had previously served was now fully integrated. Despite Robinson's overall inclination to minimize race at the personal level, he was, however, conscious of the systemic impact of segregation on the outlook of African Americans in the military. From his perspective, integration was "the best thing that could have happened" since, as he observed, it had the effect of changing the attitudes of black officers; they were now more personally responsible regarding their behavior and now had reasons to be more hopeful about future opportunities for them in the military.

Robinson's assignments were as a senior platoon leader and company executive officer, which, according to his account, were somewhat as a disappointment because he had been a company commander and battalion staff officer in Korea. However, it was made somewhat more bearable when he found out that his contemporaries had also similarly been assigned as company executive officers, not commanders. Before Robinson settled into his new assignment at Fort Campbell, he received some good news. What had been a disappointing assignment turned into an opportunity when he learned from his Regimental Commander, Colonel Davis, that he was being assigned as an instructor in the Airborne Department of the Infantry School at Fort Benning in Georgia. Expecting that his orders to Benning would come any day, he told Millie – to her disappointment -- not to think about even putting up pictures on their walls. Actually, the orders came three months later, with instructions to report in January 1954.

The selection of Robinson to the Airborne Department at Fort Benning was intentional since it was part of the Army's continuing efforts to integrate all units. Based upon someone's recommendation and for reasons – both unknown to him -- he was selected as a person of color to serve in this experimental role. Realizing that he was probably being carefully observed posed no problem to Robinson. Rather, he saw it as an opportunity to demonstrate his talents, which he did. For Millie, it meant that at least for a few years, she could now transform the officers quarters they were assigned into a real "home" for her and Robinson, including hanging pictures and home-cooked meals.

Initially, Robinson's instructional responsibilities at Benning were to teach air mobility and air transportability subjects, both of which had become increasingly important to the Army after the Korean Conflict. As his excellent instructional qualities became evident, Robinson was later assigned to the Advanced Airborne Committee to teach the advanced courses in Jump Master and Pathfinder subjects. It was during this assignment that he earned his Pathfinder patch. The specific purpose of the pathfinder course is to train parachutists to jump into enemy territory - before an assault begins - in order to mark landing, drop zones, and provide navigational assistance for aircraft and other support units. Although pathfinders who were sometimes referred to as "the first in, the last out," were used in World War II, the course was a new one in the Airborne Department. Robinson helped to write its curriculum and served as a Pathfinder Team Leader. Serving along with Robinson on the Pathfinder Committee was his friend, Joseph Clemons, who described him as an outstanding instructor, always scoring high on his performance.

Embracing the idea that instructors ought to be role models, Robinson went beyond just teaching the course. He went along with his students when they conducted practice pathfinder operations, which enabled him to determine their proficiency skills and thus grade their performance. Despite his competence as an instructor, there were still racial issues to be overcome. One incident he recalled involved a white student who was uncomfortable about having a black instructor.

> *"I remember my committee chief coming in after we had an airborne class come through and say, "Lieutenant Robinson, you have just been credited with directly influencing your first officer to quit." He was a lieutenant in the National Guard. He said he was quitting because he could not tolerate a colored officer correcting him during certain activities. My committee chief said, "That's the best thing that could have happened because with an attitude like that, we don't need him in the airborne." He was very happy to wash him out of the course."*

Robinson was not particularly offended by the officer's attitude toward him; he understood that even after desegregation of the military some racial intolerance toward blacks would linger. After all, it was still early in the 1950s and full acceptance of African Americans officers in positions of leadership was still evolving.

The Korean Conflict had also changed the way the Army viewed aviation, and Robinson would be a part of that change while at Fort Benning. Helicopters had been introduced in the latter phases of the war, primarily for medical evacuations. Now they were being viewed to be part of future tactical operations on the battlefield. While at the Airborne School, Robinson recognized the change, noting, "the biggest factor that impacted upon him was the recognition that there was a role for expanded Army Aviation." It was a strategic decision on the part of the Army that would have considerable impact in the Vietnam War.

As Robinson's duty at Fort Benning neared the end of three years, and having completed the Infantry Officers Advanced Course, he had hoped his assignment at the Airborne Department and his exemplary performance as an instructor there would lead to a bigger assignment with the 101st Airborne Division, the "Screaming Eagles," as it was known. It would have been a choice post, since the Division was one of the most prestigious and decorated units in the U.S. Army, having achieved early fame during the invasion of Normandy in World War II. The Division's elite status was only eclipsed by the 82nd Airborne Division.

When the list with the next assignment in the 101st was posted, his name was not on it. The hoped for assignment did not materialize. Only four of five of those in the Advance Course were expected to go to the 101st and he had expected to be one of them. Several of his classmates –Jack Hazelwood, Shy Meyer and Joe Clemons - however, did receive assignments with the 101st. Instead, what to him was a surprising development; Robinson was informed that he was being considered for a posting in the African country of Liberia.

Orders were orders and, as a good soldier, it was his duty to comply. While waiting for clearance from the State Department for the Liberian assignment, Robinson – now a Captain - was asked if he would consider going back to the Airborne School. He delayed responding to the offer, holding out for his preference to be a company commander in an Airborne Division. When that didn't materialize, Robinson was again asked to come back to the Airborne School, at least for a short time to work with the Pathfinder Committee in getting a new course started. It was a more appealing prospect than some other desk detail to which he might be assigned as an alternative to the Pathfinder Committee, so he voluntarily accepted the position and was there for two months while awaiting the finalization of the Liberian assignment. There was certain logic in Robinson's thinking when he accepted the interim assignment. Like most career-minded military men, he was always conscious that a good assignment, which he regarded the Pathfinder Committee to be, offered the opportunity to demonstrate the competence and leadership needed to move up in rank.

II

The brief stint with the Pathfinder Committee came to an end and in 1957, Robinson was assigned as a Training Officer in the United States Military Support Mission in Liberia, located on the Western coast of the African continent, bordered by Sierra Leone, Guinea, Cote d'Ivoire, and the Atlantic Ocean. It is small country with a population estimated to be about three million in 1950. The Support Mission's primary role involved training the Liberian Frontier Force, a small unit of about 2,000 men who were either assigned as presidential guards in the capital city of Monrovia, or they were spread out in small posts throughout the countryside. Although it was not an assignment of preferred choice on the part of Robinson, as a loyal and disciplined military man, he did not question it, even though he didn't understand the reasoning behind it.

As later events would show, the tour of duty in Liberia would have a special place in the life of the Robinson family, and it would provide him with a unique perspective on the African continent. Liberia was in the midst of undergoing major political changes, largely driven by the growing independence movements taking place on the continent. In fact, in the same year of Robinson's arrival on the African continent, Ghana was granted its independence by the United Kingdom, becoming the first sub-Saharan country to achieve that status. And by the end of 1960, eighteen other European colonies in Africa would achieve independence. This process would reshape the geo-political character of the entire continent. For a few years, Robinson would see this transformation take place. Perhaps, like other African Americans, he was pleased to see the beginning of the end of white domination of the African continent.

However, unlike many other countries in Africa, which had a long history of European colonization, Liberia had a unique historical development, primarily because of its long relationship to the United States. It was a relationship that extended back to the early 19th century when Liberia was formed and colonized by African Americans, with the aid of the American Colonization Society as a site for the resettlement of free blacks from North America and slaves granted freedom for the express purpose of immigrating to Liberia. By then, these prospective new emigrants had become convinced that the reality of their true freedom could never be achieved in America.

This elite group - who would become known as *Americo-Liberians* - would later establish in 1847 a republican form of government based on the United States, calling itself Liberia, meaning "*Land of the Free*." Although there were other indigenous ethnic groups inhabiting the region, the *Americo-Liberians* in time would dominate the cultural, social, economic and political life of the new country. Because of its long diplomatic relationship with the United States, in the early 20th century Liberia sought American help with its military organization. It was a relationship that would eventually lead to the establishment of the U. S. Military Support Mission to which Robinson had been assigned. With its location on the Atlantic Ocean, Liberia was important to the United States. As part of the Allied strategic and logistics plan, Roberts International Airport, built by U.S. personnel early in World War II, served as a refueling base for American war planes enroute to Europe for troop and materiel transport purposes or for bombing missions.

While the assignment was pending, Robinson admitted that he knew little about Liberia, and his own research did not generate much information. Unbeknownst to Robinson, there were two direct, historical connections between Liberia and his St. Louis roots. John Milton Turner, who was born a slave in St. Louis and was one of John Meachum's students on the "Floating Freedom School," and who later became a prominent attorney in St. Louis, was appointed in 1871 by President Ulysses S. Grant as Ambassador to Liberia. He was the first African American to represent the United States in any foreign country. In 1934, Lester Walton, also a native of St. Louis and a graduate of Sumner High School, was appointed as Ambassador to Liberia. His term ended in 1946, the year before Robinson entered West Point. Then, from a military perspective, Benjamin O. Davis, Sr., the first African American to achieve the rank of general, served as military attaché in Liberia during the years 1910-11.

The Liberian assignment was the first time as a couple that he and Millie lived together outside the United States. It would test their capacity to adjust as a married couple. Getting acclimated to the year round hot climate with heavy rainfalls from May to October was challenging, but the least of their initial worries. Even before they could begin to set up housekeeping in Liberia, like other military families, the Robinsons first had to secure certain amenities that were difficult to find in Liberia. For them, this meant having to have a freezer shipped from the United States, ordering frozen foods, which also had to be shipped from New York, and either bringing your own cooking stove or trying to find a second-hand one in Monrovia. In the Robinsons' case, Millie was able to find a used - but adequate for her needs - stove and bought it for $30.00. The house that they were assigned to live in leaked, and except for panoramic view of the Atlantic Ocean, it had few redeeming qualities – but it was home. Once settled, Millie - aside from taking care of the house - found time to affiliate with the Military Mission Wives Auxiliary where a major pre-occupation was playing bridge.

Things would change, however, and soon the house would become very much alive with baby tears, diaper changing, and a lot of love. It all started one day when a Liberian mother came into the Mission Office with a baby and was looking for someone to adopt her. Millie saw her and she described her as "the prettiest baby" one could imagine. The child was the offspring of a racially mixed couple. Childless and not certain of having one of their own, the Robinsons seized the opportunity and immediately began the process of adopting the baby whose name was Carol. Without the voluminous paper work often required for adoption in the United States, the process was handled by local officials and quickly expedited. Within a few weeks, the Robinsons were now parents.

The Liberian mission was staffed by a contingent of seven military personnel, four officers and three sergeants, all of whom were African American. Although it cannot be substantiated, this particular racial deployment pattern in Liberia was viewed by some African Americans in the military as "assignment by default," or what happened to black military officers when the Army couldn't find another place to send you. As with other assignments he was given that were not to his liking, he would not, however, question them *publicly*. On the other hand, in private conversations with his close friends, Robinson perceived that the Liberian assignment would ruin his career since he did not see it as particularly career enhancing.

His personal feelings aside, Robinson, in his usual professional manner, treated the Liberian assignment seriously and tried to make the experience as a Training Officer a meaningful one and do the best job he could at it. However, for some among the Liberian military corps, the training was not as valued as Robinson thought it should be. It was a conclusion he came to when one of the Liberian captains said to him, in an obvious reference to the country's economy, which was heavily dependent upon the export of natural rubber.

> *"Captain Robinson, I can't see why you get as excited as you do about getting us trained. We had World War I and Liberia gave rubber. We had World War II and Liberia gave rubber. If we have World War III, Liberia is going to give rubber."*

Rubber was, indeed, the country's primary source of wealth because of the 1926 concession of land to the American-owned Firestone Plantation Company. Rather than ignore the Liberian captain's rather cynical remarks, Robinson – in his usual calm manner – simply responded with the following strategic observation:

> "*You never know what might happen, especially with what's going on here in the continent of Africa. You are a member of the United Nations. The United Nations has certain responsibilities. Who knows when your President may say that he is going to give some forces to a UN command?*"

Little did Robinson realize, at the time, the prescient nature of his response. Just three years later in 1960, and only a few days after having been granted its independence from Belgium, a civil conflict broke out in its former colony known then as the Belgium Congo, a country with immense natural resources in copper, diamonds, and uranium. To mitigate the conflict, and hoping to avoid a full-scale civil war there, the United Nations – at the request of the Congo Prime Minister, Patrice Lumumba, sent a military force to the Congo. Following the UN authorization to commit troops, Liberian President Tubman let it be known that Liberia was prepared, if asked, to give forces to the UN Command which had been set up to oversee operations in the Congo. He was asked. And, as a good friend of the United States which had a strategic interest in containing the conflict, President Tubman made the decision to commit two battalions to the Congo conflict that lasted over a period of four years. That fact alone, Robinson had reasoned meant the training of the Liberian troops had its benefits despite the short and narrow-sightedness on the part of the Liberian captain.

When the Liberian assignment ended after two years, Robinson was delighted at the possibility of now getting an assignment to an airborne division, which is what he really wanted. To him, a new assignment was even more imperative since he let it be known that he never wanted to be in Liberia. In taking this position, he said, *"I felt I was there (Liberia) too early. Many of the other officers there were getting toward retirement. Many of them were very interested in some of the social activities that go with an assignment like that, which I had absolutely no interest in."*

The Liberian experience, however, was not without benefits to Robinson. It offered him the opportunity to learn about the important activities carried out by some of the other U.S governmental agencies with operations in Liberia. For example, United States Agency for International Development (USAID), provided assistance in the training of military and civilian police forces, and United States Information Agency (USIA) that provided Voice of America broadcasts throughout the African continent as well as the world. Most importantly, the Liberian assignment provided Robinson with the opportunity to reflect on what should be the role of the United States military in Africa and from a political perspective, what our relationship in general should be towards Africans.

> *"I think primarily our role should be to encourage stability there....I don't think we have an African policy when you speak quite frankly about it. I think our emphasis should be on trying to keep stability in the region and providing whatever kind of assistance we can. I think the best thing that we can do is to try to educate the military of the various countries by having*

them come to our schools....because when those officers come to the United States they learn a lot about our country and they can't help but gain some appreciation for the democratic type of values in the country, some of which may be a little bit foreign to them......

"I am not a proponent of the United States being a policeman for the world, but we need to develop a policy and take an interest in what is going on there (Africa), because it does have an impact on us. It has an impact on perceptions of the United States among the leaders of those countries and I think that is important."

We now know this observation on the part of Robinson, though it came years after his tour of duty in Liberia was not only appropriate, but also relevant for two reasons. First, the post-independence rise of one-party states in Africa, governed by dictatorial regimes, while creating an "image" of stability, has impaired the Continent's economic and social development. Second, while substantial American economic and military aid has been forthcoming to many African nations, the perception remained throughout much of the 1960s and 70s that the United States was the leader among the neo-colonists in the post-independence period seeking to exploit the vast resources of the newly independent countries. To support this view, many of the underdeveloped countries in Africa often cite the rise of U.S.-based multi-national corporations and their control of global markets.

Robinson acknowledged later that he was never asked by people in government when he had achieved a higher rank in the Army about his perspective of African-U.S. affairs, which he gained through his experience in Liberia and from later historical developments on the African continent. While not "personally" disappointed by this, he had expected otherwise.

III

When Robinson graduated from West Point in1951, he would have preferred being assigned to the 82nd Airborne Division, but if not, then any Airborne unit would have been acceptable. As it was, it was the 11th Airborne Division to which he was assigned; later assignment to the 82nd would come in December 1959, after the Liberian tour of duty. Undoubtedly, his early preference for the 82nd stemmed in large measure from the storied history of the division from the time it was first formed in August 1917, and as time would show, the 82nd would become one of the most legendary units in the annals of American military history. The aura surrounding the 82nd was compelling to Robinson. Known by its nickname "All-Americans" since its members came from all the states, the unit, which was then called the 82nd Infantry Division, immediately gained a reputation for courage and bravery during World War I when it engaged the German Army in several major campaigns. After a brief period following World War I when it was deactivated, the Division was called back into service during World War II and was redesignated the 82nd Airborne Division.

The Division participated in the campaign to invade Italy during World War II, and when the historic invasion of Normandy, France was launched on June 5-6, 1944 under the code name "Overlord" (referred to by the Allies as D-Day), paratroopers of the 82nd Airborne Division would be among the first to land and help to secure the area for the massive land invasion that would follow. Against huge losses of personnel and unfavorable weather conditions, the 82nd rose to the occasion and took control of Sainte-Mere-Eglise, a major

German communications hub, and then held it against counterattack by the Germans. After the surrender of Germany, the 82nd was ordered to Berlin for occupation duty, and in January 1946, returned to the United States and to Fort Bragg, North Carolina, which would become its permanent home.

So when the assignment to the 82nd was made known to Robinson in 1959, it was well received and clearly worth the wait – even though the position of a company commander in the Division was not initially forthcoming as he had hoped. It was not that he didn't ask for it; a company command position just was not what they had in mind for him - at least not then. Instead, he joined the 2nd Battle Group, 503rd Regiment and was assigned as the assistant S4 to help with logistics. Taking on the responsibilities of an assistant S4 was a bit deflating, especially when Robinson, now a senior captain, was confident that he could do just as good, if not a better job of commanding a company than those then in command positions.

The 2nd Battle Group was at the time commanded by Colonel George Blanchard, a consummate leader who had risen from the ranks of the District of Columbia National Guard from where he received an appointment to West Point. After graduating in the class of 1944, his remarkable career would include tours of duty as a platoon leader and a company commander in France and Germany, serving as an Assistant to the chairman of the Joint Chiefs of Staff, General Omar Bradley, and as a G-3 with the I Corps in Korea. Blanchard's subsequent military career would be marked by holding leadership positions during the Vietnam War where he advanced the use of helicopters in combat. Later, he would serve as commander of the United States Army, Europe.

Serving under Blanchard was the beginning of a relationship of mutual respect and admiration between the two that lasted throughout Robinson's career. He most admired the way Blanchard commanded the unit; doing things according to the procedures spelled out in the operations manual, and for his insistence upon excellence in performance. In addition to their common background as paratroopers, they shared a strong sense of caring for the well-being of the individual soldier.

> *"I don't think I ever admired any individual, certainly not at that stage of my career, anymore than I did General Blanchard when he was Commander of the 2nd Battle Group, 503rd, as a colonel. It was a real joy to serve under General Blanchard."*

Their mutual admiration, notwithstanding, Robinson continued nevertheless to express to Blanchard his preference for a company command position. However, with officers in the 503rd being replaced and their assignments being moved, the opportunity to command a company in the 2nd Battle Group was increasingly becoming a long shot. Robinson's persistence eventually paid off when the 2nd Battle Group in the 504th Regiment was activated and Robinson was assigned as the S4 officer, and then later moved to the position of assistant G4 for the division.

The Division Chief of Staff was Colonel F.K. Mearns, with whom Robinson also developed a good working relationship. And as he did with Blanchard, Robinson made it clear to Mearns that he – now a senior captain and one with prior command experience -- preferred being a company commander rather than having an assignment at the Division Headquarters. It didn't take Mearns long to get the message and he said to Robinson, *"If you want a company, I'm sure that you can get a company."* With Mearns' repeated intercessions on Robinson's behalf with other Battle Group Commanders, eventually a position opened in the 504th and Robinson was given command of E Company, 2nd Battle Group, 504th Regiment, 82nd Airborne Division.

Robinson's experience with getting action on his preference was instructive, and in the following years of his military career, he would learn that if you wanted a particular assignment, you had to ask for it directly or someone in a command position would have to ask for you. In either case - particularly the latter – the assignment would determine if you had become a part of what some military observers have called the "old boy network."

During what would be a two-year assignment with the 82nd from 1960-1962, the nation was at peace and Robinson's activities as a company commander with the Division consisted of training exercises, conducting mock operations in places such as Panama. He also conducted some large-scale maneuvers like the Swift Strike exercises; all designed to strengthen the Army's aviation capacity from being just transporters to tactical deployment capability. But, for Robinson, two memorable events that occurred during the two-year assignment stood out. On January 20, 1961 President John F. Kennedy, whose youthful magnetism (then the youngest to be elected to this office) and call for sacrifices at home and for resoluteness abroad, fueled excitement and promise of a "New Frontier" was inaugurated as the nation's 35th President. The 82nd Airborne Division was a participant in the inaugural parade. Despite the bitterly cold day, the emotional impact of this historic event on Robinson was apparent:

> *"It was one of the most spectacular events that I've been involved in. We did that, we were in his parade. My battle group went up for that. If you have participated in something like that, the amount of pride that you have walking down Pennsylvania Avenue saluting your*

Commander-in-Chief, it is difficult to describe the feeling you get. Especially in this case with President Kennedy. Standing at his side was General Gavin, who, of course, had been the wartime commander of the 82nd and was later to be appointed Ambassador to France. As we marched down, we could hear the speaker talking about the division and the fact that it was General Gavin's old outfit. But just the sense of pride you get – it's unmatched."

Robinson certainly didn't realize it, but there was a good possibility that the President "saw" him. In a personal memoir of the Kennedy Presidency, Arthur Schlesinger, Jr. wrote the following about how remarkably observant the President was throughout the parade:

"And the new President himself savored every moment of it. He watched the parade from beginning to end, saluting the marchers and applauding the floats. Noting that there were no ***Negroes*** (bold mine) *in the Coast Guard contingent, he demanded an immediate explanation and was shocked to discover that the Coast Guard Academy had no Negro students, a condition he ordered changed forthwith."*

The new President brought a changed atmosphere to Washington and a hopeful and expectant nation awaited his leadership at home and abroad. To capture the minds and energies of the young, he established the Peace Corps and encouraged them to volunteer in areas of economic hardship around the world. He would signal his resoluteness towards the Soviet Union by visiting West Germany where he proclaimed to enthusiastic crowds, "Ich bin ein Berliner." ("I am a Berliner").

It was in the aftermath of these and other initiatives that the second event involving the President took place during Robinson's early years with the 82nd. It was no less spectacular than the inauguration.

The President, never having seen an entire division and all its equipment, handpicked the 82nd for an official visit. He had assumed the presidency during the height of the Cold War, when the danger of nuclear war with the Soviet Union was still, albeit, a remote possibility, yet he feared the prospect of one, even with U.S. superiority in its nuclear arsenal. So it was not surprising that early in his administration, Kennedy, in an effort to raise "the threshold for the use of atomic weapons," proposed that the United States and NATO increase their conventional arms to levels that could stop Soviet forces in the event of an act of aggression against our European allies. The 82nd would give the President a firsthand look at a "conventional" unit.

To accommodate the President's wishes, Major General Theodore John Conway, who was then Commander of the 82nd, decided to have a full display of an Airborne Division, and a demonstration of how it could be deployed. He divided the Division into five groups, each with different uniforms to display their capability of deployment wherever they were needed. For possible Europe deployment, one group was in the traditional fatigues, for possible deployment to Vietnam, the uniform was jungle camouflage fatigues, and for a desert operation, it was desert camouflage. The two other groups were either dressed in winter uniforms or white ski suits (and carried skis) to demonstrate their arctic capability.

When President Kennedy arrived for the visit on that hot summer day, the battle groups were smartly dressed in their uniforms and equipped with special gear, including parachute gear, as Conway wanted. It was an impressive display put on by the Division for the President. Later, upon reflection on

President Kennedy's interest, Robinson said: "*We all thought that it (referring to the visit) marked the beginning of the comeback for our Army as far as our conventional forces were concerned, and the emphasis that would now be placed on conventional forces.*" Historical evidence suggests that what the President really wanted to see occur was disarmament, especially in light of the Soviet resumption of nuclear testing. The danger he saw was eloquently stated in a speech the President gave to the U.N. General Assembly in September 1962.

> *"Mankind must put an end to war – or war will put an end to mankind. Let us call a truce to terror. The goal of disarmament is no longer a dream – it is a practical matter of life or death. The risks inherent in disarmament pale in comparison to the risks inherent in an unlimited arms race."*

The impact of a visit to the 82nd by the Commander in Chief was, like the Inaugural Parade, an experience of a lifetime from Robinson's perspective. To be so close to the President of the United States, to see him in person, and to hear him speak was something few in the military ever experience.

> *"It was spectacular. The troops were in front, right along the edge of the runway with all of the equipment to the rear. There was more excitement. The fact that the troops worked for days to get ready for this, drawing the equipment out, moving out from the division area at early morning for a layout that was to take place in early afternoon meant absolutely nothing to them. They were so enthusiastic about being able to put themselves*

and the unit on display for the President. It was really spectacular."

President Kennedy gave a speech that day in which he talked about his administration's departure from the Eisenhower/Dulles policy of massive deterrents, including nuclear strikes, to repel aggression. That policy, he said was being replaced by a policy of what he called flexible response "*by strengthening and modernizing the nation's ability to wage non-nuclear war,*" which is why he had a strong interest in conventional warfare capability. Robinson understood the President's focus on conventionality, but he admitted later that he was so caught up with the entire activity of that day that he didn't remember the speech all that much.

CHAPTER FIVE

PATHWAYS TO SENIOR COMMAND

I

Robinson's initial assignment with the 82nd ended in 1962. He would then begin what would become a series of programs in advanced military training. From the time dating back to his teenage years when he was a Boy Scout and Senior Class President, Robinson exhibited early signs of leadership. He not only embraced the Boy Scout Motto, "Be Prepared" but it became a standard by which he led and motivated others. His personal leadership philosophy *"Always do the best job that you can at whatever you do,"* became the creed by which he lived and served throughout his military career. Over a thirty-four year period, he held several staff and command positions in the United States Army. These required leadership skills that he first acquired at West Point and later through both troop assignments, academic and professional training in highly competitive military service schools and at a university.

Robinson had other interpersonal characteristics, which helped to shape his working style with people, and helped define him as a leader. His colleagues knew him as a quiet person, not given to boisterous displays of intemperance in speech or actions. Lieutenant Colonel Duane E. Hardesty once served as a captain under his command and described Robinson's leadership style as personable, always having time for everybody, and with deep and sincere concern for those around him. Lieutenant Colonel John "Red" Leffler, a West Point classmate described him by his qualities of honesty and integrity, a man of his word.

"Do the right thing" and doing it with attention to ethical considerations was almost instinctive with Robinson. His wife, who knew him best, of course, described Robinson as a man who would rather quietly sit and talk out problems than castigate a person for having made a mistake. To him, a mistake was a "teachable moment, an opportunity to learn from them." He was savvy and smart, with a good measure of self-confidence in his ability to get the job done, whatever it was.

With these characteristics evident, Robinson began a process of advanced leadership training, beginning with specialized training in 1963 when he was selected to attend the United States Army Command and General Staff College (C&GSC) at Fort Leavenworth, Kansas. Located in the northeast corridor of the state and overlooking the Missouri River, the grounds of the college are campus-like in their setting with abundant open green space. Fort Leavenworth was established in 1827 and is the oldest active Army post west of the Mississippi River. As a student of history, Robinson was undoubtedly aware that it was at Fort Leavenworth in 1866, a year after the end of the Civil War, that the U.S. Congress authorized the formation of four black regiments. They were the 24th and 25th Infantry Regiments and the 9th and 10th Cavalry Regiments; the latter two were deployed to fight in the western wars against Native American tribes in the late 19th century. The Indians called these all black regiments "Buffalo Soldiers," allegedly for the fierce fighting during encounters with them. Legend also has it that the Buffalo Soldiers reminded the Indians of the large and ferocious buffalo herds that roamed the western plains. Myth or not, for their bravery, the Buffalo Soldiers earned a place in American military history.

The Army C&GSC is a graduate school for United States (and foreign) military leaders and a highly renowned center of excellence in the study of military operations of division and higher-level units. Robinson's selection was meritorious and highly competitive as evidenced by the fact that only about fifty percent of eligible officers are selected. The college educates and trains intermediate-level officers from the Army and other services to function in the full spectrum of multi-national operations as field-grade commanders and senior staff officers. Considered the "intellectual center of the Army," and to some the "Harvard" of the post- graduate military training institutions, the course of studies at the College is rigorous and demanding. Graduates of the college are expected to at some point in their career assume command of no less than a division or serve at an even higher rank. Clearly, those on the selection committee had determined that Robinson met those criteria.

Leavenworth is a small city, and there was not much to do there outside of the post to distract Robinson's attention from the reason he was there. Besides, he had family responsibilities- continuing and emerging - to take up any non-academic time he might have. Two years prior to coming to Fort Leavenworth, the Robinsons had been seriously thinking about adopting a second child, particularly a son who would be a companion to their daughter Carol. The adoption process had started when they were at Fort Bragg, but without success. They continued expressing their interest in adoption when they arrived at Fort Leavenworth, and shortly there afterwards they were told by adoption services in the nearby county of Jackson that there was a four-month old baby boy named Bruce who was available.

After meeting with the adoption agency and seeing the child – who just happened to be Caucasian -- they were able to take him home. Though it took several months before the final adoption papers were signed, for all practical purposes, the Robinsons were parents for the second time, with another child to love and to rear. While white couples frequently adopted a child of a different race, it was very uncommon in those days for African American couples to do so. But the Robinsons were an uncommon couple and perhaps nothing speaks more about the warm and embracing character of both Robinson and Millie than adopting two children, especially one of a different ethnic background than theirs. They understood that the capacity to love a child transcends race or parentage.

After a grueling thirty-eight weeks of training and instruction, participation in war games and a heavy dose of military history, Robinson graduated from the C&GSS in 1963, joining a long list of other illustrative military graduates including Generals Dwight D. Eisenhower, Omar H. Bradley, and George S. Patton. During his time at Fort Leavenworth, Robinson was promoted to the rank of Major.

From Fort Leavenworth, Robinson's advanced academic training path would take him back east to the Graduate School of Public and International Affairs at the University of Pittsburgh where he had been admitted in September 1963 to study international affairs. Like its own graduate schools, academic training at traditional American universities was also part of a continuing emphasis of the military to ensure its future leaders were prepared professionally and academically for a changing world. For those officers expected to rise in the ranks, a graduate degree, preferably in international relations, was tantamount to being a requirement.

But unlike the semi-rustic setting of Fort Leavenworth, the University of Pittsburgh was an urban campus located in the cultural heart of the city and physically dominated by its majestic forty-story Cathedral of Learning. On the first floor of this unique structure was the Commons Room surrounded by classrooms that had been constructed in the traditional architectural styles of many of the diverse nationalities that populated the city. GSPIA, the shorthand term used to refer to the school, had been in existence only for eight years and was housed in cramped spaces in a former apartment building that had been converted into classrooms and offices for faculty and administration. Bruce Hall, as the building was named, housed a good public affairs library, which helped to ease student research pursuits. The selection of GSPIA was a good choice on the part of Army as the School was quickly gaining a reputation for academic excellence in preparing its students for public service careers. Fortunately, Robinson would not be alone, as four other Army officers – Arthur Pence Jr., Lorne Black, Corky Corcoran, and Arthur Brown, Jr. - were also admitted to the School in 1963. He was the only African American officer in this group.

Though he was many miles away from St. Louis, the city of Pittsburgh has some characteristics that reminded him of his birthplace. Pittsburgh was an industrial city much like St. Louis and the early growth of both was influenced by river transportation. In the case of St. Louis, it was the Mississippi. For Pittsburgh, it was the Allegheny and the Monongahela that merge to become the Ohio at their confluence, which is called the Point. Perhaps, most important to Robinson – being a fan of baseball - it was the home of the Pittsburgh Pirates with whom his beloved St. Louis Cardinals were rivals in the National Baseball League. Moreover, the Pirates then played their home games at Forbes Field located a block away from where he would be attending classes. No doubt, the field's proximity was an inviting escape venue from the rigors of the classroom, if ever time would permit it.

However, getting settled in Pittsburgh and finding a suitable house to rent posed an initial problem since Pittsburgh was then largely a residentially segregated city. This made it difficult for Robinson to quickly find a house he wanted for his family. Under the illusion that racial barriers in accessing rental housing were something one would expect to encounter in St. Louis, but not in Pittsburgh, he continued to pursue his search. Eventually he and his wife did find a house to rent on Travella Boulevard in the predominantly African American Lincoln-Lemington neighborhood. It was a neat two-story house tucked away on a somewhat secluded street where other middle-class and professional African American families were living, including Alex Hawkins, a professor in the School of Social Work at the University of Pittsburgh, Luther Johnson, a well-known photographer, and Carl Arter, a local musician.

Life as a graduate student took on a patterned routine. Millie got Carol ready for day care at Corpus Christi Roman Catholic School located a few blocks from their home, and then returned to care for their infant son Bruce. On a daily basis, Robinson would take an early morning bus (which had a convenient stop just one block away from their home) to the University where he would spend his days in intensive study. With their common military background, the five Army officers would take turns having their families in their home for dinner, after which the men would retire to a separate room to discuss their school projects. These officers had been, carefully selected of course, and they held their own against their younger classmates, many of whom had some decidedly different views about the conduct of U.S. foreign affairs.

A former professor at the school, Alex Weilenmann, who taught many of the international affairs courses in which Robinson and the other officers were enrolled, described them as very good students. As expected, they were disciplined and had a clear academic mission to accomplish since the program had to be completed within the period set by the Army. In speaking about his classmates, Arthur Brown, who like Robinson would later have a distinguished military career and achieve the rank of four-star general, described Robinson as the "easiest going, never rattled or overly concerned about the workload and, among the group of officers, always the one most prepared."

Robinson was a consummate and disciplined student who always wanted to be prepared for his classes. This attribute was evident by an occasion that his wife recalls. An evening after three months of not having gone out, she suggested he should take a "break" and they should go to see a movie. Since she was largely confined to caring for children, Millie also needed a break. He agreed to her suggestion, but half-way through the movie, Robinson nudged Millie and said, "I don't feel comfortable being here, I have so much work (referring to school assignments) I should be doing." As an understanding wife, she consented to his request and so they left before the movie was over.

After one and a half years of course work which covered classes in Diplomacy, International Relations Theory, and Asian Political Systems, among others, Robinson completed the requirements for a Master's Degree in International Affairs, including writing a Thesis, which was entitled: *U.S. Alliance Policy, Southeast Asia Treaty Organization (SEATO): An Appraisal.* The Thesis was a systematic analysis of the overall alliance policy of the United States, with a focus on military aspects of the SEATO alliance, which was intended to provide for the collective defense of the region against the surging tide of Communist aggression.

Robinson's academic discipline paid off, and in 1964, he graduated from the Graduate School of Public and International Affairs with a Masters Degree in International Affairs. Considering the demands of being a full-time student, the constant juggling of family and home responsibilities, and the highly competitive environment of the School, Robinson earned close to a B+ average.

During the last several months of his academic years at the University of Pittsburgh, Robinson was alerted to some surprising information about what might be in his immediate future. He learned he was being considered for an assignment as an instructor in the Social Science Department at West Point, which at the time was chaired by Colonel Abe Lincoln. Robinson was excited about that prospect, which, if it came to fruition, would position him to become the first African American in that Department. Unfortunately, Robinson was not selected. He was obviously disappointed, but not dispirited. The reality was that West Point wasn't quite ready to have an African American on the instructional faculty. In reflecting upon this missed opportunity and other similar experiences he would later encounter, he would prophetically say, "When a door closes; a window opens."

As his later instructional competence would demonstrate, he probably would have been an excellent teacher at the Academy. He had a zest for learning and the skills for challenging others to realize their full potential. However, without the foresight of knowing the path his long-term military career would eventually lead, he did not realize that not having the West Point academic assignment probably worked to his advantage since instructors at the Academy seldom rise above the rank of Colonel.

II

With the option of going to West Point no longer on the table, Robinson wanted to be immediately assigned to a unit where he could utilize his graduate training in international affairs. He thought that might mean being assigned to be on a utilization tour. But the Army had other plans for him, and he was assigned to a three-year tour of duty in the Infantry branch of the Office of Personnel Operations on the staff of the Department of the Army in Washington, D.C. In that capacity, he was responsible for managing the large cadre of officers on matters of eliminations, separations, adverse actions and promotions. Perhaps to his surprise, it turned out to be an interesting assignment, and he reasoned that no matter what you think about the appropriateness of the assignment, each one has some opportunities to advance your career. He would later note the Personnel Operations assignment provided him with an administrative experience and some extraordinarily valuable insight that was useful later when he was in a command position that required sensitivity to personnel issues.

A critical and important component of the work of the Office of Personnel is to ensure the Army has in place the quality and number of officers, in particular, which might be needed. Within two and half years of Robinson's assignment, the buildup of forces in Vietnam began; heightening the responsibilities of the Office of Personnel as the number of officers coming into the commission ranks that the branch had to manage increased significantly. For him, one of the unpleasant aspects of the office during the Vietnam buildup was denying resignations to officers based on need for their continued service. As the scale of the war in Vietnam continued to escalate, even more troops were becoming necessary to counter the military strength of North Vietnam. It would not be long before Robinson would find himself in that war.

CHAPTER SIX

THE VIETNAM WAR AND AFTERWARDS

I

From the end of World War II through the 1970s, the relationship between the United States and the Soviet Union has been described as the "Cold War;" a period marked by United States efforts to contain the spread of Soviet-dominated Communism. Nowhere was this more apparent than in Southeast Asia where, since the 1950s, the Democratic Republic of Vietnam, recognized by communist nations as the government of Vietnam, had been engaged in conflict with the French-backed State of Vietnam, based in Saigon. That conflict over time would bring about United States military involvement in what would become the Vietnam War. The decision to enter the conflict stemmed from the Gulf of Tonkin Resolution passed by the U.S. Congress on August 10, 1964, which authorized President Lyndon B. Johnson, without a formal declaration of war, to use military force in Southeast Asia to protect American national interest. As one authority on American diplomacy noted, Johnson "believed (as had Truman and Eisenhower before him) that preventing a communist victory in Vietnam was a vital American interest"- despite the lack of clarity as to what really constituted American interest.

While conflicting views about the wisdom of entering the conflict were widespread throughout the United States, nevertheless, by July 1965, a major increase in American troops in Vietnam was already underway and the numbers would continue to grow in the following four years. It was a decision based upon the Johnson premise that "the necessary victory could be achieved only by the swift and massive use of military power against North Vietnam." Unfortunately, as history would show, Johnson' premise was untenable, unattainable, and costly.

If the impending engagement in the Far East was not enough to incite and consume the passions of Americans, then certainly the civil rights movement to end racial discrimination at home, which intensified in the mid 1960s, added more fuel to those passions. Race rioting during late July 1967 in Detroit, which led Michigan's Governor George Romney to declare the city in a "state of insurrection," heightened concerns that the face of the Civil Rights Movement was changing. The situation in Detroit fueled fear that race riots in other inner-city neighborhoods would follow and would lead to unprecedented chaos and violence in cities across the country. Ironically, the very unit that Robinson would later head – the 82nd Airborne Division, then under the command of Lieutenant General John Throckmorton, was called to duty in Detroit to restore civil order.

For many African Americans, the Vietnam conflict, commencing when it did during the height of the Civil Rights Movement, was a source of considerable ambiguity. The movement's acknowledged leader, Martin Luther King, Jr., chastised the nation for its willingness to spend thirty-five billion dollars a year to fight, in his words, "an unjust, evil war in Vietnam", but was reluctant to spend billions of dollars take care of those at home who needed help. It was an indirect, but clear, reference to the plight of the poor in America who were disproportionately people of color. Some of the more radicalized voices in the black community considered the war strictly political, and if drafted, urged African Americans to "stand up and say I will not follow law and order, I will follow my own conscience."

It was in the midst of this turbulent political and social environment that Robinson, now a Lieutenant Colonel, was posted to Vietnam, where he initially served as G-4 (Assistant Chief of Staff, Logistics) with the First Cavalry Division. Whatever personal views Robinson had towards the Detroit riot or the legitimacy of black grievances and rising militancy that fueled the situation, Vietnam was not the place to express them. Like other African American soldiers in that combat zone, he was there because he believed as Wallace Terry, author of *Bloods: An Oral History of the Vietnam War by Black Veterans, "that America was guaranteeing the sovereignty of the democratically constituted government of South Vietnam and halting the spread of communism in Southeast Asia."*

Like some other assignments that Robinson had been given during his career thus far, if he were given the choice, serving as a G-4 would not have been his preference. When he knew the Vietnam assignment was imminent, he had hopes of going to the Division to serve as commander of a battalion, and if not a commander, then he hoped for an assignment as a G-1 in the personnel area. His preferred choice was not the plan for his initial deployment in Vietnam. Rather, Robinson was informed that it was decision of General John J. Tolson, Commander of the 1st Cavalry Division, to have incoming officers first work in a staff position and then, if he decided mid-way during their tour they were ready, assign them to a command position.

As had been exemplified throughout his career – even when the assignment was not what he expected or wanted, Robinson, when assigned as the G4, took it as yet another challenge, with a determination to do the best job he could. From a logistics perspective, this meant spending time in helicopters to see how resupply operations were conducted, visiting battalion units in the combat zone to determine what kind of support they had and what they needed, and setting up supply locations to cover the needs of a division spread over a wide area. The Vietnam War, as Robinson knew, was the first large combat test of the air mobility concept that envisaged the use of Army aerial vehicles to assure the balance of mobility, firepower, intelligence, support and command, and control. Since the learning process of how to employ the air mobility concept was still is progress, the actual operation of it became a challenge for Robinson – from a logistics perspective. In the end, however, air mobility would prove to be an invaluable deployment strategy as the war progressed.

Anxious to get closer to combat in a command position, throughout his time in the G4 position, Robinson would frequently go to Tolson's Chief of Staff and make known his availability – at any point – to assume a position as a battalion commander. In February of 1968, Robinson's desire for a battalion commander position came to fruition – in a somewhat amusing way. General Richard Erby, who had replaced General Tolson as Acting Commander of the 1st Cavalry Division, asked Robinson if he had been told by Tolson that he going to take command of a battalion. Robinson responded that he had not been so informed. General Erby replied, "Well, I will ask you a question. How would you like to be the mayor of Phan Thiet?" Robinson responded, "I'd love to be the mayor of Phan Thiet," knowing that it just happened to be the site where the 2nd Battalion was operating.

His wish was granted, but he wasn't going to be the "mayor" of Phan Thiet; rather on February 1, 1968 – after a stint of six months in the G4 position, Robinson took command of the 2nd battalion in the 7th Cavalry Regiment, First Cavalry Division, replacing Lieutenant Colonel Joe Griffen. The date of the change of command would be long remembered by Robinson since just the day before – in the early hours of

January 31, the Tet Offensive – a coordinated attack by the North Vietnamese and the Viet Cong (The National Front for the Liberation of South Vietnam) – was launched throughout South Vietnam.

The Tet Offensive would last until September 1968. Often called one of the greatest and bloodiest military campaigns in United States history, the Tet Offensive would mark a major turning point in the war, with some 50,000 North Vietnamese and over 7,000 United States and South Vietnamese killed or wounded. So horrific was the death count, especially for the North Vietnamese, that one military person would later observe, "*In all the wars I've been in I've never seen so many dead people stacked up.*"

In the early months of the Offensive, Robinson's battalion, which would become a part of the 3rd Brigade, was involved in several operations. One notable operation was called "*Street Without Joy,*" a stretch of Road 1 along the central Annam coast running along the west coast of Vietnam. The area was so named by the French soldiers during the First Indochina War in 1953 when the French suffered heavy casualties in an effort to reduce the threat from Communist units. The labeling of the area "*Street Without Joy*" would become so infamous that it later became the title of a book by Bernard Fall, which after it was published in 1961, would become one of the best-known expose's of the Indochina War.

As operational plans were being discussed for addressing the then present threat in the "*Street of Joy*" area, Robinson's battalion was assigned the mission of bringing the area under control. The route was heavily sympathetic to the North Vietnamese Army. His battalion, though it was subsequently able to bring the area under control, was often the object of sniper fire from insurgents operating in the area. It was a difficult combat operation, leading Robinson to make the following observation about the difference between fighting in the Korean War and Vietnam,

> *"We knew who the enemy was in Korea, essentially it was anybody north of where we were. In Vietnam we knew who the uniformed enemy was as far as the North Vietnamese were concerned, but we didn't know who the little old lady in tennis shoes was, who might be operating a hand held mortar or firing a sniper weapon at you. We didn't know who was who because we were really involved in insurgency operations.....An area that you thought you had totally pacified one day may turn up to be a hot bed of enemy activity the next day."*

Robinson's analysis of the way combat was conducted– at least on the part of a guerrilla army that numbered tens of thousands - affirmed a description of this type of war made by Henry Kissinger, who was U.S. Secretary of State during part of the Vietnam War. As an astute observer of diplomacy and war, he held the view that Vietnam was a guerilla war and difficult to execute as "the guerilla army wins as long as it can keep from losing; it continues to engage in hit-and-run tactics for a long time even with greatly diminished forces."

Even that assessment did not fully describe the guerilla character of the Vietnam War, especially when the guerillas were able to draw upon support from the local population. It was situations like this that led Staff Sergeant Don F. Browne, who served in Vietnam from 1967 to 1968, to recall the following episode:

> *"When we passed through those villages, we really had to watch out for the kids. They would pick up arms and shoot at you. And we had to fire right back. When we*

> *were going out from an operation not very far from Vung Tau, we went through a hamlet we were told was friendly. Quite naturally, you see the women and children. Never see the men. The men were out conducting the war. We had hooked up with some Army guys, so it was about a company of us. As soon as we got about a half mile out down the road, we got hit from the rear. Automatic gunfire. It's the women and children. They just opened up. And a couple of our guys got wasted."*

Despite the "unconventional" combat in which he was engaged, once Robinson's battalion had pacified the area near Hue. The 2nd Squadron, 17th Cavalry, 101st Airborne Division, which was commanded by his friend, Lieutenant Colonel Julius Becton, Jr., was ordered to take relief of his battalion. One afternoon while sitting outside Robinson's command site, the two men discussed the military situation in the area, and when Robinson was asked by Becton about any contact with the enemy, he replied: "*A piece of cake, Julius. No real problems. No activity up here, everything is just pacified, and peaceful. We have everything under control."* Becton replied, "*Great Roscoe, this is going to be a joy, because we have been having a hell of a fight down south. We're looking forward to taking a break.*"

Robinson's description of the situation would soon change when Becton was in command, as within the first twenty-four hours, intense fighting broke out and continued every few days for the next sixty days. Becton's task of holding the area and keeping it under control was successful, but the battles continued until Robinson's battalion returned to occupy their position. Later in life, both Robinson and Becton, who would later become a Lieutenant General, would reminisce and even laugh about the exchange of the command and the differences in the level of fighting each experienced.

The second major operation in which Robinson's battalion was involved was called Operation Delaware, which began on the 19th of April 1968 and lasted for approximately one month. The operation was centered in the A Shau Valley – a narrow stretch of land running north-south along the Laotian and Cambodian borders, with 5,000-foot mountains on one side and a dense jungle on the other. The valley was strategically important to the North Vietnamese and the Viet Cong as it was interspersed with an elaborate system of roads and paths used to transport their troops from the north to the south, infamously named the Ho Chi Minh Trail. Sparsely populated, the area was virtually a sanctuary for the North Vietnam army, and with huge supply depots used as a staging area for preparing attacks against South Vietnam coastal provinces. The battle for control of the A Shau Valley was a major undertaking under the direction of Major General John Tolson. Robinson's battalion was tasked with going into a major North Vietnam logistics base in the Valley, which was heavily fortified with anti-aircraft weapons. This required the clearing of a landing zone, using helicopter landings carrying personnel equipped with chain saws to enable safe and fortified landing areas to bring in troops.

Encountering dense jungle, adverse weather conditions, and unseen enemies, Robinson described the Delaware Operation as a "very difficult" one. It was also a costly operation as several helicopters crashed either upon landing or upon take-off. His unit was able to uncover and destroy supply caches and weapons. Robinson's battalion, with massive air and land support of the 1st Cavalry Division, did manage to deny the use of the Valley to the North Vietnamese Army for a time. However, since Operation Delaware was not completely successful and definitive, control of the A Shau Valley continued to be problematic and would be followed by other operations, most notably, the battle for "Hamburger Hill" (Dong Ap Bia) in May 1969.

Throughout the Vietnam War, amidst the growing and bitter anti-war protests, the media clamored for news about the course of the war and the attitudes of those serving. Robinson would have an occasion in the midst of Operation Delaware to respond the interest of the media - albeit reluctantly. Upon receiving a directive from division headquarters, he was told to allow a news crew from a British company called Granada Productions, which intended to make a film, to come to his battalion and speak with some of his men. To make the filming as "painless" as possible, Robinson assigned the crew to cover A Company, the last unit going into the A Shau Valley, which he did to lessen the possibility of the crew encountering any stiff action. The filming with A Company took place over several days and was, of course, uncensored. Upon viewing the film for the first time, which was shortly after he had left the Battalion command, Robinson expressed ambivalent feelings about the film.

> "*I reviewed it with a great deal of apprehension, I guess, because I had no idea the type of footage that they had made of the comments that my soldiers had made. So as I watched that film, I was very proud of my soldiers, because they made comments that you would hope that a young soldier would make about his responsibility to his country. They were there because it happened to be in the best interest of the United States for them to be there. They had no reservations about what their mission was all about and on and on in that theme.*

> "*Notwithstanding what I said about my soldiers, the type of shots they made in this case.....Just the selection of the background music they used ---anti-war music as a background –they took some shots that I thought were very unfortunate of some of our casualties. That did come through, and how the press could use what they wanted to show the public. The story they wanted to present---this does come through. Obviously their anti-war attitudes were apparent when you look at the film, but they still couldn't change what my soldiers said about their role in Vietnam.*"

The Vietnam War is regarded as the first major war in which television played a crucial role in shaping public opinion. Robinson, like other high-ranking military officers and those under their command, was well aware of the anti-war movement and the role certain segments of the press took in opposition to the war. Across the country, news accounts increased about the growing number of American casualties, which by 1968 had reached 130,000 – dead or wounded. Open criticism of the war would soon ensue, coming from major newspapers as the *Wall Street Journal,* the New York *Post,* and the St. Louis *Dispatch.* In the midst of this spiraling opposition – from both the press and the public - whatever Robinson might have felt "privately" about the war and American policy; he kept his thoughts and his political views to himself - in keeping with the honored tradition of respecting civilian authority over the military. Appropriately so, he believed: if asked, the military can advise, but it is up to the Commander-in-Chief to decide. Moreover, he understood that public opinion was always a concern during wars regardless of the legitimate reasons why they were being fought. Certainly, that was the case throughout the 20th century. But what bothered him most was that he knew that some of the members of the press corps were looking to sensationalize or were reporting out of context. The "truth," he reasoned, is often the first casualty of war.

Robinson recalled an operation when one of his companies was on the ground when a village had been set afire and all the cameras of the press were focused on a burning hut, which, in his view, had nothing to do with the operation. The reality of the war in Vietnam, however, was different as huts and crops were intentionally burned by American forces when there was a tactical necessity to do. As one young officer who served in the Vietnam War candidly and without apology said about a village, his men encountered during an operation: "*We burned down the thatched huts, starting the blaze with Ronson and Zippo cigarette lighters....I had no qualms about what we were doing.*"

"Search and destroy" missions like the one described by this officer were common during the Vietnam War. Some of these missions, however, had disastrous consequences as the one that later became known as the My Lai Massacre on March 16, 1968. It was a village in the South Vietnam which was heavily mined and where the Viet Cong were deeply entrenched. When the men of Charlie Company, 11th Brigade entered My Lai, the shooting began, resulting in over 300 apparently unarmed women, children and the elderly being killed.

Even if combat incidents as burning huts could be justified as a tactical necessity, Robinson nevertheless concluded that focusing on the burning hut was seized upon by the media since it would make the "best copy" to be shown back home on the 6:00 o'clock evening news and only further inflame the opposition. It was incidents like this why Robinson preferred to distance himself from some of the prevailing and often negative sentiments by avoiding the press whenever he could – even though he recognized the military's responsibility to the press in an open society. Further, he understood that along with equality of opportunity and freedom of speech, freedom of the press had deep roots in American society since the founding days of the Republic. Nor should he have been surprised that the oft-times tensions between the military and the media during periods of war or conflict would surface during the Vietnam War. Tension between the two institutions was not a new phenomenon. The source of that tension is inevitable because each – the military and the media – have a different mission. For the military, the mission is to win; for the media, the mission is to ostensibly seek and find the truth and report it.

Despite his understandable reluctance to engage with the press, Robinson – given his knowledge of U.S. military history – also understood that there will be opposition to any war (as was also the case with the Korean War in which he had served), given the horrors and pain associated with them. Schooled as he was in the nature of war, Robinson understood as long as nations compete for territory, where there are conflicting and rival political ideologies at stake, and when control over natural resources are a consideration, that war was an inevitable and unpleasant reality of human existence. Quite possibly, from his studies at the West Point, he was reminded of the observation of the 19th century military philosopher Carl Von Clausewicz that "war is nothing but the continuation of political intercourse."

That understanding, notwithstanding, rather than directly engage with the press, Robinson would use his Public Affairs Officer as a source of communications with the media. Allowing information to come from someone trained in media communications was a wise and pragmatic decision on the part of Robinson. His avoidance of direct personal contact with the press, however, was not limited to periods of combat, but it was a stance he took throughout his career, and, as he reasoned, it was safer to do it that way. Besides, he simply disliked giving interviews:

> "*I have always taken the view that if you give an interview and it doesn't go the way you want it to go, you have nobody to blame but yourself, because you are the one who agreed to the interview. We all know that some of the members of press corps are looking to sensationalize; they are looking to report out of context. I know that is not the way all of them operate. I would say if you know an individual and you have dealt with him before, it would change the way you would deal with that particular individual. But short of that, I didn't want to deal with any of them.*"

But no matter how Robinson felt about the press, it remained a constant shaper of public attitudes throughout the war. Convinced that Vietnam was a hopeless and futile exercise, disengagement from the war was what the press and the public wanted. On March 31, 1968, a beginning step in that direction was taken when President Johnson, in a broadcast to the nation, said: "*Tonight, I have ordered our aircraft and our naval vessels to make no attacks on North Vietnam, except in the area north of the demilitarized zone, where continuing enemy build-up directly threatens allied forward positions and where the movement of their troops and supplies are clearly related to that threat.*"

Johnson would also make an equally dramatic (though not a totally surprising one, given the growing opposition to his re-election) statement that with domestic challenges right here at home, he did not believe that he should devote an hour or a day more of his time to personal partisan causes. His statement was followed by an announcement that he would not seek nor accept the nomination of his party for another term as President. Despite his early defense of the necessity of the war to protect democracy, the anti-war movement had taken its toll on his presidency.

Almost to the date of the announced bombing halt and the President's withdrawal from the nomination, three months later as June was nearing its end, Robinson's six-month command of the battalion had concluded and he returned to the United States. Despite Johnson's overture to Hanoi, a peaceful resolution of the war and soon was still, however, a distant reality. By Robinson's own admission, the amount of effort exerted and what a battalion commander was expected to do during combat was a tiring experience. He was happy when the command ended. It would be his last direct combat experience.

Neither during the course of his Vietnam command or when it ended did he speak about himself. With equal reluctance would he talk about the critical combat encounters he was involved in during the war. To this quiet and unassuming man, if there was valor to be associated with his leadership during combat, he preferred to assign it to those who fought and died along side of him. To him, they were the brave ones for having given their lives for their country, and for making the ultimate sacrifice. His reluctance to speak of himself was, no doubt, inspired by the words of the *Paratroopers Creed* he embraced: "I shall prove my ability as a fighting man against the enemy on the field of battle not by quarreling with my comrades in arms or by bragging about my deeds…..I shall always realize that battles are won by an Army fighting as a team…"

However, others who knew about his command and his individual courage under fire would speak about him. As one officer who knew Robinson and had followed his career said:

> *"I subsequently learned that of the remarkable things he had done in Vietnam, two involved his personally landing in the thick of firefights when his battalion was engaged, refusing to leave until all of his wounded were evacuated from the field. On another occasion he was personally involved in the killing of one enemy soldier and the capture of another when the odds against him were particularly heavy."*

While these words could suffice to tell of Robinson's Vietnam War experience, the Army went further. For his outstanding leadership during a period of close and intense combat during the Vietnam War, he was awarded two Silver Stars, the Distinguished Flying Cross, eleven Air Medals and the Legion of Merit.

II

Upon returning from Vietnam and with a career trajectory that was clearly heading upwards, in 1968 Robinson was selected to attend the National War College located in Theodore Roosevelt Hall on the grounds of Fort McNair. Situated in southeast Washington, DC near the confluence of the Anacostia and Potomac rivers, McNair is one of the nation's oldest active Army posts, West Point being the oldest. Regarded as one of the most prestigious of the advanced military schools, the National War College was established in 1946, and its military training importance is best stated in the words of one of its founders, Lieutenant General Leonard G. Gerow: *"The College is concerned with grand strategy and the utilization of the national resources necessary to implement that strategy. Its graduates will exercise a significant influence on the formulation of national and foreign policy in peace and war."*

While the College's students come from various federal government departments such as State, Treasury and Defense, those military officers selected by the Senior Service College Selection Board are mid-level and senior military officers likely to be promoted to the most senior ranks. Since only about ten percent of eligible officers are selected, Robinson was deemed to be among those likely to be promoted to a senior rank. When the Pentagon announced that a total of 281 Army officers were selected for the school year 1968-69 for attendance at the senior service colleges, which include the Army War College, Industrial College of the Armed Forces, the Naval War and the Air War Colleges, only thirty-five were selected to attend the National War College. Knowing that he was among a rare and privileged group, when the announcement of his selection was posted, he was excited, as attendance at the College is often a critical juncture in the lives of career officers.

In keeping with the practice of making sure that attendees were personally prepared for the vigorous schedule they would have to follow, he was informed by the College's administrator about what was expected of him (as was true for other attendees). He was told that his schedule would be crowded for the first few weeks, and because of the amount of time required, the Commandant does not look kindly on excusing members of the class from College activities, except for the most pressing reasons. For some the Commandant's warning might have been necessary but not Robinson. As evidenced by his performance at the other advanced schools, he was too disciplined to take his training less than serious and he always wanted to be successful regardless of the undertaking.

But the rigorous standards of the College had one waiver Robinson found appealing, which was that except for certain official occasions and for the first few weeks, he could exchange his usual military attire for civilian clothes, preferably business suits. It was a small measure of consolation, but civilian clothes would be more relaxing.

Robinson's class at the National War College included only one other African American officer – Fred Clifton Sheffey, Jr., who like Robinson had served in an infantry combat position in the Korean and Vietnam Wars. He began his military career first as a Distinguished Graduate of the Reserve Officers Training Corps (ROTC) program at Central State University where he was commissioned as a Second Lieutenant, and then rose through the regular officer ranks and later became a Major General in the Army. Sheffey would distinguish himself as the first African American to command Fort Lee, Virginia, the Quartermaster Training Command and the Quartermaster School.

West Point was also well represented in that class, as Richard Wells, a company mate of Robinson at the academy, was also in the entering class. They would reconnect and when not burdened with class attendance and study, the two men, their wives and other couples would spend time together socializing. Being a very charming and engaging couple, the Robinsons would be among the most respected and well liked at the College.

Similar to the Army Command and General Staff College, the academic program at the National War College is equally rigorous and demanding. The courses include military history, politics, and diplomacy, and are taught by seasoned scholars, military persons, and others of first rank. The attendees engaged in varied discussions about national security and related subjects, while also preparing oral presentations on some subject relevant to the course of studies. Robinson used one of his presentations to address the provocative and re-emerging subject of Black Nationalism, with the intent of discussing its impact on the national security of the United

States. In a somewhat surprising analysis, he noted, "the principal implication of black nationalism on the nation's security is clear. The development of black nationalism could lead to an increase in violence and polarization that could result in serious demands for partitioning of the country." With careful attention to historical data, Robinson traced the evolution of Black Nationalism in the United States through the personages of Marcus Garvey in the early 20th century and Malcolm X in the 1960s, and then examined some of the major influences shaping the movement in the late 1960s.

Robinson concluded the presentation saying, "*Black Nationalism at the close of the decade of the 1960s has been primarily a voice of protest and alienation.*" From his perspective, he further concluded that there were militants in the movement willing to disrupt and destroy, if necessary, to bring about changes in the structure of society. Robinson had previously written two other papers on the subject while a student at the University of Pittsburgh, one that was entitled "*Nationalism and Minorities*" and the other entitled "*Negro Nationalism.*" So his interest in Black Nationalism was piqued during this period of his career. He could hardly escape being drawn to the subject since nationalism was a topic of considerable discussion in the African American community as many blacks were becoming increasingly disenchanted with their ability to improve their conditions through normal political channels.

This disenchantment took many views among the African American intelligentsia, ranging from extreme separatist positions to those that were more moderate in tone and in the objectives they sought to achieve. It was the latter group that represented the majority of African Americans, particularly those of middle or upper class status. Viewed, as a radical manifestation of Black Nationalism, the more extremist position on the spectrum was the Black Panther Party, which emerged during the 1960s, which some described as "nationalists with guns and uniforms." The Party's advocacy of "armed rebellion" was most likely what prompted Robinson's cautionary assessment of Black Nationalism. He was not alone in his fear about the movement. For some, the ideological basis of the movement was socialist, and hence potentially was seen as destructive of certain core American values and principles. Clearly, Robinson's views about the movement were conservative, but understandable given his military and highly educated status.

The year Robinson spent at the National War College culminated with him, along with 139 others, receiving their certificates of completion when graduation exercises were held in Washington, D.C., on June 6, 1969. At least for the time being, his formal preparation for command was now complete, but command and leadership were subjects of continuing interest to Robinson, and they would be topics, which he would address many times in speeches during the various commands he held. While the "formal" leadership training that Robinson received at the advanced military schools and at the University of Pittsburgh helped him hone his leadership skills, he studied and observed the leadership styles of other officers whom he admired and under whom he served. He said about two such individuals - General George Blanchard and General Frederick Kroesen – "*When I consider those two officers, I see them both as being very, very special people. Their methods were different. When I try to assess my leadership style, I am sure that there is a lot of Blanchard in it, but there is also a lot of Kroesen in it. They were both great teachers.*"

Robinson, mindful of the influence of these two men on him, nevertheless developed his own leadership philosophy. It was, "Do it your way and lead in a manner you are comfortable with, and never try to imitate anyone else." The core characteristics of that leadership philosophy – as a mirror of himself – were plain and simple: "Take responsibility for those under you, set goals, be willing to listen, be decisive and tough when necessary, always be positive and don't be afraid to delegate authority when it is appropriate to do so." If there was one dominant theme that characterized Robinson's leadership, it was his concern for unit morale, taking the view that if troops believe there is a "problem," then the leader needed to address it. This sometimes meant having to cross the line between leadership and followership by talking directly to and listening to the troops since - in the final analysis - their performance depended upon gaining their trust.

As his subsequent performance in command positions would indicate, Robinson's views of leadership were not merely intellectual thoughts, but ones that had to be put into practice, and those who would serve under him would attest to the veracity and authenticity of his leadership style. His views on leadership went beyond what he expected of himself; they extended to others who had supervisory responsibilities and whom he tried to influence. Using a teachable moment during a speech at the Noncommissioned Officers Academy in 1973, he said,

> *"The attitude a leader has toward his job and those under him greatly influence his effectiveness as a leader, and how he does his job. All of you to some degree are supervisors, the people under you deserve to be treated with dignity, and they deserve to be treated as individuals. Be firm with them, but be fair, and don't think that the same technique will work for every man under you. Set the example, and exercise self-control and considerations of others."*

While clearly, the leadership principles and behaviors about which Robinson was speaking might have different implications and meaning in a military context, it is equally true that crafting his views of leadership as he did meant that they could easily have broader application across organizational environments outside of the military.

CHAPTER SEVEN

THE PACIFIC COMMAND AND OKINAWA

I

After attending the National War College from 1968 to 1969, Robinson's next assignment would again be in the Pacific region. But this time it was not a direct combat assignment, but rather a strategic planning position with the United States Pacific Command (USPACOM); the headquarters of which were located at Camp H.M. Smith on the island of Oahu, Hawaii. In broad terms, the Command's mission is to protect and defend, in cooperation with other U.S. Government agencies, the territory of the United States, its people, and its interests, while, at the same time, enhancing stability in the Asia-Pacific region by responding to contingencies, deterring aggression, and engaging in combat when necessary. Established on January 1, 1947, USPACOM (commonly referred to as CINCPAC) is the oldest and largest of the United States' unified combatant commands. It has a geographic territorial reach that covers an area about half of the earth's surface, stretching from the West Coast of the United States to the western border of the India, and from Antarctica to the North Pole.

When Robinson arrived at the Command Headquarters, the first order of business was getting his family settled. Fortunately, as a Vietnam veteran, he was able to get preference for housing, and the Robinsons rented a house for the six months near Fort Shafter, on the island of Oahu. Later, they moved to another rented a house in a beautiful area of Schofield Barracks, the largest military base in Hawaii. The house – one of only six located on a cul-de-sac was surrounded by lush Hawaiian vegetation including avocado, banana, and papaya trees; the produce of which would find its way to the breakfast table. It was among the most pleasant of the many houses the Robinsons lived during his military career. Once again, the children would be changing schools. Carole was enrolled in a Catholic High School and Bruce was enrolled in second grade at the base school.

Over the course of their married life whenever and wherever it was possible, Millie would be alongside her husband. While Robinson and his wife would have loved having a permanent home somewhere in the states, his frequent reassignments made that improbable. Instead, home was wherever he was stationed, which meant living in Army quarters or in civilian housing at several bases in the United States and abroad. For many military families like the Robinsons, living in so many different places creates a sense of "rootlessness" requiring an adaptability and resilience of the highest order. When parenting under these circumstances, Millie's response was, "You do what you have to do." And she did.

But no matter where they lived, Millie was a gracious hostess when guests and foreign dignitaries were received at their home for a reception or dinner, or when she was by his side welcoming guests at public or community events. Millie not only loved to cook, but she was a good one, and hosting a dinner party was never thought of as a chore, but something she enjoyed. When the social demands and caring for the children did not occupy her time, she would join with the wives of other officers for a variety of activities, including volunteering in the local communities where their husbands were stationed.

Robinson's military obligations did not allow him as much time as he would have liked to have had with Carol and

Bruce, so child rearing became the major responsibility of Millie – a not an uncommon practice. Even outside the military, men in those days didn't do as much day-to-day caring for children, as later generations would begin to do. Yet, despite his military obligations, he made it a practice to spend his evenings at home with his family whenever possible. Robinson was a good and devoted father to his children, strict when necessary, but always caring and available when they needed his attention. Robinson loved sports, whether it was football or baseball, and it was with Carol, the other sports aficionado in the family, that he spent time watching the games. Carol also participated in horseback riding and competitive swimming, and as a dutiful father, he was supportive as much as possible.

Similarly, he would take Bruce to his sporting activities and, like his father; Bruce was a Boy Scout. Together, they would attend Boy Scout events, even those activities such as overnight camping when common sense might be the better part of valor. Robinson and his son were faced with that choice when they went out to a Boy Scout campsite for an overnight camping experience during very adverse weather conditions of cold and rain. After spending a few hours at the site, and when it seemed the weather was not going to improve, the choice had to be made to either stick it out or leave; it was the latter option that prevailed.

When it came to matters of learning and education, Robinson, reaching back to his own parents' insistence on being academically prepared, was uncompromising with his own children. When he was away on a temporary military assignment, he would give them "homework" assignments or papers to write on specific, handpicked subjects, with the expectation that the assignment or the paper would be finished and ready for his critique when he came home.

In a manner not unlike many other parents who hold highly visible and very public positions, Robinson's military career obviously had its effect on his children. A strong sense of family pervaded the household so the children were made aware they "lived in a glass house," and that others would be constantly observing them, perhaps sometimes with unrealistic expectations of how they should behave. Regardless, they were encouraged not to do something that would be an embarrassment to the family. But there was no confusion on their part. They knew what was expected of them by their father, and as is so often the case, their mother was at home to reinforce those expectations. According to Millie, the children were also fortunate in being able, when Robinson was not at home, to turn to "surrogate" fathers who lived on the various bases with the Robinsons and with whom they were friends, if they needed to talk to a male figure. Military bases on which personnel live with their families are often thought of as "shared interest communities," where there is a sense of shared responsibility for each other. In many respects, the availability of having other responsible adults with whom to talk was reminiscent of the concept of the "extended family" and the African proverb: "It takes a village to raise a child."

As a father, Robinson also had his religious faith to draw on while raising his children. Although he was Methodist, the children were raised in the Catholic faith of their mother. He made it a practice to insist that Carol and Bruce attend their Confraternity of Christian Doctrine (CCD) classes, which serve as a means of providing religious education, as well as a channel for instructing children in the faith, and practices of the Catholic Church. Frequently, the children would attend Methodist services with their father.

II

At the start of his duty assignment with CINCPAC, Robinson was assigned to the Southeast Asia Plans Branch (J5 -Strategic Plans and Policy Directorate), with specific responsibility for updating one of the major plans for that sub-region, which included some of the most populous countries - Indonesia, Philippines, Vietnam, Thailand, and Cambodia. The purpose of these plans is to provide strategic and policy guidance relative to current and future military strategy, how to respond to contingencies and, if necessary, provide guidance for deterring aggression. Robinson did not find this initial assignment particularly challenging since he regarded the updating process, itself, to be obsolete, given the major changes that had already occurred in Southeast Asia.

With his normal inclination to fully utilize his experiences and training, Robinson began to assume other duties, which eventually led to taking on responsibility for Thailand planning and later, after being asked, to include Cambodia under his planning responsibilities. The latter assignment was especially important. Bordering on Vietnam, Cambodia - although officially neutral throughout the Vietnam War while under the rule of Prince Norodom Sihanouk, its former king and later Prime Minister - was becoming a strategic military problem. The thinly populated Cambodia/South Vietnam border areas were used by the North Vietnamese as a supply route and a staging area that prompted the initial, but secret, U.S. bombing raids in 1965 ordered by President Johnson. Later, the North Vietnamese Army, with the aid of its Communist sympathizers, used the Cambodian/South Vietnam border area to prepare for the Tet Offensive of 1968.

In March 1970, regime changes were underway in Cambodia, with the overthrow of Sihanouk by his former aide,

General Lon Nol, who was pro-American and democratic leaning. To prepare for the possible expanded operations in Cambodia, Robinson was given the task of coordinating a conference – later known as "Save Cambodia Operation" - in Bangkok, Thailand for doing some initial planning. Given the increasing political turbulence in Cambodia and the imminent threat to its neutrality from the North Vietnamese, coordinating and planning the conference was an important assignment for Robinson. When convened, the conference brought together political leaders as well as military planners from Southeast Asia, Hawaii, and Washington. When the conference adjourned, Robinson was given the task of preparing the final report which was delivered to Admiral John S. McCain, Jr., Commander in Chief, Pacific Command, who was then in Saigon. Robinson also participated in the briefing on the report, which contained recommendations that covered political, military, and civic actions to bring some stability to Cambodia.

In Washington, with full knowledge that Cambodian "sanctuaries" were still being used as staging areas for North Vietnamese troops, which, if not destroyed, would lead to a complete takeover of Cambodia and be catastrophic for South Vietnam, options on how to address the threat were being discussed by the Nixon administration. The options included the possibility of an invasion of Cambodia, a choice that was unsettling to some key administration officials.

With the Cambodia report that Robinson helped prepare in hand, on April 18, Admiral McCain briefed President Richard Nixon; the effect of which Henry Kissinger, who was then Secretary of State, described that it "gave focus to the President's hitherto inchoate anxieties about Cambodia." The continuing threat posed by the actions of the North Vietnamese over the next two weeks would set the stage for Nixon's decision on April 30, 1970 to authorize the sending of 12,000

U.S. ground troops along with 8,000 ARVN troops into Cambodian base areas used by the North Vietnamese and the Vietcong. To convince the public of the temporary nature of this action, Nixon announced that the troops would be withdrawn "once enemy forces are driven out of these sanctuaries and their military supplies are destroyed."

That announcement did little to assuage skeptics; rather it sparked anti-war protests across the country, including the May 1970 student-led protest on the campus of Kent State University during which, in a clash with Ohio National Guardsmen, four students were killed. The scene of that protest – with its extensive media coverage - would become deeply etched in the memory of many Americans.

The Cambodian crisis would linger on, but Robinson was now feeling that his role with Cambodia planning had been completed and that the J5 position in Southeast Asia Planning branch had run its course – at least as far as he was concerned. And so Robinson sought and secured the position of Executive Officer to Major General Charles A. Corcoran, Chief of Staff, CINCPAC. It was a good assignment as it was Robinson's first real exposure to that operations level of the military. Moreover, it was one that provided him with considerable understanding of practically all that goes on in a headquarters operation especially during wartime. He was able to do so because General Corcoran allowed him to sit in on all the high-level briefing conferences that took place in his office. Afterwards Robinson would prepare a memorandum for Corcoran on the substance of those conferences.

Being so close to the operations of CINCPAC, however, provided Robinson with a particular vantage point of how the Command really functioned. He would later suggest that the Pacific Command, which was intended to be a joint headquarters for all the military branches, i.e., Army, Navy,

Marine Corp, and Air Force, did not function as a joint command, but rather was run by the Navy – using many of its operational methods. Robinson's assessment, it should be noted, had some historical roots, as most of the Commanders of the Pacific Command had been naval admirals. Inter-service rivalries notwithstanding, like others in the Army branch of the Command, Robinson subscribed to the view that Admiral McCain suffered from what they called a kind of the "ship captain syndrome," never wanting to relinquish total control.

> *"We joked about the fact that we were really assigned to a Navy command and not a joint headquarters. It was (only) joint from the extent that you had a Chief who was Army, you had Air Force personnel there and it was joint from the point of assignment."*

In the context of how the Command operated, Robinson's characterization of Admiral McCain's leadership was understandable, and even perhaps accurate. On the other hand, Admiral McCain had achieved a distinguished record in the Navy where he specialized in amphibious warfare, commanded submarines in several theaters of operations and fought during several wars, including World War II and the Vietnam War. He also held several naval posts in Washington, and apparently enjoyed the support of President Nixon.

While at CINCPAC, as was the case with some of his other assignments, Robinson again had the opportunity to reconnect and serve with one of his former West Point classmates. In this instance, Edward Matney was also assigned to CINCPAC as a J5 in the Planning Division. During their time together they became good friends – and even more important - tennis rivals. Matney, whose nickname was "Moose," described a three-hour grueling match between the two of them that went back and forth until Robinson finally won. Matney attributed Robinson's victory – his skill at the game, notwithstanding - to his sheer determination to do well at everything.

Matney also described Robinson as "very reserved and not one to attract attention to himself" – at least most of the time. But as many knew, Robinson also had a great sense of humor, which on occasions would be demonstrated. Matney would be involved in one of those occasions. Both men were Lieutenant Colonels when they came to CINCPAC, and both were up at the same time for promotion to Colonel. However, on February 22, 1972, Robinson was promoted to that rank one day ahead of Matney, and, in a light-hearted and unpretentious manner, quietly approached his friend and suggested that it would be protocol if Matney saluted him. He did, but later both laughed about the incident.

Robinson considered his time at CINCPAC as an important boost in his career, as it gave him an opportunity to work with General Corcoran from whom he learned some valuable lessons. One of which was the need to give staff some leeway and the importance of being protective of the person in the field who has responsibility and knows what is happening on the ground. Since the Vietnam War was still in progress, the person on the ground, in this instance, was General Creighton Abrams, Jr., who was- at that time - commander of U.S. military operations in Vietnam. Robinson admired General Corcoran's persistence in making sure that General Abrams' position was represented at the highest command level at CINCPAC, which in this case was Admiral McCain.

Later in life, when asked to reflect on some of the difficulties with the CINCPAC command structure, Robinson took the position that General Abrams' Headquarters should probably have been a separate command, which - he believed - would have been a more effective structure than having command decisions emanating from Hawaii where CINCPAC was headquartered. Robinson's position on this matter was not based on any notion of abdication of command responsibility; rather it was rooted in his belief that sometimes delegation of authority is not only appropriate, but also essential in carrying out a particular assignment in order to get the results you want.

III

During and after Robinson's first assignment with the 82nd, his affinity and fond attachment to the division would only grow stronger, and even though he knew the need for different assignments, the opportunity to return someday to the 82nd was something that he looked forward to in the not-too-distant future. Clearly, it was where his military heart lay. Fortunately, the opportunity to return came in early 1972 in the form of a letter while at CINCPAC. The letter was from his old friend General Blanchard, now Commander of the 82nd Airborne Division, telling him about an impending commander vacancy in one of the Brigades, and asking him if he was interested in coming back to Fort Bragg.

What Robinson did not know at the time was that Blanchard had already asked his colonels to recommend officers for his consideration for two brigade commander vacancies. They came up with a list of nineteen infantry colonels for Blanchard's review; Robinson was one of them. Blanchard then asked Julius Becton whose judgment he respected if he thought Robinson had the capacity and interest in commanding a brigade. As his old friend, and knowing of Robinson's competence and leadership skills, Becton responded in the affirmative. This helped to seal the decision to offer the brigade command to Robinson.

General Blanchard wanted and expected a quick answer to his offer, which he got. Robinson accepted the assignment offer immediately, and to move the process along as quickly as possible, he met with General Corcoran to let him know that he had the opportunity to return to the 82nd to command a brigade. He also made the request that he be allowed to leave a few months short of his three-year tour with the Pacific Command. General Corcoran knew that a brigade commander has significant responsibilities, with between 2,500 and 4,000 personnel under his command, and he understood what this opportunity would mean to Robinson. He approved the request, much to Robinson's delight.

Perhaps anticipating he would someday be returning to an airborne unit that would require him to be in good physical condition, during his time in Hawaii, he kept up a steady routine of playing tennis, handball and running. It paid off – so much so that when he got back to Fort Bragg in May, 1972, where he was assigned by General Blanchard to the 2nd Brigade to replace a classmate from his days at West Point, Colonel Sandy Weyant, his colleagues, after running with him one morning, remarked about how "good a shape he was in." Little did they realize that being in a fit condition was in Robinson's DNA; it was something that came natural to him.

Blanchard's decision to bring Robinson to Fort Bragg was part of a long time effort on his part to make affirmative action and equal opportunity a reality in the Army. It was a reputation that African Americans in the military valued and appreciated – so much so that Blanchard in 2001 would become the first white general officer to be a recipient of the Honorary Rock of the Year. It was quite a distinct honor, inasmuch as the award was given by The Rock, Inc. – a nonprofit organization founded by a group of African American Army officers in the

1960s to provide professional and social interaction and development to strengthen the officer corps.

When Robinson assumed his duties at Fort Bragg, a decade had passed since he was last at that facility, and critical events had taken place in the nation and the world. He had been a witness to and a participant in what is often described as the most turbulent decade in American history. It was a decade during which three prominent and revered American leaders were assassinated. The sitting President, John Kennedy, was assassinated in 1963, dashing the hopes of many. Five years later, Dr. Martin Luther King, Jr., a powerful exponent of non-violence was killed by an assassin's bullet in Memphis, Tennessee and two months later, Kennedy's Robert, an aspirant to the Presidency was assassinated. The Vietnam War was full blown, bringing with it considerable domestic unrest, partisan divisions, and protests against what was being called the "unwinnable war." The civil rights movement had been unleashed, bringing in its wake, with the passage of the Civil Rights Act of 1964, the most sweeping civil rights legislation in the history of the nation. And in July 1969, America's goal to be the first nation to land a man on the moon was achieved.

Yet, like most Americans, Robinson was undaunted by the events and remained optimistic about America's future. While unquestionably these events changed America in countless ways, the 82nd'semphasis on readiness for immediate deployment did not change, though Robinson was aware that there had been morale problems in the 82nd Airborne Division in the late 1960s. It was also experiencing the infusion of airborne soldiers who had returned from Vietnam – many with combat-related problems and post-traumatic stress disorders. To his surprise, Robinson even found that the Division had some of the same soldiers that were there in the early 1960s, yet the "espirit de corps" was much the same as when he was a company commander. But Robinson was now a Brigade Commander which brought increased leadership and management responsibilities; one of which he noted was simply setting priorities.

> *"Well, even though everything is always number one priority, we know that when it comes down to time management, something has to be less than number one priority. Where the individual does his job well, is recognizing what that item might be. Don't neglect the one that really is number one priority, but in your mind, sort out what may be stated as number one priority. You can't give the resources and time to all of them. You had better figure out which one it is that you can have less emphasis on and still perform your mission."*

During his Brigade Command assignment, one of his priorities was the introduction of some innovative programs, including the off-post deployment for parachuting exercises – often involving the use of "live" ammunition. Under his command, the Brigade would conduct simulated deployment exercises against hypothetical opposing forces, often times in different environments outside of Fort Bragg as were the case with jungle exercises in Panama and Puerto Rico. Even though he recognized the risks of such exercises, which sometimes resulted in accidents, Robinson saw them as necessary to ensure that the Airborne Division met its readiness and deployment requirements. And that was a status which he saw no room for compromise. Whether he ever read the book "*The Art of War,*" written by the ancient Chinese military strategist, Sun Tzu, is uncertain, but Robinson's focus on readiness certainly subscribed to one of Tzu military principles: "*The art of war teaches us to rely not on the likelihood of the enemy's not coming, but on our own readiness to receive him; not in the chance of his not attacking, but rather on the fact that we have made our position unassailable."*

But readiness was something that has to be worked at, and Robinson had a way of doing just that. An officer who worked for him during his command of the brigade, described Robinson as an "on the ground" leader. He would personally talk to the company commanders to get a first-hand feel for what was happening in their companies, and he would talk directly with the soldiers under their command. Knowing the climate of the companies was important to him. But it was also part of the information he used to rate his companies, their leadership, and their readiness. After the ratings were done, he would call the commanders in and in face-to-face conversation discuss their rating with them. He did so to avoid what some considered an unpleasant task and choose to send their negative or low rating via written communications. So knowledgeable about the companies and their quality, he would not hesitate to say, "These are my four best companies, and these are my four worst companies." Ratings were important and Robinson took them seriously. A good rating, particularly one given by him, could become a "career accelerator" for one aspiring to become a general officer, or it could become a career decelerator.

From Robinson's vantage point, having the Airborne Division "ready," did not only apply to potential international situations that might develop, but to domestic ones as well. The latter test of readiness was about to happen when on July 14, and August 22, 1972, respectively, the Democratic and the Republican Parties held their conventions in Miami Beach, Florida. With still fresh memories of the 1968 Democratic Party Convention in Chicago during which violent rioting broke out among demonstrators protesting the Party's nomination of Vice President Hubert Humphrey who won on a plank supporting the

Vietnam War, two Brigades of the 82nd Division, including the Robinson's 2nd Brigade, were put on alert – ostensibly for riot-control purposes. It was a reminder that at the 1968 Democratic Convention 7,500 Illinois National Guard had to be called out by Chicago Mayor Richard Daley to help quell the disturbances. With anti-war sentiment still at a high point, some officials thought that direct military support might also be required for riot-control at the Miami conventions.

The prospects of having to potentially use his unit for a similar type of riot-control in Miami was something Robinson would long remember. His brigade had been deployed to Indiantown Gap Military Reservation in Pennsylvania for ROTC summer camp support where paratroop training exercises for the benefit of the ROTC cadets were being conducted. It had been a pleasant summer, for when not in training exercises, the soldiers played handball and with Robinson's intervention, even secured free tickets to baseball games in Philadelphia and Baltimore. It was another example of his caring for his men by getting them away from the base in order to have some fun. But when the alert came for possible riot control deployment, his brigade was ready. He gave this account of the situation he faced:

> *"We stood at alert. My brigade was at Indiantown Gap. The First Brigade, under Ed Partain, had the mission of deploying to an airfield near Miami. They actually had a little tent city there using television for their sources of information....I flew down with some of my command group. We did all of the reconnaissance work. We got our routes and selected our landing zones. We picked out schoolhouses that could be used as our CPs along the route. Fortunately, we did not have to deploy. I was going to be the second unit to deploy. The First Brigade*

was already there. I would be the follow-on and would come in as soon as they had been deployed. Fortunately, there were no major incidents there that caused the troops to have to react. Most of us felt very good about that, because if there was a no win situation, we would have been in one. To have our soldiers going into a situation like that would not have been good. We knew that the eyes of the world would have been on us. We would have been on every television screen in the country."

Fortunately, the need for deployment never materialized, as there were no convention-related riots as in 1968. The well-organized anti-Vietnam war movement that had been a key force behind the 1968 demonstrations had weakened. The movement also had a candidate for the Democratic nomination who had built his campaign around the anti-war movement. Nevertheless, Robinson probably would have been right about television coverage since, in 1968, the Chicago episode drew extensive media coverage and the same would likely to have happened in 1972. In the end, however, the 1972 Democratic Convention went off as planned – peacefully, with Senator George McGovern chosen as the party's presidential nominee. The only excitement that Convention generated was the decision – a few days afterwards – of McGovern's Vice Presidential running mate, Thomas Eagleton, to withdraw from the race after revelations of his prior mental health problems surfaced.

Robinson always considered the time he spent as Commander of the 2nd Brigade a high point in career. It was something he enjoyed as it gave him an opportunity to be involved directly with soldiers and their families in a way that was not possible in other assignments. In one of the many notebooks in which he recorded his thoughts, he said, *"During my career, the most interesting, the most challenging and the most enjoyable assignments, I've had were troop assignments, especially those I had been in command."* As a man of considerable insight into the thinking of the ordinary soldier, Robinson learned a valuable lesson during his time as a brigade commander, one that would resonate with him throughout the remainder of his career. It was the importance of senior officers keeping their identity with their soldiers. He said, "*Soldiers are very perceptive. You can't be phony as far as they are concerned. You can't turn something on for an hour and off for something else. You've got to maintain your identity with soldiers. If you lose your identity with your soldiers, they go through the motions for you.*"

For Robinson, maintaining identity with the soldiers did not mean diminishing your command and leadership responsibility, rather it meant caring about those under your command, being approachable, and showing compassion and understanding especially when soldiers are faced with family difficulties. Colonel Frederick Black, who Robinson had known since he was eight years old and the son of Gorham Black, a U.S. Army Colonel, served under his command of the 2nd Brigade and recalled one experience he had with Robinson's display of concern. Knowing that Black's wife was in the hospital awaiting the delivery of their first child, Robinson told him to forget about his duties for the time being and go to the hospital and check on his wife. Black did that and when the child was born that evening, Robinson and Millie were the first visitors to see the couple's new son. When Black's father passed, it was Robinson who he heard from immediately afterwards.

These displays of caring on the part of Robinson were common occurrences with those with whom he worked. But

Robinson was doing only what he believed as important when in a command or leadership position. He was taking care of his soldiers; it didn't require technical or tactical competence, rather it required a sense of compassion and caring. A contemporary moral philosopher and theologian said it this way about one who possesses these qualities, "The recognition of oneness of humanity and the need of actively brotherly concern for the welfare of others is the breath of a man's life." At a pragmatic level, Robinson, on the other hand, said it this way, "Our soldier want leaders who are willing to share their hardships, who are totally concerned with their welfare, and who are willing to place personal ambitions secondary to the needs of their troops or units." It was precisely these qualities of character and sensitivity why Colonel Black later remarked about Robinson's time as brigade commander, "It was a special unit experience because we had a special commander."

I V

On July 2, 1973 while still commanding the 2nd Brigade, Robinson was promoted to Brigadier General. As always, Millie was there, along with General Kroesen, the 82nd Division Commander, helping to pin the stars. Soon there afterwards his second tour of duty at Fort Bragg ended and for his service, he was again awarded the Legion of Merit. The tour would be followed by orders for Okinawa where he was assigned as Deputy Commanding General, Okinawa Base Command. There was – at the time of this assignment – not much in the way of preparation for what the position entailed. Again, if he had a choice, he would have liked becoming an Assistant Division Commander some place; preferably with the 82nd which he had just left. But there were other recently appointed Brigadier

Generals on the list awaiting and hoping for that assignment with the 82nd.

When his Okinawa orders were published, Robinson was serving on a Command Selection Board and had only a couple of weeks before his scheduled departure – leaving little time to think about his upcoming assignment, and particularly what he needed to do in preparing his family for the move. His first thought was the short lead-time was not the way to treat a general officer. But having heard of similar cases of where officers didn't have adequate preparation time for their new deployment, Robinson had no choice but to accept the situation as it was. He reasoned that - at least - making such a quick adjustment was easier now that he had achieved the rank of general officer. Okinawa would become another place where the Robinson family would settle in and make their new home; this time in a humid subtropical climate with its unusual and beautiful species of flora and fauna, white beaches, magnificent coral reefs, and majestic mountains. There could be less desirable places, Robinson thought.

During his briefing, Robinson was made aware that the primary mission of the Okinawa Garrison was to operate as a depot, which entailed the storage of materials and providing military logistics services in the fields of supply, maintenance, and property disposal. But having responsibility for operating depot was not something in which he was terribly interested, whether it was in Okinawa or any other location for that matter. In his mind, he was first, and foremost, a combat soldier.

In the larger context, however, Robinson's assignment to Okinawa, his subsequent duties there, and the issues he would have to confront, must be viewed in the context of the changes in the relationship between Japan and the United States over several preceding decades relative to Okinawa. The relationship had long historical roots, beginning as early as the

19th century. Although it had engaged for years in trade with China, Japan and Korea, for most of its thousand-year history, Okinawa remained an isolated kingdom until Commodore Matthew Perry – an American - visited the Royal palace at Shuri in 1854. This was during the time when the United States and other western nations were attempting to expand their relationship with the island. The island's independence changed when in 1879, with Japanese nationalism and modernization in ascendancy, Okinawa was formally annexed by the Japanese government and organized as one of the country's prefectures and became an integral part of that nation-state.

In preparing for the Okinawa assignment, Robinson did his homework. He knew from military history that it was the largest of the Ryukus Islands and that it had taken on increased importance during the campaign for the Pacific during World War II. For example, as the war with Japan was reaching its final stages resulting from American victories in the Philippines and on Iwo Jima, Okinawa – located strategically in the East China Sea and within 400 miles of the southern tip of Japan – became the site for launching direct attacks on Japan itself. On April 1, 1945, in a historic battle deeply etched in the memories of those who fought during the campaign for the Pacific, American Marine and Army troops swarmed ashore on Okinawa. Against strong Japanese military resistance and aided by the use of suicide pilots targeted at the American naval fleet, the battle for Okinawa raged on for three months. Though in the end America succeeded in gaining control of the island, it was one of most costly military victories of World War II, resulting in 40,000 American casualties.

On August 15, 1945, two months after the battle for Okinawa and with their country devastated by the bombing of Hiroshima and Nagasaki Japan unconditionally surrendered to the Allies; an event marked by the acceptance of the Potsdam

Declaration. It was also the beginning of a six-year period of occupation of Japan by the Allied Powers, with the U.S. in the leadership role. In the United States, however, the long-term future status of Okinawa, including the length of U. S. occupation of the island had become, even before the end of the war, a subject of considerable policy debate – given its strategic location. The debate ranged from those who pressed for full annexation to those favoring reversion of the island to Japan. During the period of U.S. occupation – even while the debate continued, American Navy commanders became increasingly disenchanted with conditions on the island and its prospects as a base for naval operations, but subsequently agreed to transfer administrative control of the island to the U. S. Army. It was because of the Army's administrative role why Robinson was there.

For a variety of reasons, which included the perceived need for surveillance of Japan after the termination of occupation - indecision on what to do with Okinawa continued throughout the immediate post-war period to permeate U.S. foreign policy in the Pacific. It was not until September 8, 1951 with the signing of the Peace Treaty between Japan and the United States, which ended the American occupation of Japan, and the simultaneous signing of the Japan-U.S. Security Treaty that the status of Okinawa was resolved. Under the Peace Treaty, Japan was restored as a sovereign nation and permitted to retain residual sovereignty over the Ryukus Islands. Under the security treaty, Japan granted the rights to the United States to dispose land, air, and sea forces in and about Japan, which had the effect of enabling the U.S. to continue to administer and rule Okinawa – almost as though it were a colonial possession - at least until reversion would be considered. Parenthetically, using comedy as the setting for his characterization of American rule over the Japanese citizens of Okinawa inspired the 1953 prize-winning play called *The Teahouse of the August Moon* by John Patrick.

A more realistic characterization would show that, in fact, before and after 1951, U.S. administration was accompanied with substantial investment in Okinawa as schools, recreational facilities and houses were built, and new military bases were constructed, with the latter estimated to have cost over $600 million. As "Keystone of the Pacific" - the nickname given to Okinawa because it was viewed as the key geographic perimeter for the defense of the free world in the Pacific area -American investment, though very costly, could be justified. This investment was demonstrated during the period between 1950 and 1953 when Okinawa was a base of operations in the initial defense of South Korea during the time Robinson was there.

After years of consultations between the United States and Japan, the *Agreement between the United States and Japan Concerning the Ryukyu Islands and the Daito Islands (Okinawa)* was signed on June 17, 1971. Under the Agreement, the United States relinquished responsibility and authority over the islands to Japan. This Agreement, which took official effect on May 15, 1972 at ceremonies held in Naha and Tokyo, made official the reversion of these islands to Japan. However, under Article III of the Agreement, Japan agreed to grant the United States the continued use of facilities and areas in the Ryukyu Islands and the Daito Islands. The return of the islands marked the end of United States civil administration of the Ryukyu Islands and the re-designation of a new Army command on Okinawa. The command was later reorganized on July 1, 1974 to become the U.S. Army Garrison, Okinawa with the status as a subordinate unit of the U.S. Army, Japan. It was at this time that Okinawa's primary status as an Army Depot began to emerge. A status that required the U.S. to develop an administrative infrastructure to manage the depot's activities.

V

While Okinawa's important military status was known to Robinson, when he arrived on the island, he nevertheless made it known to General Herron Maples, the Commanding General of the Okinawa Garrison, that he was not particularly interested in overseeing depot activities. Rather, he let it be known that he preferred taking on responsibility for some other activity that would be more to his liking. Fortunately, Robinson's desire fit well with Maples' plan for how he wanted to utilize Robinson anyway, as it was precisely because of his good troop background why he had been selected by General Maples. After conferring with Robinson, Maples told him he wanted him to focus on some critical troop issues in Okinawa that were emerging from the reversion of control of the island to the Japanese.

That decision was to Robinson's liking since being responsible for personnel related issues, next to combat, was clearly one of his preferences throughout his military career, and it was something at which he excelled. In the context of Okinawa, however, personnel issues would be somewhat more complex as they related directly to the reduction of U.S. troop units (e.g., Military Police, Air Defense, Special Forces) on the island and their subsequent transfer back to the states. This required considerable coordination with the Japanese Self Defense Forces, which were taking over defense responsibilities for Okinawa.

The reversion also created some financial and morale issues for the base command that required Robinson's attention. Some of the officers and enlisted personnel clubs were on the verge of bankruptcy and had to be closed or kept open on a limited basis due to the Garrison having to absorb the unplanned for costs of benefits, retirement and severance pay due to the Japanese work force under the Status of Forces Agreement. Prior to reversion, these costs had not been considered as future liabilities that would eventually come due.

Clearly, as he became involved in his duties, Robinson was enjoying addressing troop issues on Okinawa. Always wanting to improve the quality of life for soldiers, the personnel area of responsibility gave him the opportunity to do so. But before long, the logistics of depot management would reenter the picture when the Major General Bert David replaced Maples as commanding officer less than a year after Robinson arrived in Okinawa. David, like Robinson, also wanted to be involved in troop activities. So in his scheme of management, he and Robinson would share responsibilities in all (including of course, depot management) the activities associated with the command. As time would show, having shared responsibility would become important to Robinson since after serving in the Deputy Commanding General position for two years, on August 14, 1975, after David' brief six month stint as Commanding General, Robinson was appointed the Commanding General of the United States Army Garrison, Okinawa.

This position would be the first time – in a noncombat situation - that Robinson was in direct charge of a unit with considerable responsibilities. It would be an occasion when the qualities of a "diplomat" would be equally as important as military leadership. In the course of the command of the Okinawa Garrison, Robinson's diplomatic persona would be characterized by employing tact to find mutually acceptable solutions to common challenges, to listening to what others were saying, and to exhibiting patience and calmness during periods of sometimes-hostile negotiations with the Okinawans and the Japanese.

However, just as Robinson had settled into his new position as commander and had begun to address the weighty problems with which he was confronted, his hometown and the high school of his youth beckoned. He was asked by the Principal of Sumner High School, Samuel Miller, to serve as a Vice Chairman of the Sumner Centennial Observance. Remembering the school's *alma mater* -"Live in Our Hearts-----Sumner High," Robinson agreed to accept the invitation, even though his participation in the major event – the Centennial Alumni Banquet - was problematic. As much as he would have liked to take a break from his duties on Okinawa, he could not attend the observance, given that he had just assumed his new duties.

But, a few years later, Robinson would respond to the call to return to Sumner High School, this time to speak to its graduates. It was also a rare opportunity to visit with his mother, now 78 years of age, and his sister. Realizing that it was a new generation of African Americans about to enter responsible adulthood and remembering the words of encouragement he had received while when he was about to graduate, he urged the graduates not to dwell on the possible injustices of the past, but to look to the future, "Your future will be no larger than your dreams. Continue to dream great dreams so our society can be dynamic and alive." These were not just poetic words; they spoke to his view of the opportunities that were becoming increasingly open to African Americans.

When Robinson took over the top Army job on Okinawa, some of the same issues that he addressed as Deputy Commander continued to occupy his time. As expected, however, some new activities began to emerge, largely brought on as the Vietnam War was coming to an end and from the reversion of control activities that still had to be undertaken. As the central Pacific area depot, the Okinawa Base Command, under Robinson, would have the major responsibility for handling, inventorying, and disposing of retrograde military equipment and supplies being brought back from Vietnam. Unlike after World War II when the U.S. would simply leave equipment and supplies, the Department of the Army now wanted a retrograde operation undertaken. This meant that whatever kind of equipment and supplies could be salvaged were to be returned to property disposal offices in the United States or redistributed, depending upon the disposition instructions Robinson received.

The retrograde operation was a huge undertaking and, from Robinson's perspective, it overtaxed the installation due to manpower downsizing resulting from troop withdrawals. Being short-handed in terms of personnel required him to seek help and technical assistance from the United States Army Materiel Command, which was eventually called in to manage much of the workload. When the disposition activities were finished, for the most part, Robinson could take credit for having directed the retrograding of over 24,000 tons of equipment, valued at 50 million dollars, that was subsequently sent back to CONUS (Continental United States).

Implementing the reversion agreement would also bring to the surface, at the urging of the Japanese local government responsible for the Okinawa Prefecture, the issue of the environment. From the local Okinawa government's perspective, the environmental issues stemmed from the pollution emanating from Army installations as well as the unresolved question as to how the U.S would handle the disposal of a considerable amount of industrial chemicals used as pesticides, insecticides, and cleaning compounds. There were also concerns about potential toxic leaks from the petroleum pipelines and their storage facilities.

The environmental issues, and having to address them, would come as no surprise since by the time Robinson assumed command of the Okinawa Garrison these issues had already taken on considerable urgency in Japan. On the mainland, the Japanese had moved the environment issue to the forefront of its domestic agenda with the establishment of the Environment Agency in 1970. In the process of setting up this agency, the Japanese government had promulgated some stringent environmental regulations, which meant that the Army would have to dispose of these chemical materials through destruction, neutralization, sale or moving them to other locations. With diplomatic tact, Robinson made it clear that he understood the concern on the part of the Japanese and the Department of the Army about the political sensitivity of ensuring that Okinawa was "cleaned up." Moreover, he had first-hand experience with environmental hazards and their effects, having had during his command an accidental spill of a used cleaning compound in the summer of 1975 that flowed out into the sea. Although small in volume, both sides feared the spill's potential damage to aquatic life.

Robinson took his environmental cleanup responsibilities seriously and with the authority to do so, and with close attention from General John R. Guthrie, Commander of United States Army Japan, he proceeded to supervise the task of disposing of the depot's excess industrial chemicals while, at the same time, attending to other environmental abatement activities. It was his way to "find common ground" by demonstrating the Garrison's strong commitment to ensure Japanese environmental standards would be met. These environmental actions were taken even though, under Article IV of the Status of Forces Agreement, the United States was not obligated to return the lands to the conditions they were in when they became available to the U.S. But environmental remediation did comply with Department of Defense policy that called for the removal of imminent and substantial dangers to health and safety due to operations of DOD installations and facilities.

The environment remediation activities (as well as others) were further complicated by severe labor problems that Robinson had to negotiate relative to pay and safety standards being demanded by the local nationals who constituted the majority of the work force employed by the base command. To press their grievances and demands, worker demonstrations and strikes were common occurrences. Maneuvering through the mine-field of labor problems and addressing the clean-up and environmental problems was a test of Robinson's diplomatic leadership – but in end the clean-up was more successful than Washington anticipated. *"I really think that there were a lot of people back in Washington that never thought we would get the place cleaned up in Okinawa. I think there was a great amount of surprise when we did get it cleaned up. A lot of hard work went into that cleanup operation out there."*

Throughout the time he was discharging his duties, Robinson acknowledged that General Guthrie "kept his pulse" on what was going on in Okinawa through his frequent visits and their telephone conversations. The frequency of their contact was, as Robinson understood, due to the fact Okinawa was a hot spot at that time, and that he was sitting in the "hot seat." Guthrie's oversight, notwithstanding, Robinson acknowledged that the General let them do their thing and didn't interfere; rather, whenever help was needed, it was provided. As evidence of his respect and admiration for Guthrie, and in keeping with his tendency to give praise when it was due, Robinson called him probably the smartest guy for whom he ever worked, very fair-minded and concerned about troop issues and the quality of life they deserved.

But apart from the clean up and management activities, Robinson's command of the Okinawa Garrison was equally a test of his leadership on other dimensions. He was also faced with carrying out the Department of the Army's decision to reduce U.S. troop strength on Okinawa, and, at the same, reduce the Army's responsibility to maintain certain facilities as recreation areas, housing, and storage facilities. This required some skillful negotiations with the Air Force and the Marines (who were the big users of these facilities) to take over the maintenance responsibilities, but without having his troops suffer. He succeeded in convincing them to do so, albeit, with some reluctance on the part of the other service branches.

One of the more challenging leadership issues Robinson faced was dealing with Mr. Yara, the Governor of Okinawa, who let it be known that he didn't care for either the Japanese or the Americans. With a clear understanding that Okinawans spoke a different language and had a culture that was different even from mainland Japan, Yara was quoted as saying that, "Okinawa is for Okinawans," and, if he had his way, he wanted both the Japanese and the Americans out of their country. Considering that ever since the end of World War II, the prefecture government of Okinawa had made numerous demands calling for withdrawal of the U.S. military, Yara was not alone in his hostility toward the American presence; it was a presence with continuing problems as violent crimes committed by U.S. military personnel against Okinawan citizens, the disproportionate amount of land occupied by the U. S. military, and what some referred to simply as an unwanted intrusion in their daily lives. Even the American rationale that its military presence on the island would deter external threats to Japan was not sufficient to moderate the opposition; and that opposition would endure beyond Robinson's time on the island.

Whenever Robinson had to go and see Yara, as was frequently the case, he regarded him as not a very pleasant person to visit. But, as Commander, he had to on matters that strictly involved the Army, or when Yara requested a meeting to discuss some issue. That was what his leadership responsibilities required, but to Robinson's delight, there would be no purely "social encounters" with Governor Yara. Robinson would subsequently learn that Yara's "unpleasantness" was deep-seated and very personal; he had apparently lost a child during the battle for Okinawa in World War II.

Personal relations with Yara aside, Robinson was nevertheless always fully cognizant of his diplomatic role to help to bridge the cultural and sometime tense divide between the Island's ethnic groups and the U.S military establishment. He was not conversant in Japanese, which he admits had he known he would in Okinawa for three years; he would have tried to learn the language. Instead, he relied on one of his aides, Lieutenant George Sankey, who spoke excellent Japanese, as his translator and interpreter. But, as not one inclined to let language be a barrier, Robinson still made it a regular practice to attend cultural and social events as Laymen's Sunday observances sponsored by the Chaplains Association. After one such observance, at which Robinson spoke, the Administrative Chaplain, Lieutenant James Hynek, was prompted to say to Robinson, "Many people feel that Generals live in a different galaxy and certainly you dispelled that notion for all who were present." Robinson was different; his mindset was one conditioned by a genuine respect for all people, regardless of their cultural or ethnic backgrounds.

But his engagement with the local community would be extended to even "low profile" events that included participating in judging a Beauty Queen Contests sponsored by the Filipino Community and in Homecoming Ceremonies held by various high schools on the island. Robinson's receptivity and responsiveness to the Japanese (and other indigenous groups) on Okinawa was enduring, so much so that one observer is quoted as having said "He had never seen people that were loved more by the Japanese people than Robinson and his wife, and when he (Robinson) left there, they cried." Considering that hostile feelings among Japanese about Americans being on Okinawa often ran deep, it is apparent that Robinson – through the warmth of his personality and his openness to other cultures- managed to mitigate some of those feelings.

Robinson's diplomatic role, however, extended beyond interacting with the local community. With his accommodating wife as the "official hostess," they also received, welcomed, and entertained American visitors and governmental officials who visited the island in order to learn about Okinawa or who came on official assignment. On one occasion in August 1975, the Robinsons were visited in their home by Lieutenant General Guthrie. He was invited for breakfast but arrived much before the scheduled time and before Millie had it prepared. In her stoic and unflappable manner, she simply went about finishing what she had to do while the General sat talking to Robinson. He later thanked her gracious hospitality and apologized for arriving too early for breakfast.

During his command of the Garrison, another of the most prominent visitors who the Robinsons hosted was James Farmer, Jr., Co-founder of the Committee for Racial Equality (CORE), who was one of the best-known leaders of the civil rights movement in the United States, and certainly one of its most eloquent spokesmen. It was a quality that Farmer had developed when he was a member of the all-black Wiley

College debate team, which in 1935 defeated the reigning national debate team, the University of Southern California. Farmer had been invited by Robinson to speak at the 1976 Dr. Martin Luther King, Jr. Commemorative Service at the Garrison. Farmer's charismatic and eloquent address was well received by those in attendance. Robinson had obviously followed Farmer's career and expected no less, but the impact of the speech was greater than he expected as talk about it continued long after Farmer's departure. In appreciation to Farmer, Robinson sent him a letter in which he wrote:

> *"Your visit to the United States Army Garrison, Okinawa will certainly be remembered as one of the very significant events of our Bicentennial Year. It is obvious that you have made a positive impact upon this Command.*
>
> *The lecture you presented to our Race Relations Discussion Leaders Course provided the students with a broader knowledge base of the social injustices of American society and created a learning desire never before experienced in this course."*
>
> *I also thank you for making our 1976 Dr. Martin Luther King, Jr. Commemorative Service a dynamic, meaningful experience for everyone in attendance."*

The speaking engagement was part of Robinson's pattern to promote, wherever he was assigned, racial understanding among those under his command. As to his personal attitude toward racial issues in the military, Robinson preferred to let his performance demonstrate what he could do, thereby challenging racial myths about African Americans. However, it was also clear to Robinson that when he was a commanding officer, he should use his authoritative position to promote racial understanding, tolerance and diversity within the military. It was a top-down approach that was becoming increasingly used by others in executive and leadership positions in other social institutions during the 1960s and 70s.

It was this contextual frame of thinking why he not only enthusiastically embraced the Army new approach to addressing racial tensions, but why he willingly took responsibility to address the issue of race by promoting and encouraging race relations education. Authentic leadership required nothing less. But he made it clear that while a healthier racial climate and destroying some of the racial stereotypes that still existed were highly desirable ends in themselves, they had a larger purpose – to increase the effectiveness of the Army.

In a 1973 speech to the 9th and 10th Cavalry Regiments, he eloquently summarized his views on race relations:

> *"Race relations education in the army has been established to increase interracial communication and awareness, and to develop rapport among all personnel, thereby reducing the potential for racial tension. The objective of the race relations education program is to maintain the highest degree of organizational and combat readiness through the creation of harmonious relations among all military personnel……it aims to provide a uniform level of understanding of the Army's race relations and equal opportunity programs and it represents the initial effort to counter the causes of racial tension through education. It also set the scene for an individual's army service in an atmosphere of teamwork and racial harmony."*

In the same speech – out of an obvious concern for more racial diversity in the military – he made the following observation about blacks in leadership roles in the Army at that time and what should be done to ensure continued diversity:

> "*We are making great strides in race relations, but there is one thing very disturbing. There is a great shortage of black junior officers. While 5.3% of all Lieutenant Colonels and 5.0% of all majors are black, the number of black Captains drops to 3.5% and only 2.8% of our Lieutenants army wide are black. Obviously, major recruiting efforts are needed. Your membership can help by encouraging black youth to seek ROTC scholarships and appointments to the military academy.*"

Robinson understood that the social injustices he referred to in his letter to Farmer had their manifestations in the military as well. It was evident that these manifestations applied to the recruitment of African Americans and promotions, but to the treatment of African American personnel residing in communities surrounding military bases. When Robinson was assigned to the Garrison, he recalled that during the earlier days in Okinawa, black troops had to establish their own off-base clubs in an area called Koza Four Corners. This was done because blacks were not welcomed in clubs frequented by white soldiers. Despite the acknowledged racial separation during off-duty hours, it was still a source of contention. Later, however, as Robinson would observe during his command of the Okinawa Garrison, the racially separate clubs had become outdated due, in large measure, to the broad social changes that had already taken place back home.

During his time as commander of the Okinawa Garrison when the diplomatic role did not make demands upon his time, it was equally important to Robinson that he attend to other official duties as making frequent visits to military sites under his command and giving support to various projects to improve facilities used by military personnel. It was a responsibility in which he took a personal interest out of his passionate concern for the welfare of those under his command, and their families. One such site where his personal efforts were cited as being particularly valuable was the Army Security Field Station and Communications Site at Sobe where several "people-related" projects as the upgrading of the dining facility, construction of a hand-ball court, improvements to an enlisted men's club, and modernization of the base's barracks were started and brought to completion. Upon Robinson's departure from the command position, the Commander of the Sobe base, Colonel David Wisyanski, noted in a congratulatory letter "never before had this station (Sobe) enjoyed such attention and appreciation from a host." Further, he expressed the "deep sense of loss that his (Robinson's) impending departure gives us."

While Robinson regarded the Okinawa assignment as interesting, he always hoped that he would not "be left there too long." As it would be, Robinson's command of the Okinawa Garrison ended in 1976, three years after his first assignment as Deputy Commander. He had successfully carried out his mission and responsibilities, and drew from them several insights that would be valuable in future command assignments. Having worked with the Marines to whom many facilities and operations were being transferred, and with the Air Force and the Navy (though to a lesser extent) during the transition, he learned how essential it was to coordinate services and activities with other service branches which sometimes had competing interests. Equally important, Robinson, when he was faced with the sensitive environmental and labor issues during the reversion, learned how to deal with the anxieties of people who felt oppressed as did the native Okinawans and how to work with the Japanese people under adverse conditions when

American motives were sometimes suspect. The latter skill would be very important when he was later assigned to the Japanese mainland in 1980.

On a personal level, however, for the Robinsons, Okinawa would have a special place in their lives. It would be remembered as the place where their oldest child, Carol, graduated from Kubasaki High School; one of the several Department of Defense schools on the island for dependent children of military personnel. Like so many other parents, for the Robinson's seeing a child complete high school represents a threshold accomplishment and the recognition that they are now adults.

CHAPTER EIGHT

BACK HOME AGAIN: THE 82ND AIRBORNE DIVISION

I

As a career officer, Robinson was aware that the next assignment was always fraught with uncertainties, some good, bad, or indifferent. So it came with both surprise and elation while in Okinawa when he received a call from his superior, Lieutenant General John R. Guthrie that he should expect to receive orders – at any moment – to go back to Fort Bragg, this time to command the 82nd Airborne Division. At that point, in his career, it was the kind of assignment that he was prepared to assume, and needed no convincing. He had all the requisite characteristics needed in a commander – intelligence, leadership skills, and fortitude.

When the official order was received, Robinson was ready and so, in 1976, Robinson, having been promoted to Major General, was back at Fort Bragg where he assumed command of the 82nd Airborne Division. If there was ever a place the Robinsons could call "home," it was Fort Bragg where they spent the most years. Though their daughter Carol was now an "emancipated adult" for all practical purposes, Bruce was fourteen and would soon be entering high school, and being back in familiar surroundings, at least for a couple of years, was important and refreshing. This was especially so since Fort Bragg, one of the largest military bases in the world had many of the amenities found in a large city, shopping malls, good schools, and abundant recreational and cultural facilities. While service abroad had its rewards, they paled in comparison to being back home, especially for wives and children.

Robinson always considered the 82nd Airborne Division as a unique unit in which to serve, but its uniqueness would become even more apparent during the change in command – from General Tom Tackaberry, the then Commander of the 82nd -- to himself. It was an operation that was described as "something out of Hollywood," and, as Robinson recounted the event, it certainly had the makings of a scene from a movie script.

> *"He [General Tackaberry] had planned a change of command that involved a parachute operation. We had 16 C-130 aircraft and 900 troops that included all the commanders. The plan was to make a parachute jump on Sicily Drop Zone, get out of our equipment, and assemble on the drop zone. We were able to do that behind a little rise at Sicily so the people in the stands couldn't see what was going on. During the period of assembly, the band and our very fine Airborne chorus entertained them. We picked up our flags, which had been prepositioned on the drop zone, formed up in battalion mass, marched up in front of the reviewing stand, and conducted the change of command ceremony. We did it without incident. Tom and I were in the lead aircraft as we were flying. He was in one door and I was in the other door."*

In assuming the command of the 82nd Airborne Division, Robinson became the first African American to hold that position which had previously been held by such legendary military figures as Generals Omar N. Bradley, Matthew Ridgway, James A. Gavin, and, of course, his mentor and friend, General Blanchard. The honor of returning to the 82nd and an opportunity to bask in its elite status was something

Robinson clearly relished. It was not surprising that one of the first issues with which he was confronted with had to do with getting authorization for the soldiers of the division to wear the maroon beret, which had become a visual symbol to the troops of their elite status. Moreover, the wearing of the beret represented a great tradition of elite airborne divisions around the world, including Great Britain, France, Italy, and Canada. Although the troops of the 82nd were wearing the maroon beret when Robinson took command, the Army has not officially authorized it. During his two-year period in the Commander position, the issue of getting official authorization was a constant agenda item, and one Robinson supported a hundred percent.

From Robinson's perspective, elitism was something you would not consciously want to promote, as he wanted all soldiers to be good. But the elite frame of mind embedded in the 82nd Airborne was – no matter how much you might want to eschew elitism – something to be valued. It was seen as a means of instilling pride and high expectation when the division was called upon to perform. Robinson was so committed to the maintaining the idea of elitism that - throughout his command - he protected and defended the right of the 82nd Division to continue wearing the maroon beret, even though it meant going against official Army authorization. It was his way of keeping the Division's elite status present in his thinking and those of his soldiers, even if his position on the berets might have been considered as bordering on insubordination.

But aside from the beret issue, Robinson's saw his major challenge as how to ensure that the 82nd remained consistent with the mission followed by his predecessors - to be prepared to deploy to any place in world for combat purposes and on no prior notice. Therefore, a good deal of Robinson's time in the command post was spent on ensuring proper readiness by emphasizing continuous and realistic training of the division's soldiers to ensure that they could operate well in combat—both in terms of professional skills and mental and physical toughness. In a speech on Training Management in Battalions, he made clear the importance of realism in training and the role of battalion commanders.

> *"I am personally very concerned with realism in training. Realism is one of the most important ingredients of tactical individual and collective training. It is realism that will maintain our soldiers' interest and make them as combat ready as possible under peacetime conditions. All we need are well-trained, enthusiastic leaders at all levels who are genuinely concerned about their men and their units. Leaders who are not interested with themselves and their careers, but with making their units better; leaders who are interested in making the units more combat ready."*

For Robinson, realism in training also meant having his soldiers getting live ammunition issued to them when they were called to be on alert for possible deployment. To not be given live ammunition, Robinson reasoned, would send the message to his men that they really weren't going to deploy somewhere and thereby undermine their mental state of readiness. However, getting the ammunition depot personnel to make the same shift in their thinking required some assistance, so he enlisted his friend, Elmer Pendleton, who was in charge of the Corps Support Command at Fort Bragg, in the effort. They succeeded, and the ammo depot issued the live ammo as requested.

About a year after Robinson assumed command, the readiness of the 82nd for live deployment would be tested. It was in May 1978 when Katangese rebels in the southern region of the large African country Zaire, with backing from the Soviet Union, infiltrated the country, trapping 3,000 foreigners – some of whom were massacred. This was the second time that the U.S. was involved in Zaire (formerly called the Democratic Republic of the Congo) during the post-independence period. In 1964, a Belgian-American coalition – supplying combat aircraft and transport planes - was involved in the rescue of over 1,600 foreigners who were held hostage in Stanleyville where former supporters of Patrice Lumumba had set up a "People's Republic of the Congo." Lumumba, who was the first Prime Minister of the Republic of the Congo, had been mysteriously assassinated in 1961, but he remained a martyr and a hero to his followers.

When the crisis in this troubled and restive country erupted again in 1978, the 82nd Division was put on alert to go to Zaire to ensure the safety of Americans living there, and under Robinson's command, Division troops from two battalions were marshaled and moved to an airfield for possible deployment. While intelligence information was being sorted out, and after three days of active readiness, the 82nd was pulled off alert when on May 18 French and Belgian parachute battalions entered Zaire to quell the disturbance. Their actions were followed by a decision by President Jimmy Carter to dispatch 18 Air Force C-141 transport planes to assist in the evacuation, rather than directly intervene. Up to that time, it was the first and biggest military challenge of the Carter administration. Later Robinson would acknowledge that the Zaire operation would have been difficult due to the uncertainties as to whether the proper logistics would have been in place at the time and the distances involved in the operation that would have taken the 82nd deep into the heart of the African continent. In expressing this concern, Robinson was echoing the same that U.S. commanders had expressed in 1964 during the airlift of Stanleyville.

If preparation for the possible deployment to Zaire would be a challenge to Robinson, it was equally a challenge to address one of the pressing current domestic issues facing the military establishment as a whole. It was the question of how to implement the Women's Armed Services Integration Act of 1948, passed by Congress and signed by President Truman, under which women were allowed to serve as regular members of the armed forces of the United States for the first time. Prior to the Act, most women in the military could only serve in special segregated units designed for women only, or in an emergency capacity, but they could not serve in direct combat. Though the Act was intended to change the military status of women (with the prohibition on combat service to be maintained) with all due speed, as late as the 1960, women represented only about one percent of the Armed Forces. And even where women served, their roles were often limited.

When Robinson assumed the Division Commander position, the 82nd Airborne had no women. Frankly, it was a situation that did not disappoint him, as he was not – at the time – a supporter of having women in the division because of how he viewed the importance of the unit's deployment status. As an African American who had witnessed the benefits of racial integration, his position on gender integration might have seemed as a contradiction. But like many of his male contemporaries in the military, white and black, racial integration was one thing, but gender integration was very different.

Despite, however, his reservations about having women in the division, the climate for gender integration of the military had changed, largely due to the increased political activism on the part of women – throughout 1960s and 70s - to end discrimination in all areas of American life. That was settled by the passage of the Equal Rights Amendment (ERA) in 1972, which, in part, stated, "*Equality of rights under the law shall not be denied or abridged by the United States or by any state on account of sex.*" Moreover, the need to move more quickly on the issue of gender integration was quite apparent at the highest levels of the Army bureaucracy in Washington, especially since all military occupation specialties had been opened– at least by law to enlisted women since 1972, including parachuting. In fact, a number of female soldiers had, by the mid 1970s, already graduated from parachute rigger courses and were "jump-qualified." Further, when the Women's Army Corp (WAC) was formally disestablished in 1978, the direction the Army was taking was patently clear.

With pressures from the Department of the Army, in 1978, Robinson was directed to develop a plan for bringing women into the division. In many respects, the directive on gender integration was similar to what occurred during the early period when racial integration of U.S. military forces was at issue. In the case of women, however, the need to integrate was driven by not only growing demands for gender equality in all facets of American life, but also by the end of the draft in 1973 and the move toward an All-Volunteer Force. Together, these changes were raising concerns about how to maintain U.S. military strength in the absence of conscription, and hence pointed to the need to increase the number of the women coming into the Army. Nowhere was this need better evidenced than when Army Reserve Officers Training Programs (ROTC) on the campuses of American colleges and universities began admitting women. Even the all male bastions, the service academies would feel the effect of change when Congress passed a law in 1975 that directed them to begin admitting women. Faced with implementing the law, West Point admitted 119 female cadets in 1976.

With the inevitability of having women in the 82nd now confronting him, Robinson, after conferring with his battalion commanders as to what would be the maximum number of women they could absorb, without the number having an adverse impact on their readiness, they arrived at 285 for the whole division. Though the number was conservative, and with doubts expressed by his Assistant Chief of Staff for Personnel as to its acceptability by the Department of the Army, Robinson nevertheless submitted his plan. While it was a carefully thought out plan, he wasn't sure how it would play in Washington. To his surprise, the plan was approved - but with the following caveat: *"Your plan is approved, but once you reach the figure of 285, it must be reevaluated so that you do not consider that figure as a ceiling for the number of women that you have in the division."*

The plan for integration of women into the 82nd was now underway. The question of the availability of qualified women was not an issue. Within six months after the Army approved Robinson's plan the screening and selection process began, and the number of women – airborne qualified having completed jump school - brought into the division numbered about fifty-five. Most of the women were assigned to the division support command, to the Signal Battalion, the Military Intelligence Battalion, or to the Maintenance Battalion.

It was a new era in the history of the 82nd, and if Robinson had any lingering reservations about having women in the division they were, to his credit, quickly dissipated. He described the women as "very, very good," and in excellent physical condition. Being "very good" meant to Robinson that the women had been carefully screened and had demonstrated to his satisfaction they met exactly the same qualifications, as did the men coming into the 82nd. Later, when asked what he meant by his comments, Robinson said, "*Because, just as I didn't want any non-airborne qualified men in that division, I didn't want any non-airborne qualified women in the division either.*"

Further, any adverse morale problems that he thought might surface because of the inclusion of women in a previously all-male division did not materialize. Rather, contrary to his expectations, the women were readily accepted by the men in the division – not because it was politically correct to do so – but because the women could perform and embraced the airborne "mystique" without hesitation. Despite their qualifications, however, there would be no relaxation on the prohibition of women in the 82nd serving in a direct combat zone; and on that issue, Robinson remained – like others in command positions in the Army – adamant.

During his command of the 82nd, race still entered the picture, even when it sometimes took on an embarrassing quality. An incident occurred when Robinson and a white Sergeant Major were making a field visit to Nellis Air Force Base in Nevada, the home of the U.S. Air Force Air War Warfare Center. When they deplaned, both dressed in fatigues, they were met by a white officer who walked toward the Sergeant Major and said "Welcome General Robinson." To the consternation, surprise, and perhaps embarrassment on the part of the white officer, Robinson corrected him, saying, "I'm General Robinson." Having been only informed that one of the visitors was a General Robinson, the officer never anticipated that the General would be an African American.

As his command of the 82nd was ending, there remained that unsettled issue of wearing the maroon beret. Since it was still important to him, Robinson urged his successor, General Guy Meloy, to keep pressing for official authorization. He was not alone in his concern about the red beret, as his position was also supported by General Matthew Ridgway, a former commander of the division. In a compelling letter to the *New York Times,* Ridgway wrote:

> "*Espirit in a military unit….is a delicate intangible, nurtured over a long period of time in many seemingly trivial ways. The result translates into far-reaching positive benefits in times of crisis, above all in war, and those benefits to the country concerned can endure for generations…..They can also be destroyed at a stroke, and what was an elite unit become just another run-of-the mill organization.*
>
> *"Our Airborne is an elite corps, envied and feared by our foes and admired by our friends. Its members are imbued with the highest concepts of dedicated service, proud of its achievements and its uniform, proud of the Airborne image in the public eye, and proud of the red beret, which marked them at once for all who saw them. Without them, as both Eisenhower and Bradley said, the D-Day invasion of Europe in June 1944 would have failed."*

Despite Robinson's efforts and those of others in defense of the maroon beret, they were to no avail. On January 1, 1979 - a month after Robinson's command ended – the ban on wearing the maroon beret was made official when the Army introduced a policy of standardized headgear and designated the wearing of the black beret – not the maroon colored one. However, to the delight of many airborne troops, the ban was rescinded in 1980 when the Department of the Army allowed Airborne divisions to resume wearing the maroon beret.

By all accounts, Robinson's time as Commander of the 82nd was a success; in large measure due to his leadership style, which was characterized by a willingness to delegate to staff – particularly his Chief of Staff - much of the burden of carrying out his priorities. He left to the staff the day-to-day managerial and routine tasks associated with those implementing those priorities. This approach fits well with his philosophy of command, and with good and insightful reasoning, he concluded:

> *"We are not all brilliant people, and even if we were, we would still need some help in executing our brilliant ideas. Let your subordinates do their job. Commanders must not become their own operations officer or their own personnel officer. There is not much satisfaction when your boss is doing your job."*

But, Robinson also understood the importance of having good officers in place who would work as a team to help in managing operations. He would frequently say the key to a good unit is good people; all units have their share of good and not so good, but the leader must learn his people when he takes over for the first time. He must learn who can take broad guidance, who must be given more detailed tasking, and he must learn how to coach his subordinates. Robinson acknowledged that while commanding the 82nd Airborne Division he had the some good people in subordinate roles.

> *"Over the period of my command, I had two sets of fine officers. Jim Lindsey and Dick Boyle comprised the first set. Bobby Porter was my Chief of Staff. An excellent team. They all were very experienced in Airborne operations. We thought a lot alike and it made it an*

excellent opportunity....I used those guys. I used them a great amount of time. We got along very well together. They were able to come in and we could talk about our problems. We did that very well. I think it helped me in managing.

Robinson also understood that leadership required visibility and involvement in the Division's daily activities. He made it a practice to try to spend much of his workday out of the office participating as an observer during intensive training, frequently visiting the battalions, occasionally participating in parachute jumps with the troops, and personally welcoming replacements coming into the division. Though always mindful of the breadth of the managerial responsibilities of as a division commander, Robinson's defining leadership characteristic was his desire to spend – as he did – as much time as possible with the soldiers. It was his way of getting to know the total climate of the unit and, to him, knowing included the state of discipline in the unit, the racial climate and the morale level. As he viewed it, only when this kind of information is known can the person in charge determine what the unit needed and where the commander must apply pressure or ease up to correct certain conditions.

In December 1978, after two years in the position of Division Commander of the 82nd Airborne, Robinson was reassigned. He always referred to those two years as the commander of this elite unit as the highlight of his military career. In a speech to the 82nd Airborne Division Convention in Scottsdale, Arizona on August 12, 1978, Robinson affirmed how he viewed and felt about the division.

"It's always a source of special pride for me to be able to talk to people about this favorite subject of mine. . .to

> *talk about the 82nd Airborne Division and the men who make it...a Special Division....I am often asked, "What makes your airborne troopers special?" Well, when you're 'different', when you're something not of the ordinary, you're frequently singled out for unearned criticism. Some accuse us of "elitism," that of being more than Ordinary Soldiers. Well, that's true. In fact, I'm sure that everyone here realizes that there's an entire philosophy dedicated to creating and promoting ourselves as being "the best soldiers in the Army. We are ready to HIT THE BLAST," anywhere in the world. And we know that we can do any job they give us. We have a spirit that makes our airborne troopers....something special."*

He also made it a point - in that same speech - to acknowledge the foundation laid by his family and religious faith, which brought him to this stage of his career. He said:

> *"We are in large part a reflection of our homes...The places we were born....Home, for most of us, includes some notion of God. It's a relationship, which includes our belief that God is good. ....We will need his help....that He will be with us....That we will never be alone. We also have strong ties to the past. In fact, we owe much of our present to our past...and we have no hope of securing our future without attending the lessons of that past".*

The profundity of his remarks about valuing the past and the lessons it teaches and his bold statement about dependency upon the goodness of a Divine Being spoke much about the depth of his character, his beliefs and his willingness to express them openly. An individual who was close to Robinson said he was not religious, which was perhaps a reference to his lack of close identity to the institutional church, although in his military records, he lists Methodism as his faith affiliation. Yet, those who frequently cited the strength of his moral and ethical principles, his deep sense of caring for the welfare of others, the tendency to see the good in people, and his strong support for religious instruction of his children discerned a depth of "spirituality" in Robinson. First and foremost, his spirituality began with and ends with God. The spiritual characteristics that Robinson exemplified were neither innate nor accidental. Rather they were the product of his belief in God, how he chose consciously to live with God in the world, and how, together, they determined the choices he made when faced with ethical and moral decisions.

CHAPTER NINE

THE UNITED STATES ARMY EUROPE

I

In the late 1970s, Robinson would begin the first of two tours of duty on the European Continent, the first being with the United States Army Europe (USAREUR). It was now some thirty years since the end of World War II, and the European theatre in which Robinson found himself had changed. From the "bewildered, baffled, and breathless world" as it was described by Churchill in the immediate post-war period, Western European countries were being transformed into vibrant economies. The countries of Eastern Europe, on the other hand, remained "satellites," under Soviet Union domination. Though the "iron curtain" which had after World War II descended upon the continent and separated the two areas remained in place, Europe was clearly different from what Robinson's predecessors in USAREUR witnessed immediately after the war. Nevertheless, the two dominant world powers - the United States and the Soviet Union - still feared that the stronger would use its superiority to annihilate the other.

The USAREUR to which Robinson was assigned occupies a unique status in twentieth century American military history. It was first organized on June 8, 1942 in London to prepare for the assault on the European continent during World War II. In the following years, under the command of the General Dwight D. Eisenhower, ETOUSA (and the Seventh Army) participated in the campaigns in Sicily, Southern France, and the Rhineland. When World War II ended, the U.S. European Command (later to be better known as USAREUR) assumed duties of administration and control of the U.S. occupational zone of West Germany – one of three zones created by the Allied powers. It was the beginning of a long-term American military presence on the European continent; in particular in West Germany where U.S. military forces were stationed throughout the Cold War until the formal occupation of West Germany ended. The city of Stuttgart became the home of the U.S. command in Europe

Once occupation ended, USAREUR would become the keeper of peace. It was premised on the notion that the presence of a strong combat capacity was the best strategy to ensure peace and security in Europe – and to respond to any Soviet threat. It is in this context that Robinson's role would be when in December 1978, following his command of the 82nd Airborne Division; he was assigned to serve as Deputy Chief of Staff, Operations, United States Army Europe. Because of many restructurings and reorganizations, USAREUR has been known by other names, including the European Theater of Operations, U.S. Army (ETOUSA) and the Seventh United States Army.

The Commander in Chief of U.S Army Europe and the Seventh Army when Robinson first arrived was his old friend, General George Blanchard. Six months into his tour, Blanchard was succeeded in June 1979 by General Frederick J. Kroesen, Jr. who was also Robinson's friend. It was under Kroesen that Robinson's role and responsibilities as Deputy Chief of Staff, Operations would be most clearly executed. Kroesen had previously served as Vice Chief of Staff of the Army, and had commanded troops in World War II, the Korean War and the Vietnam War. Working under Kroesen and learning his leadership style would be one of the highlights of Robinson's career.

Being assigned to USAREUR headquarters, which were located in Heidelberg, Germany, was likely to have been considered by Robinson a good place to spend a tour of duty. The city, one of the few major Germany cities that were not significantly damaged by Allied bombing during World War II, lies on the Neckar River. On its wooded hillsides, ancient church steeples and the picturesque ruins of the historic Heidelberg Castle, which was built in the 13th century, dominate the landscape. Old cobblestone streets laced with buildings erected during the Baroque period and quaint sidewalk cafes provide plenty opportunity for one to spend some leisure time. The city is also the home of Heidelberg University – one of the oldest in Europe, and the setting for one of the best-loved operettas, the Student Prince. With music composed by Sigmund Romberg, it is a story of youthful romance during college. Other than when he was assigned to the Army's Personnel Office or was attending the National War College in Washington, D.C., Heidelberg would be the most cosmopolitan city in which the Robinson family had lived.

While the attractiveness and the romantic quality of Heidelberg were compelling features of the assignment, they would give way to the reality of the responsibilities Robinson would face. For when Robinson assumed his duties with USAREUR, the Cold War between the United States and the Soviet Union still existed – alternating between periods of heightened tensions and relative calm. The period of calm had begun to emerge three years before Robinson arrived at USAREUR when the Helsinki Accords were signed by all of the countries of Europe, the Soviet Union, the United States and Canada. To the signatories to the Accords, they represented the formal end of World War II since the agreement recognized all of the European national frontiers, including the East-West division of Germany.

In effect, the Accords were a codification of the European spheres of influence controlled by Washington and

Moscow. Later, the period of calm was marked by the continuing negotiations between President Jimmy Carter and Leonid Brezhnev, the Soviet Prime Minister, to curtail the spread of strategic nuclear weapons. However, despite the expression of cooperation on security and the nuclear weapons negotiations, a potential confrontation between the two superpowers on the European continent- the U.S. and the Soviet Union - was still seen by some as a distinct possibility, and one that would remain a constant until the late 1980s.

This possibility would heighten Robinson's role as Deputy Chief of Staff for Operations in USAREUR and Seventh Army to ensure a constant state of readiness for possible conflict. To do so, Robinson and the USAREUR staff had responsibility for receiving re-enforcements sent via sea or by air into the European theatre and drawing the POMCUS, (Prepositioned Overseas Materiel Configured for Unit Sets). It is a system designed to assemble American equipment and supply sites (i.e., have prepositioned) to enable as quickly as possible the reconstitution and combat readiness of an European ground force in the event of the breakout of hostilities.

To ensure the readiness of the POMCUS as well as the readiness of American troops, Robinson had responsibility for overseeing maneuvers and training exercises with various units as the V and VII Corps, which were stationed in Europe. One of the major preparedness-ready exercises involving POMCUS was known by the term "REFORGER" (Return of U.S. Forces to Germany); an exercise in which an entire unit of division size from the United States would be moved to Germany. The decision to initiate REFORGER exercises started in 1967 when the United States announced plans to withdraw 28,000 troops from Europe in the following year as part of what was, at the time, planned to be a gradual reduction of U.S. military presence. With access to the huge prepositioned supplies and materials, the purpose of REFORGER exercises, which were held annually, was to demonstrate U.S. capability to quickly deploy conventional military forces to Germany in the event of a conflict between NATO forces and the Soviet Union.

During Robinson's time at USAREUR and while carrying out his responsibilities with REFORGER exercises, he would reconnect with Julius Becton, one of his close friends and a fellow combatant during the Vietnam War. By then Becton had been promoted to the rank of Lieutenant General– the first African American to be promoted to that rank in the Army. Becton was in Germany, serving as the Commander of VII Corps; one of the two Army corps having major combat responsibility during the Cold War should there be an attack. When he assumed VII Corps command, Becton became the first African American in United States military history to command a corps. A gifted and talented man, Becton would – after retiring from military service – later head the Federal Emergency Management Agency, become President of Prairie View A&M University in Texas, and then Superintendent of the Public Schools in Washington.

Under Becton's command, the VII Corps – headquartered just outside Stuttgart, Germany - would be one of the units assigned to participate in a REFORGER exercise during Robinson's tenure with USAREUR. That exercise started in February 1979 and would last for several weeks. A typical REFORGER exercise, based upon Becton's description of the one in which the VII Corps participated, involved - once the equipment had been drawn from their prepositioned storage sites – moving the aggressor force and the friendly force (both of which were U.S. military personnel) to their assembly areas where a simulated encounter would begin.

The exercise would require thousands of vehicles and hundreds of tanks and, of course, the deployment of thousands of military personnel on each side of the line. During this particular exercise, which was held during the winter, adverse weather, conditions were encountered, making it difficult to continue, and so it had to be terminated earlier than planned. According to Becton, the decision to terminate was a matter of some controversy as to who should have the authority to do so, should it be Becton himself as exercise director or General Blanchard. In the end, it was neither, but rather General Alexander Haig, then Supreme Allied Commander in Europe, who in that role was the final authority on all NATO related military matters.

In addition to REFORGER exercises, a major part of Robinson's readiness effort also involved overseeing the modernization of the full range of weapons and equipment, with a major focus on replacing the obsolescent tanks with newer, more sophisticated ones. The Deputy Chief of Staff for Operations' office was also responsible for monitoring daily operations throughout the European theatre and for reporting those to Operations Center. It was a task that required considerable coordination with the Central Army Group (CENTAG) – the central military planning group for the North Atlantic Treaty Organization, but which was also under the command of Kroesen, Commander in Chief, USAREUR.

While Robinson had no direct combat decision-making responsibilities at USAREUR, his role in preparing for the initial stages of a war was critical. It entailed making sure that U.S. Forces were "properly received, and the actions were taken in the assembly areas before transferring them to their fighting units or their fighting headquarters." This responsibility also included doing considerable preparatory work on protecting the USAREUR headquarters – including its possible relocation – in the event of a war. Much of the determination of where the headquarters would be relocated required attention on

Robinson's part, particularly since any decision had to consider locations that would take advantage of existing facilities with easy access to communications lines.

Like so many of his other assignments at the staff level, carrying out his duties required coordination with other operational units and the ability to get along with others – a personality trait he always exhibited. His former classmate at West Point, Edward Atkeson, who was also on the staff of USAREUR and who was responsible for the intelligence operation, described their two operations as "meshing like a hand in glove," largely because of their mutual confidence and warm personal ties.

During his time in the Deputy Chief of Staff position, there was, of course, the usual spate of prominent visitors from the United States who Robinson had to meet and sometimes entertain. One of the visitors was John Silber, President of Boston University. The purpose of the visit was to promote continued collaboration between Boston University and the Seventh Army. An entrepreneurial-minded university president, Silber was in the process of rebuilding the institution's national and international reputation, including offering degree courses on military bases. As a strong proponent of continued education and training for members of the Armed Forces and recalling the value of his advanced training at the University of Pittsburgh, Robinson expressed his commitment to President Silber to strengthen their collaboration.

Although tensions between the United States and the Soviet Union remained high throughout Robinson's year and a half tour of duty with USAREUR, they never escalated into a military conflict in the European theatre – even though both the United States and the Soviet Union continued to deploy medium range missiles in their respective spheres of influence. While security and concern for their common defense remained the high priority for Western Europeans, increasingly the economic integration of Europe was also seen as means of preventing future war. It was an initiative that began as early as 1957 with the creation of the European Economic Community (commonly referred to as the Common Market), whose initial membership included Belgium, France, Germany, Italy, Luxembourg and the Netherlands. In the course of the years that followed, continental Western European countries were being transformed. A resurgent West Germany had become the economic leader.

For Robinson – though USAREUR had been exciting - time had now come for yet another new assignment; the unveiling of which began in April 1980 when Robinson was summoned to the office of General Kroesen. Robinson was told that he was to go to Washington to meet with his boss, General Edward "Shy" Meyer, Chief of Staff of the United States Army, the Secretary of Defense, and some other officials. Since the nature of the meeting was not revealed to Robinson, he did not know what to expect, or how to prepare for the meeting. When he arrived in Washington, Robinson met with General Meyer, at which time he received the news; that he wanted him to go to Japan as the Commander of the United States Army Japan. In terms of U.S. military structure in the Pacific, Robinson knew it was an important assignment and a good one when promotions are being considered. As plans were being made to leave USAREUR, Robinson received the news there indeed, would be a change in his rank. And so, just three months after meeting with the Chief of Staff, Robinson was promoted to the rank of lieutenant general on June 12, at a public ceremony held in Heidelberg.

After General Kroesen - who had been his commander at the 82nd division when he was commander of the 2nd brigade there, read the official appointment, Kroesen and Mrs. Robinson pinned the third star to Robinson's epaulets. The military farewell commenced with the playing of the American and German anthems. And in his honor and following a long military tradition, the troops passed in review. It was an impressive and memorable event. Soon after, the Robinsons were on their way to Japan - the "land of the rising sun," where militarism once predominated but where now pacifism was in ascendancy. It was a change that would set the stage for his next challenge.

CHAPTER TEN

THE U.S. ARMY, JAPAN AND THE IX CORPS: BECOMING A FOUR-STAR GENERAL

I

When Robinson met with General Meyer regarding assuming command of U.S. Army, Japan, he indicated he expected Robinson to be in place by the first of June. That date posed a problem for Robinson since his son, Bruce, was graduating from high school in Heidelberg on June 10, and as a caring father, that was something he did not want or plan to miss, if possible. So after telling General Meyer that he wanted to delay the arrival until after the graduation, the actual time of Robinson's arrival in Japan was set for June 15, 1980; just enough time to help Millie set up housekeeping. By now, however, having moved up in rank, the housing choices available to the Robinsons were considerably more varied and nicer in quality; a sign of the "perks" of being a commander.

Unlike some parents, the Robinsons were not worried about which college Bruce would apply to and be accepted. Bruce had determined that during his senior year in high school, as Robinson's military career had an unexpected influence on his son. Bruce had decided he would follow his father's example and entered West Point in 1980. Bruce was no different in this regard from many other sons (and later daughters) who would follow their fathers to West Point. But for Bruce, it was more than tradition that motivated him; his dad was his idol. But according to Robinson, Bruce's decision was not something he initially encouraged, nor did he push him in that direction. It all started one day when Bruce came home from school after one of those typical post-high school counseling sessions when students are asked what they plan to do after high school. When his father asked what he said, Bruce said, "I told them that I wanted to be an Army officer, and that I wanted to go to West Point." That Bruce was even thinking about West Point was a surprise to Robinson, so they talked about it. But Bruce was unwavering in his decision, and once he made it, Robinson, like any parent would do, gave him encouragement and helped him to make sure it was the right decision, including making sure Bruce understood the "pros and cons" of military life.

For Bruce, however, the decision was further confirmed when, at his father's suggestion, they took a weekend trip to visit the Academy in order to have him experience what it was to be a student at West Point. It was also a good opportunity for father and son to spend some quality time together; something that Robinson always wished he had been able to do more frequently. Most important, however, it was an opportunity to for Bruce to "get a feel" for the Academy. Accompanied by a member of the faculty, Bruce visited some classes and attended a football game at the historic Michie Stadium. As the home field of the "Army Black Knights," the stadium – the site where many legendary Army football greats carved their names in college sports history - sits on high plateau with a magnificent view of the Hudson River. Being there in the midst of a crowd of enthusiastic cadets was, for Bruce, an awe-inspiring experience. Now that Bruce's decision- aided by the visit - was definite, his father saw his role of making sure that Bruce, on his own initiative, did what he needed to complete the application process.

Securing a nomination to West Point – even when one's father or grandfather is a graduate – is not a given. For the reality is that West Point has fewer second and third generation students than is found to be the case at other American collegiate institutions. But Bruce had demonstrated during his high school years that he was a good student, and it was on his own merit that he was admitted to West Point and where he would began the same journey that his father had traveled several decades before. In one respect, Bruce was more fortunate than his father was when he entered the academy and knew no one. For Bruce it was different. During his plebe year, the Deputy Superintendent of West Point was Arthur Brown - Robinson's old classmate at the University of Pittsburgh. He took advantage of their relationship, and, on occasion, Bruce would stop in the Brown's quarters for a chat, and perhaps some "friendly" advice. It certainly didn't hurt to have a family acquaintance to talk to when the going got tough at the Academy.

II

The United States Army, Japan, which Robinson commanded, was at one time a component of United States Army, Pacific before it was disestablished in the 1970s. It was now a separate major command under U.S. Forces Japan. In taking on the Commander assignment, Robinson viewed himself as part of the country team, working alongside the then U.S. Ambassador to Japan, Mike Mansfield who he knew would be a key figure in helping to strengthen further the relationships between the two countries. An avid proponent of strong bilateral relationships between the U.S. and Japan, Ambassador Mansfield, a former United Senator from Montana and a highly respected leader during his time in the Senate, had held that position since April 1977 when he was first appointed by President Jimmy Carter and then later re-appointed by President Ronald Reagan.

One of Robinson's responsibilities as part of the country team was to represent the Army at team meetings and keep the Ambassador fully informed on Army activities. In turn, Ambassador Mansfield viewed his role as part of the team to help Robinson in any way he could to solve problems, particularly those that might have political implications. In dealing with military issues involving American relations with Japan, he couldn't have had a more knowledgeable person than Mansfield. Not only did he have extensive experience in Asia, including China, he had become, in many respects, an authority on U.S-Japan relations. Even prior to becoming ambassador, Mansfield had taken the position – as early as the 1955 - that Japan needed to taken as a major world player and be seen as the "key to war or peace in the Far East." Together, Robinson and Mansfield made a formidable team in representing U.S. interests in Japan during a particularly sensitive time.

In his new assignment, Robinson would hold two command positions, as in addition to being the Commander of the U.S. Army Japan, he was commander of the IX Army Corps based at Camp Zama, Japan which is located about twenty-five miles southwest of central Tokyo. Known as the "Jewel of the Orient" – a characterization attributed to its campus-like grounds lined with beautiful cherry blossom trees, having a well-manicured golf course and other high quality facilities – Zama is one of the choice military bases in the Pacific.

Like other commands with which Robinson had been associated, the IX Corps had a proud history. Since it was originally activated in 1940, the Corps had been involved in two Asian military campaigns. After the Japanese bombing of Pearl Harbor in December 1941, the unit was assigned to the Tenth Army with the mission of preparing plans for the invasion of the Japanese controlled territory on the China coast, which included the major port city of Shanghai. As the war against

Japan was nearing its end, the Corps was engaged in the initial invasion of Kyushu, Japan, and once Japan surrendered, the unit was responsible for the occupation of Japan. After the war, the IX Corps was then assigned to the Far East United States Army Forces, and in 1961, it became a separate headquarters of the U.S. Army Pacific; the status it was upon Robinson's command.

After World War II, the military complexion of Japan changed since under its new Constitution of 1947, it declared – with some pressure from the United States - that it would never again maintain land, sea, or air forces. However, also with American encouragement, Japan was permitted to provide for its own internal security through a Self Defense Force. So when the Chief of Staff of the Army briefed Robinson on his primary assignment as Commander of U.S. Army Japan, he suggested that Robinson focus his attention on the Japanese Ground Self Defense Force; one of three services into which the Force was divided – the others being Maritime and Air.

Even though under the 1960 Mutual Defense Treaty, the United States was committed to defend Japan, for many years there was pressure from Washington on Japan to increase the size of its defense forces – hence the reason for this new charge given to Robinson. To move the Japan toward a greater commitment to its own self-defense would mean having to convince Japan, with all the diplomatic skill Robinson could muster, it would have to devote more of its own resources for defense purposes. It was a position taken on pragmatic grounds since by the time Robinson arrived in Japan, it had emerged as a strong industrial nation, out-producing other major industrial nations in electronics, computer chips, and was making significant gains in the automobile manufacturing area. The economy was continuing to expand rapidly and at a growth rate higher than the United States. Old plants that had been destroyed during the war were being replaced by ones that were more efficient. On the social level, the country's standard of living –measured by indicators of family incomes, health care, and education - had also risen phenomenally. The political reforms brought about by the new Constitution of 1946 calling for a democratic polity were now broadly accepted. Japan was a nation quite at peace with its newfound economic and political status and its "remarkable success" in the global environment.

However, it was the very strength of the Japanese economy – much of which had been restored by American financial and technical assistance after World War II - that prompted some in Washington to accuse Japan of getting a "free ride," while the United States was being burdened with the expense of defending the country. But for Robinson, convincing the Japanese to increase their defense spending would not be easy. Although the Self Defense Force had been in existence since 1954, political opposition among segments of the population against any revival of "militarism" forced the Japanese government into setting a limit – for many years – of a ceiling of 1 percent of Gross National Product (GNP) for defense spending. The opposition had reasoned that it was precisely the dominance of militarism within the nation's political culture that resulted in the destruction the nation suffered during the war. Despite the opposition, by the time Robinson assumed command, Japan has already begun to increase its military spending – through still not at the level that Pentagon officials wanted to see.

It was in this context that Meyer urged Robinson to engage in bilateral activities in training and planning as a strategy for moving Japan toward a greater commitment to its own defense. In the area of training - which before his arrival has been limited to studies and observer exchanges where American officers would spend a week or so with a Japanese unit, Robinson began initiating training called "command post exercises" with the Japanese Ground Defense Force in which they took an active role in planning and executing. Initially, to avoid too much adverse publicity from the Japanese public, these exercises were conducted at Camp Zama. Later, the Japanese Ground Self Defense Force, after gaining some acceptance of the training idea, took the leadership and began hosting the training exercises on a Japanese installation.

However, it was moving Japan toward taking a greater role in planning for their defense that represented the major breakthrough. In this regard, Robinson was successful in bringing American troop units from the 25th Division in Hawaii - first a squad and then elevating the unit level to company strength, to participate with the Japanese Ground Self Defense Force in defense planning. Indirectly, these defense-planning activities would help the Ground Self Defense Force to make the case with the Japanese government for an increase in the Force's budget and the need to modernize their forces.

The response on the part of the Japanese government was positive, and under Robinson's watch, they began a 53 million dollar facilities improvement program for construction and modernization of new family housing, bachelor-enlisted quarters, a new community center at Camp Zama, and other facilities. Only three million of this cost was U.S. money. Having succeeded – with continuing pressure from the Washington military and congressional establishment - in convincing the Japanese to devote more resources to their own defense and modernization, Robinson made it clear to his superior that, as a matter of principle, the United States must, in turn, make "a conscious commitment to live up to our end of the bargain," which he understood meant providing American troops for defense planning with the Japanese.

It was a commitment that was frequently resisted by commanders in United States Army Forces Command

(FORSCOM), as Robinson noted, it didn't always fit into their scheme of things. However, on an occasion when General Robert M. Shoemaker, Commander of FORSCOM, made a visit to Japan, the problem was resolved once he observed Robinson's performance. *"From what you are doing out here, to have a FORSCOM unit come out and participate in some of your bilateral activities is a very small price to pay for the type of relationships that you are trying to build out here in the Pacific."* Aside from the fact that Shoemaker and Robinson had several common experiences they shared as infantrymen and having served in the 82nd Airborne Division, this was a reassuring and welcomed comment.

During his time in Japan, Robinson, whose passion for physical fitness was always paramount in his thinking, devoted considerable attention to making sure his troops were in good physical condition by putting in place remedial physical fitness tests. Robinson - a stern and tough taskmaster - ordered those soldiers who were unable to pass certain fitness tests to report to the gym at 5:50 or 6:00 in the morning. Robinson's directive was not received initially, with overwhelming enthusiasm, but those affected respected his reputation for caring for those under his command and they complied.

But Robinson went one step further. To avoid the seduction of having his soldiers think that playing nine or eighteen holes on the well-manicured and challenging golf course at Camp Zama was the "way to exercise," Robinson initiated – to the surprise of those under his command – what he called the Commanding General's two-mile run which was held every month during his time in Japan. Over time, it became extremely popular with the troops, clerical personnel, and frequently even high school students would join in the run. But Robinson had one rule about the run and that was nobody was allowed to pass him. It was not a rule made with rank as an issue, nor because Robinson simply didn't run very fast, but because running in formation was a means of strengthening morale and cohesion among the troops.

Faced, as he was, with the need to bring diverse operational units, which were spread throughout Japan, together in pursuit of a common goal, Robinson began to convene quarterly meetings of the representatives of all the Army units to discuss their concerns. The highly popular monthly runs were also used as means for promoting the kind of togetherness he wanted to achieve.

But his monthly runs were not the only vehicle for building togetherness and addressing the fitness issue, he even used his reputation for proficiency in handball to accomplish a fitness objective. On one occasion, he was approached by a Major on his staff who, through observation, Robinson concluded was a bit overweight. He asked Robinson to play a game of racquetball with him. While racquetball required some different skills than handball, Robinson knew how to play the game, and said to the Major "If you lose twenty pounds, I'll play you a game of racquetball." The Major took him up on the challenge and lost the pounds. They played, and though Robinson still beat him, it was not about winning, but it was about challenging the person to become fit that motivated Robinson.

The United States Army, Japan – given the significant reductions in force size by the time Robinson arrived – was a small command and one where most of the soldiers were higher-ranking officers. This had its benefits, as it reduced the kind of troop problems found in larger units. Despite Robinson's deep affection for his time as Commander of the 82nd Airborne Division, his command of United States Army, Japan was also one of his most pleasant and enjoyable assignments. He was impressed with the professionalism of the

Japanese Self Defense Forces, their superb officers and the commitment they exhibited to improve their readiness to assume more responsibility for their country's defense. Not only had the bilateral military activities in which he was engaged been successful in gaining acceptance, but also he was impressed with the Japanese responsiveness to Americans in general. He held the view that "*The Japanese people, once you get to know them, are very friendly and enjoy being around Americans.*"

Building relationships and establishing good rapport with the Japanese was something that Robinson took seriously. He helped to cultivate and nurture those relationships by opening Camp Zama to festivals such as the traditional Cherry Blossom Festival, the Bon Adori Festival and by hosting open houses, which sometimes would bring as many as 50,000 Japanese to the post.

The Bon-Adori Festival, Camp Zama, Japan

Participating in the Cherry Blossom Festival was not an especially unique event for Robinson, as during the spring of each year, the city of Washington DC has its own Cherry Blossom Festival to celebrate the beautiful and colorful renewal blooming of cherry trees, which had been donated in 1912 by the Japanese to the nation's capital. But the Bon Adori Festival was something quite different, and with sensitivity and respect for the Japanese culture, he not only hosted the Festival, but also actually, along with his wife, participated in it. With its focus on the dead, the event is the greatest and most revered festival in Japan. Colorful lanterns or torches are lit to escort the spirits of the dead from cemeteries to the houses that were once theirs. During the several days of the festival, the spirits, together with everyone else, are feasted, invited to dance and otherwise made to feel at home. Then under the full moon, the spirits are escorted back to their resting places. Considering that Bon Adori was "foreign" to anything he knew or had previously participated in, Robinson, nevertheless, enjoyed the event and treasured the photos taken of him during the festival – one of which he and Millie are pictured dressed in traditional Japanese clothing. Clearly, Robinson – not as a General, but simply as a culturally sensitive person - knew how to win friends.

However, Robinson was not alone in helping to build relationships with the Japanese. Millie, his wife, took on the responsibility of agreeing to be the Chairman of Volunteers for the Japan-Okinawa District of the American Red Cross. Having been a Red Cross volunteer since 1972, she knew – first hand - the valued services the Red Cross provides during natural and man-made disasters, and carried out her duties enthusiastically. They were a unique couple who mixed well socially with others. They were unpretentious and friendly. Considering that by custom and culture, the Japanese are a people with whom open and uninhibited social relationships are not easy to establish, Robinson and his wife constituted a partnership that was enduring to the Japanese. This feeling was expressed in a simple letter they received from a Japanese girl when their departure was announced.

Dear General Robinson

Aug. 18, 1982

I am a Japanese girl, named Mimeko Suzuki, civilian member of Japan Self Defense Forces. I enjoyed the Bon-Adori held in Camp Zama, where I took many pictures. Among them, I found some pictures, in which you and your fascinating wife are posing or dancing. I want to present you these pictures.

I hear you have to leave Japan soon and I hope you and your wife will come back to Japan again. I believe that these pictures I enclosed will become good souvenirs of Japan.

To Handsome general and his fascinating wife.

Though there were many official duties that kept Robinson occupied while he was in Japan, he also took some time off to do what he always liked and that was getting even more academic training. After applying for consideration to attend an advanced course, in 1982 he was selected by the Department of the Army, Office of Chief of Staff for Personnel to attend the Program in National and International Security at the John F. Kennedy School of Government, Harvard University. The program is designed for Flag and General Officers from the armed services and for civilians of comparable status from the State, Treasury, OMB, and other organizations concerned with foreign affairs and national security.

In his application, Robinson cited three reasons for wanting to attend; to broaden his understanding of national security policy and relevant issues; to enhance personal awareness and gain insight during open exchanges with representatives of other backgrounds, and to improve his managerial/leadership skills through exposure to varying concepts and practices. It was not as though he needed these skills at this stage of his career; his interest in professional growth was motivated by his commitment to "life-long learning." It was an impulse that was one of the defining characteristics of Robinson's entire career.

The Harvard program, taught by academics and highly accomplished practitioners, ran from August 22 to September 3, 1982 and involved intensive study, with classes running all day, including weekends. The program claims, with legitimacy, that the participants leave with a better understanding of certain critical issues of national and international security policy, and with an enhanced ability to devise and implement effective solutions to today's complex and multi-faceted problems. Robinson was accustomed to rigorous academic schedules, meeting deadlines, and the like, and he successfully completed the program and then returned to Japan. It was a brief interlude from his official duties, but it was a welcomed and enriching one.

III

Among all of his previous military assignments, however, U.S. Army, Japan and the IX Corps Commands would be the most memorable and the start of a historic event. It all began with a call from General Meyer, who told Robinson that he was being sent to Brussels (Belgium). Robinson, who had been out of the continental U.S. for some time and longed to get back to the states, in good humor, responded: "What state is that in?" Meyer let the "tongue-in-cheek" comment pass, and then let it be known that he, Robinson, with whom he had shared other similar experiences as attending the Command and General Staff College, the National War College, and time with the 82nd Airborne Division, was being nominated for promotion to the rank of four-star General, and would be assigned to the North Atlantic Treaty Organization, commonly referred to as NATO.

Robinson knew that the promotion was a quite an honor, but he also knew that his nomination to the grade of four-star General would ultimately have to be approved by Congress. Then, on the other hand, he was aware that the principal action of recommending promotions to the President is a shared responsibility between the Army Chief of Staff and the Secretary of the Army, after potential candidates have been evaluated and screened by a promotions board. All of this would take place during the turbulent second year of the first term of Ronald Reagan's presidency. Not only was the nation responding to two foreign policy crises – the winding down of the British war over the Falklands and the invasion of Lebanon by Israel - but the nation was mired in the greatest economic recession since the Great Depression of the 1930s. The year before, President Reagan – described by one of his biographers as a "gambler, a bold, determined guy" - had already put his imprint on American history when he appointed Sandra Day O'Connor as the first female justice of the Supreme Court of the United States.

Reagan would again take a bold step with his nomination of Robinson. For as the grand sweep of history would show – thirty-one years after receiving his first commission as a Second Lieutenant - Robinson was promoted to the rank of four-star General. He would become the first African American in the history of the United States Army and the first African American graduate of West Point so honored.

After discussing the promotion with his wife, Robinson acknowledged – privately – that he, as an African American, never expected to achieve the rank of four-star general, remarking, "After all, they [the Army] had none." The same could not have been said about the Air Force since seven years before, an African American, Daniel "Chappie" James, had been elevated to the same rank in the Air Force, and the first of his race to achieve that rank.

Indeed, perhaps it was time for the Army to have a "four-star" African American general, but Robinson's promotion was not an act of tokenism or affirmative action; rather it was the acknowledgement on the part of his superiors that he was a proven leader of exceptional talent, that he was one who not only demonstrated high performance, but exhorted others to meeting the same high standards. In a sense, what was most important is that he placed duty to country above self. The many who knew and worked with him would acknowledge that Robinson possessed these characteristics, but it was equally true that he had earned the respect and admiration of his colleagues who control the promotion process.

While, undoubtedly, he was aware of the growing pressures for racial equality, Robinson wanted his elevation to four-star general to be based upon "color-blind" criteria and not on the rationale of preferential treatment because of his race in order to meet some quota. On this issue, his views were consistent with his practice. He applied the same qualitative and pragmatic standard when he was faced with having to admit women to the 82nd Airborne Division. However, to assume that President Reagan or the promotions board were totally oblivious to Robinson's race in their discussions about his promotion would be a misreading of American history. A more balanced interpretation of the application of a "color-blind" criterion is where race is sublimated to the consideration of other criteria such as competence and performance.

When the announcement of Robinson's promotion became public, along with the congratulatory letters from his colleagues for this signal achievement came recognition from the University of Pittsburgh's Graduate School of Public and International Affairs from which he graduated eighteen years before. He was awarded the school's Distinguished Alumni Award, the highest recognition the School gives to its alumni. Despite the fact that Robinson's elevation to four-star general in the United States Army was one of the most significant achievements of a person of color in 20th century America, it was not widely heralded in the African American community. The absence of attention was, in part, due to the ambivalent views that many African Americans held toward the military and war itself in the last quarter of the century. While on one hand, this ethnic group took considerable pride in the accomplishments of African American in the military during times of war; on the other hand, it had felt that during the long and arduous struggle for equality, the armed forces had been – for a long time, a formidable example of institutional racism.

Further, drawing inspiration from the anti-war philosophy of Dr. Martin Luther during the Vietnam War – one of the two conflicts in which Robinson participated - African Americans signed peace petitions and participated in peace demonstrations in greater numbers than in any other war in American history. Undoubtedly, the unpopularity of the war among segments of the African American community was also a contributing factor to the absence of attention to Robinson's promotion, especially since there was a "war" going on in the streets of American cities over issue of race and discrimination.

The ambivalence of the African American community toward his promotion was not particularly troubling or disheartening to Robinson. The constant reminder of his career and his achievements was that he had always attempted to avoid overdue attention to his race. Yet his racial identity was not something from which he wanted to, or could escape, and his encounters with race issues were a part of his life and his military career; indeed the latter began when the army was still segregated. The fact is that race and the status of blacks within the military were an indelible part of the history of the United States – at least for much of the 19th and 20th centuries. Their roots were deep and their consequences endured for many decades and helped to shape African Americans' views about the military, and they helped to shape white views of African Americans in the military for much of the same period.

Robinson was also aware that the changes in racial policies of which he was a beneficiary were the product of the efforts and struggles of many– both inside and outside the military - who had preceded him. For the reality is that by the time Robinson entered active military service in the spring of 1951, the status of blacks in military service had begun to change from the period during which his father served.

To understand how the status of blacks in the military in fact, had changed, and their views toward the military itself, one needs to consider that change in a historical context. Robinson's father was inducted into the Army on April 29, 1918, at age 19, while a resident of St. Louis, Missouri; almost one year after Congress passed a resolution recognizing a state of war between the United States and Germany and the mobilization of forces began. Though the threat posed by Germany to democratic systems everywhere was evident, the issue as to whether or not blacks should serve or get involved in World War I was not without controversy in the black community. The prominent intellectual W.E. B. Du Bois in August of 1918 offered the view that *"While the war lasts... forget our special grievances and close our ranks shoulder to shoulder with our own white fellow citizens and the allied nations that are fighting for democracy."* Conversely, A. Philip Randolph, an activist black labor leader, argued that blacks should stay out of the war and not fight for the American ideals of liberty, freedom and democracy, given the long history of racial injustice in America. He concluded that black involvement would do little to end racial prejudice. That tension continued to characterize African American feelings about the military for many years later.

However, when Robinson's achievement to rank of four-star general is viewed in the longer historical and cultural perspective, he, in many respects, typified what Du Bois – who is regarded as one of the most gifted black scholars of the 20th century – called the "Talented Tenth"; a kind of aristocracy based not on wealth, but talent and character. It was a term Du Bois used to describe the one in ten black men with the talent, education, and intellect to become leaders of their race, particularly in matters related to social change. The latter role – if taken to mean being a protagonist or fierce advocate on behalf of social justice for the masses of black people - would not particularly apply to Robinson. He never saw himself as – nor aspired to be - a social activist or a visible spokesperson on behalf of people of color in the U.S. military. To do that would require him to take a more public role on race that simply did not fit his personality or his views on how to bring about change. As an "insider," he could and did – quietly – use his influence and negotiating skills to make sure the Army was doing what it needed to do about race.

Whenever he spoke on matters of race - and there were many occasions when he did so, the substance of his thoughts was inspired by a sense of moral consciousness and pragmatic necessity. Holding this view of how racial equality is achieved—to some of his contemporaries—might put Robinson at odds with the popular notion of affirmative action as a political and social mechanism for righting the wrongs of racial disparities that existed in the military. Rather than personally championing affirmative action, he preferred to let on-the-job performance demonstrate the capabilities of African Americans, or any other ethnic group, to provide sufficient evidence of their ability to perform as equals. After his promotion, he was quoted as having said: "*I think what you're doing and how you go about doing it is much more important than who is doing it*."

The issue of race aside, the reality is that fewer than one-half percent of all commissioned officers make it to the rank of general, and the number of active four-star Army generals at any time is usually less than fifteen. To Robinson, achieving the rank of four-star general, however, was not the measure of success or what constituted a satisfactory military career, nor was it a personal goal. Rather, as he later said:

> *"My goals have always been to do the best job that you can. I think that is what guided me through West Point. Do the best you can. I did not see stars on the horizon. In fact, today, I don't feel that a person has the right to expect to be a general officer. At West Point, the general officer thing never came up. It was a career and if you completed your career as a colonel, you had a satisfactory career in the military. I believe that. I don't equate success necessarily with having become a general officer. I equate success in doing the best that*

> *you can at whatever you are assigned to and those kinds of things are going to take care of themselves."*

Equating success with doing the best you can at whatever you are assigned speaks to Robinson's profound sense of humility, a rare quality in a highly competitive environment where rank is often the surrogate of success. Success, as he gave meaning to the term, was about making a personal commitment to achieving excellence in whatever endeavor one finds himself, no matter how humble or highly sought after it might be.

It would be expected as a native son of St. Louis and as the first African American to achieve the rank of four-star general in the Army that Robinson's promotion would generate media attention in his hometown. It did. When his mother was asked by a reporter with a St. Louis newspaper if her son was excited about the news of his appointment, she replied, "Oh, not too much;" an obvious reference to her son's humility, his modesty, and an affirmation of his own views about success.

Four-Star General Pinning Ceremony

Robinson's promotion ceremony was held at the Pentagon on August 30, 1982, with General Meyer and his wife sharing in the pinning of the fourth star. Military wives are supportive of their husbands in many ways; they are often a sounding board about issues their husbands are facing and they are compassionate companions during periods when personal crises arise. Most important, if wives are well liked by their husband's colleagues and supervisors, they are an invaluable asset in their careers, particularly as the rise through the general officer ranks. Millie was such a person, and it is not a stretch to say that she also deserved some small measure of recognition when Robinson was awarded his fourth star.

His mother, Lillie- now 85 years of age and about whom he affectionately and always talked, was in the audience. The depths of her emotions about her son's achievement were those only a mother can describe. Forty-two years earlier, when Robinson graduated first in his class from Simmons School, she wrote a note in his autograph book. It read, "*My son, I hope to always be as proud of you as I am today.*" On that historic day in 1982, she had every reason to be as equally proud of her son. She and other family members were witnessing the results of a long and distinguished military career that carried Robinson to the highest rank of his profession.

CHAPTER ELEVEN

THE NORTH ATLANTIC TREATY ORGANIZATION: THE CULMINATING ASSIGNMENT

I

The North Atlantic Treaty Organization (NATO) where Robinson would assume his new duties was the byproduct of the devastation of the European continent during World War II and the subsequent political realignment of Europe that followed. After the war, it was a divided, unstable continent, and two spheres of influence would emerge – each fearful of the other. In Eastern Europe, the Soviet Union, aided by its large military force had taken control - directly and indirectly - of eastern and central Europe, and control would lead to the imposition of communist regimes in countries in that region. The observation made during a speech at Fulton, Missouri in May 1946 by Britain's ex-prime minister Winston Churchill warning, "From Stettin in the Baltic to Trieste in the Adriatic, an iron curtain had descended across the continent" had become a reality. Further, by early 1946, the Soviet Union had clearly given indication of its intent to give priority to rearmament. In many western European capitals, Soviet domination of Eastern Europe and the threat it represented was being felt, so much so that several of the Western European countries that bordered the Atlantic, along with the United States, were becoming increasingly concerned about Soviet Union expansionism toward the Atlantic Ocean.

In response to the perceived Soviet threat, a number of schemes for a new defense alliance were discussed and then dismissed because of differences over which countries should be invited to join. This was followed by other discussions on the possibility of creating a broader defense arrangement - an "Atlantic Alliance." The membership that would include, at least initially, those countries with Atlantic Ocean coastlines. During 1948 and early 1949 – with strong urging from Great Britain - discussions on a potential pact for the collective defense of Western Europe began in earnest in Washington, D.C.

Agreement on the alliance moved swiftly through the European capitals and, on April 4, 1949, it was signed and ratified by the foreign ministers of twelve nations – Belgium, Canada, Denmark, France, Iceland, Italy, Luxembourg, Netherlands, Norway, Portugal, United Kingdom, and the United States. The official U.S. entry into the alliance came when the Senate ratified the Treaty on July 21, 1948. With this action, the North Atlantic Treaty Organization became a reality, committing its members to come to one another's aid if attacked. For the United States, it was the nation's first peacetime military alliance. When the Treaty was signed and to signal the strong support of the U.S., President Truman declared, "That the determination of the free countries of Europe to protect themselves will be matched by an equal determination on our part to help them to protect themselves."

When NATO was birthed, Robinson was a third year cadet at West Point, yet – thirty-two years later - it would be with NATO where he would begin his last active military years. Robinson's tenure with NATO began on September 9, 1982, when General John W. Vessey, Jr. Chairman, Joint Chiefs of Staff, appointed him as the United States Representative to the NATO Military Committee. Given the challenges NATO was facing during this time, a highly competent and seasoned military person was needed to represent U.S. military interests. Robinson fit the profile needed and was chosen.

The Military Committee is one of the permanent bodies established in 1949 and initially consisted of the chiefs-of-staff of the member countries, but in order to handle the ongoing military affairs of NATO, the Committee was later reorganized to include a permanent national military representative with the rank of lieutenant general or its equivalent. When so constituted, it would be called the Military Committee in Permanent Session.

It had been thirty plus years since NATO had been created, and the alliance had changed by the time Robinson took up his duties. Unified commands had been established; the major one being SACEUR (Supreme Allied Commander Europe), and several new members had been admitted, the most historic being the admission of the Federal Republic of Germany (West Germany) in 1954. The latter's admission to the alliance was referred to by one European NATO member as "A decisive turning point in the history of our continent." Equally historic was the withdrawal in 1966 of France- one of the founding members – from NATO's integrated military structure due to conflicting views between French President, George de Gaulle, the United States and Great Britain over leadership issues within the alliance. Though France would continue to participate in the North Atlantic Council and several other NATO bodies, it would not return to NATO's unified military command until almost forty years later.

For the next three years after his arrival, Brussels, the capital of Belgium and the headquarters of NATO, would also be home for Robinson and his wife. It was also home to representatives of the many nationalities that served in NATO. The city - settled over a thousand years ago - is one of the most picturesque in Europe, with a character distinguished by the coexistence of a French and Flemish culture, and getting adjusted to the city's multilingual character would sometimes be a challenge for the Robinsons. But like other places where Robinson had served and was accompanied by his wife, their adjustment would only be a matter of time. Their children were now fully involved in their respective careers and doing well.

As the senior military authority in NATO, the Military Committee's principal responsibility is to provide direction and advice on military matters and for recommending measures that might be necessary for the common defense of the NATO area. In his capacity as the senior military representative from the U.S., Robinson's primary responsibility was to represent the Chairman of the Joint Chiefs of Staff in all deliberations and actions of the Military Committee in Permanent Session. Specifically, this meant Robinson was expected to present approved United States policies to the Military Committee and other agencies at NATO. With the directives he was given, Robinson's charge was to focus on strengthening NATO's and the United States deterrence capabilities since the Alliance was facing what Vessey described as a "Soviet Union that was strengthening every facet of its forces opposed to NATO….and was engaged in covert operations to weaken European support for NATO."

In fact, in his letter of appointment as Senior Military Representative, Robinson acknowledges that General Vessey was quite specific about his duties, while at the same time making clear that Robinson had some latitude to do things in a manner he – as the point man on the ground - considered appropriate. This included recommending to the Joint Chiefs of Staff any changes in policy that he thought met the criteria of appropriateness and would best serve American interests. Robinson was also responsible for supervising the work of the U.S. Delegation of the Military Committee whose responsibilities included coordinating military policy decisions with other NATO authorities and major NATO commanders.

Upon assuming his duties, the first major issue Robinson faced was to address the important change that was about to take place in the chairmanship of the NATO Military Committee. West Germany was pushing for their retiring Chief of Defense Staff for the position, but he was considered by Vessey and the Joint Chiefs of Staff as too "left-leaning," and one who they considered as reluctant to push for a tougher stand against the Soviet Union. Robinson, at the direction of the Chairman of Joint Chiefs of Staff, was urged to push for a chairman more attuned to U.S. and NATO's interests. And according to Vessey, Robinson, with his "Wonderfully gentlemanly qualities, his understanding of international politics, and his toughness," succeeded in negotiating the election of General de Jager, the Dutch Chief of Defense as the chairman. Having succeeded in handing this sensitive and delicate issue, Robinson was beginning to make his influence felt in the Military Committee.

Since the Military Committee met every Thursday, one of the biggest logistical maneuverings Robinson faced was being able to immediately report to General Vessey on the activities and proposed actions being considered by the Military Committee in sufficient time to allow him to receive his instructions back prior to the next weekly meeting of the Committee. Occasionally this reporting was through direct telephone conversations or visits to Washington to meet with the Chairman or, in his absence, with the Director of the Joint Staff.

While Robinson had direct reporting responsibilities to the Chairman of the Joint Chiefs of Staff, he also had to maintain communications on policy matters with the U.S. Ambassador to NATO, who, holding the title of U.S. Permanent Representative on the North Atlantic Council (NAC), is the official and chief U.S. representative to NATO. Since the

Council exercises the primary political authority within NATO and serves as a forum for consultation between member governments on all security issues, Robinson had responsibility – once a military or security decision was approved by the Joint Chiefs of Staff – of advising the Ambassador of the decision, and for working with the Ambassador's own defense advisor to resolve any differences prior to a Council meeting. The Ambassador's defense advisor at that time was Dr. Larry Lajier, with whom Robinson developed a good working relationship that facilitated their resolving any differences.

When an upcoming Council agenda included major security issues, Robinson was invited by the American Ambassador to attend the meeting, and/or be given an opportunity – in advance of the meeting - to provide input to the Ambassador on pressing issues. During Robinson's time as Military Representative, he served under two U.S. Ambassadors to NATO. When he was first appointed, the Ambassador was W. Tapley Bennett who was succeeded in 1983 by David M. Abshire who was a West Point classmate of Robinson, and who himself had achieved a distinguished career in the public service.

The flexibility that Robinson had when it came to making a decision – to be sure, not one that had major strategic implications for the United States – without having, first, to call General Vessey was a demonstration of his confidence in Robinson's judgment. It was also something that distinguished his discretionary latitude from the military representatives of other countries. With the West Germans, in particular, all decisions – even minor ones – had political implications that needed to be discussed with their superior before any decision could be taken. As Robinson would observe:

> *"The Germans, especially, are very political. They had a direct line back to Bonn, their Military Representative, and we knew that they were taking their instructions directly from Bonn. But on a private basis, we had many discussions and we talked very frankly, Military Representative to Military Representative. And many times, it would come out, "Well yes, I may agree with you on a personal basis, but you've got to understand my position. I am representing my government."*

While the Military Representatives on the Committee are expected to represent their nation's best interests, the Committee's working style often required open discussion and negotiation to break an impasse so that a consensus could be reached. Sometimes these negotiations required the assumption of "leadership" on the part of specific countries. During Robinson's time on the Committee, it was with the British Military Representative that leadership would be shared and accepted by other members.

Robinson recalled a period when tensions between the Greeks and the Turks surfaced and threatened to divide the Committee. The resurfacing of these tensions was not a surprising development considering their adversarial and even hostile relationship due to long standing boundary disputes between the two countries over the territorial waters of the Aegean Sea (which both countries bordered) and differences over control of the island of Cyprus which was populated by both Greek and Turkish settlers. Greek anger had been simmering for some years before because of the invasion of northern Cyprus by Turkey in 1974. In fact, it was the unresolved differences over Cyprus that brought about Greece's withdrawal from the Military Committee for six years, only returning in 1980.

Robinson and other members of the Military Committee knew that getting the Greek and Turkish representatives on the military committee to agree on anything would require some tough negotiations. Therefore, to prevent discussions in the military committee from becoming entangled in continuing disputes between Greece and Turkey, U.S. leadership, in concert with its British counterpart, had to be exercised. Robinson and his British representative handled these recurring disputes with the finesse that this tension required:

> "*The big issue, of course, was trying to get the Greeks and the Turks to get along, which was very difficult. The British Military Representative and I would usually get together and decide what we could do to break the impasse. One of us would usually go talk to the Turk and the other one would go talk to the Greek on a one-on-one and say, "Hey, we can't be disruptive in the deliberations of the military committee. Why don't you do this and why don't you do that and so forth."*

In most cases, this kind of "off the record" and direct approach seemed to work to remove an impasse in the Committee. Moreover, the approach fit Robinson's temperament as a "quiet" negotiator.

In 1979, four years prior to Robinson's assignment, NATO made a strategic decision to modernize its LRTNF (long-range tactical nuclear forces) which would mean the deployment of Pershing II launchers to replace the Ground-launched Cruise Missiles in Europe, with the expectation that all members of the integrated command would participate. This action was in response to an earlier Soviet Union decision to deploy mobile SS-20 intermediate range nuclear-armed ballistic missiles in the German Democratic Republic and

Czechoslovakia. And since the missiles were aimed at Western European cities and NATO forces, the decision generated considerable alarm. NATO had succeeded in gaining a commitment on the part of the Federal Republic of Germany, Britain, and Italy to accept the Pershing II and ground launched Cruise missiles. On November 23, 1983, that commitment became a *fait accompli* when the United States deployed the first Pershing II Intermediate-range ballistic missile in West Germany.

Largely for political reasons and concerns about domestic unrest, not all the NATO members – in particular, Denmark, Belgium and the Netherlands - were so enthusiastic in support of the decision to have the missiles placed on their territory, even for the prescribed purpose of deterrence. In Denmark, the resistance was particularly vocal, and was made official when its parliament voted against deployment. This reluctance, and ultimately gaining acceptance of deployment, would raise one of the continuing and strategic issues that the Military Committee (where there was broad support for the deployment decision) had to address during Robinson's tenure at NATO. While acceptance on the part of the Netherlands and Belgium would eventually come with the stationing of forty-eight cruise missiles in each country, the issue required some skillful political negotiations on the part of Robinson and the U.S. NATO Ambassador, David Abshire.

Although both sides were engaged in nuclear weapon deployment, neither NATO nor the Soviet Union wanted a nuclear confrontation. If a conflict were to erupt, the preference was for it to be fought with conventional forces. Yet, during the course of discussions in the Military Committee, even the issue of conventional defense of Europe, in the event of war, would also reveal differences among the members; each opinion emblematic of nationalistic views. Robinson and his NATO

Military Committee colleagues would be forced to wrestle with the issue, particularly when the somewhat reluctant position toward conventional forces held by the West Germans surfaced. To explain their position, Robinson said:

> *"The Germans had a very difficult position because they knew that the war was going to be fought in their country. When we talked about improving the conventional defense, everyone wanted to improve the conventional defense. The Germans had a very difficult time in expressing this because the SACEUR (Supreme Allied Commander, Europe) was interested in improving the conventional defense so that it would reduce the likelihood of going nuclear. If you have a stronger conventional defense, you wouldn't have to go nuclear as soon. The Germans, of course, did not want to be held in a position where we would take away that nuclear umbrella by improving our conventional defenses so much, but at the same time didn't want to have to slug it out in a conventional mode in their own territory."*

But for Robinson, in the final analysis, the real issue surrounding conventional warfare was about deterrence; it was about keeping the other side uncertain. "*We want to deter war. We don't ever want to get to the point where we have to fight a war. We have done this, I think, by remaining strong,*" he said. His preference for deterrence as the antidote to war placed him in the mainstream of much of American thinking. Indeed, on the issue of war, Robinson views on war were similar to those of the highly respected General Dwight D. Eisenhower who said, "*I hate war as only a soldier who has lived it can, only as one who has seen its brutality, its futility, its stupidity.*" The reality is that both Robinson's and Eisenhower's views on war mirrored what other military men have expressed throughout American history.

Yet Robinson knew that deterrence meant remaining strong by improving American conventional forces and those of the West Europeans as well. Throughout his time at NATO, he argued that if we were to be successful in a war in the European theater, the United States and its NATO partners needed to continue to modernize their conventional forces in order to improve their strength and sustainability. It was also a position, which many other U.S. military leaders – fearful of the potential reliance upon weapons of mass destruction – had also long supported. In support of conventional forces, General Matthew Ridgway, the distinguished military leader during the Korean War, said, "*The assumption that a war can be won quickly this way (i.e., the use of weapons of mass destruction) was an erroneous one*."

The breadth and range of issues that Robinson, acting under the direction of the Chairman of the Joint Chiefs of Staff, would bring before the Military Committee continued to expand. One of the new issues, which Robinson sought to get on the agenda and raise the awareness of the Military Committee, was terrorism. With growing concern about the vulnerability of military targets in Europe to terrorist attacks and the need for an improved intelligence capability on known terrorists, there was ample reason for Robinson's concern and of others in the American military establishment over terrorism. The concern was first evidenced by what had happened in the Middle East when, in April 1983, - just a few months after Robinson was at NATO - the U.S. Embassy in Beirut, Lebanon was bombed by a terrorist group, resulting in 40 deaths, including eight Americans.

Then, six months later, another terrorist assault took place in Lebanon, which resulted in 220 Marines killed when a truck driven by suicide bombers and loaded with explosives crashed into the U.S. Marine compound at the Beirut International Airport. Eighteen naval and three Army personnel also were killed. The French lost 58 soldiers who were victims of an almost simultaneous terrorist attack in the heart of Beirut. The Marines, along with French, British, and Italian soldiers, were a part of multi-national force attempting to keep peace in Lebanon during what might be termed as a civil war. In September 1984, seventeen months after the first Beirut terrorist attack, a second one on the U.S. Embassy would take place.

While these were not military targets in Europe, that fact did not allay concerns on the part of the U.S government about the vulnerability to terrorism in that region. But despite even a direct and personal appeal by General Vessey at one of the Military Committee meetings, the issue of terrorism as an action item was not accepted. The reluctance to do so, Robinson explained was because *"Our allies all seemed to think that the terrorist issue was not one that required military involvement and certainly should be handled by civilian or police authorities."* Robinson's frustration and disappointment on the getting Military Committee action on terrorism was somewhat lessened by the willingness of Committee members to engage, at a minimum, in some beneficial exchanges at their respective national level on terrorist awareness programs. However, later years would show that Robinson's stance on behalf of the American position on terrorism as a military issue for NATO consideration was vindicated when the Alliance began to make international terrorism a core issue of concern.

I I

Weighty and important military issues were not the only matters that would occupy Robinson's time while serving on the Military Committee. With Americans working on "official" matters scattered throughout Brussels – some working in the NATO Headquarters, some assigned to the International Military Staff and others assigned to the Ambassador's staff and the U.S. Embassy, Robinson took up the challenge of ensuring some kind of "togetherness." Surprisingly, he found the leverage he needed by simply ordering staff to wear their military uniforms – at least every Thursday when the Military Committee would meet. Resurrecting the rule of wearing uniforms and encouraging its application proved to be a workable strategy for building a common sense of identity.

While wearing a uniform had been the rule, it had fallen into disuse – even to where some military personnel did not even have a uniform or, if they did, it didn't fit anymore. The latter was something Robinson attributed to the "good life" that came with serving in Brussels and from the inattention to physical fitness. As was the case everywhere he served and had the authority to do so, he began to do something about it by resorting to his favorite remedy -- initiating a physical fitness program. He issued a directive requiring that Army people take a physical fitness test. It was well received, not only by Army personnel but also by Marine and Navy personnel stationed in Brussels. Robinson knew that leaders lead by example and being physically fit wasn't something for others only at the NATO headquarters; Robinson – always a good athlete - kept himself in excellent physical condition as a member of the NATO Runners, and in one race, attained the goal of completing 2000 kilometers.

In early 1984, unexpectedly, he received some good news from his home town of St. Louis. A letter from Harris-Stowe State College, which he had attended for one semester in 1946, informed him that he would be awarded an Honorary Doctor of Humane Letters at the Commencement Exercises to be held on May 17. He was humbled, yet proud of the recognition, but unfortunately, due to a scheduling conflict, he could not attend that ceremony. Five months later, on October 12 of that year, he traveled to St. Louis to receive the degree. Perhaps nothing in the citation was more heart-warming to Robinson than were the words read from it by the Vice President for Academic Affairs:

> *"Because of his outstanding examples to young men and women as a fulfiller of dreams, and because of his unusual service to both the community and nation, it is my unparalleled privilege and distinct honor, Mr. President, to recommend and present to you for the degree of Doctor of Humane Letters, honoris causa, a truly great man and officer whose records and example shine as high incentives to young people who dare to dream great dreams and hold high aspirations – General Roscoe Robinson, Jr."*

If the Honorary Degree from Stowe College was insufficient evidence that he was now recognized as distinguished leader, then the Honorary Degree he would also receive from Washington University in St. Louis in 1984 would certainly have provided enough. In that same year, an important event took place in the Robinson household. His son, Bruce, completed the same rigorous academic and physically challenging program at West Point that his father had experienced, and in doing so, would join him in the Long Gray

Line. Despite his reservations about having his son choose a military career, Robinson was immensely proud that Bruce was able to demonstrate that he had what it takes to complete the rigors and meet the demands of the Academy. With a certain bit of nostalgia and remembering that same event in which he participated, Robinson and Millie traveled to West Point to pin the lieutenant bars on Bruce. Perhaps Bruce's performance at West Point was due, certainly in part, to the fact that he had in his father a good role model. Since 1984 was also the year Robinson started the process toward retirement, Bruce's commission as a second lieutenant was the beginning of the third generation of Robinson men who would serve their country in the military. But unlike his father, Bruce's military career would not become a lifelong enterprise, as he would later make the decision to enter the private sector.

General Robinson and wife Millie, pinning 2nd Lt. bars on their son Bruce

★★★★

In reflecting upon the NATO assignment, Robinson was of the opinion that the most significant event that occurred during his time there did not occur in Brussels, but rather, interestingly, in the United States and Canada. In 1985, it was the United States' turn to co-host with Canada a meeting of the Military Committee and the Chiefs of Staff of the NATO countries. This annual event involves a tour of one or more NATO countries held in conjunction with the meeting. When it convened in 1985, it began with a visit to Washington, DC and a meeting with President Ronald Reagan, followed by addresses by the Secretary of Defense, Caspar Weinberger, and the Secretary of State, George Shultz.

The U.S. tour – designed in part to showcase the U.S. commitment to NATO - also consisted of visits to the Strategic Air Command base in North Dakota, the Army's National Training Center in California, and the Trident submarine facility at Bangor, Washington. The remaining days of the tour were spent in Canada where the Military Committee and Chiefs of Staff visited facilities in Calgary, Edmonton, and Banff. At the conclusion of the meeting, which he played an essential coordinating and planning role, Robinson and his staff received many compliments from his colleagues and the Chiefs of Staff about the warm and informative treatment they received.

When Robinson was not involved in discussing military matters during the monthly working meetings of the Military Committee, he was also involved with providing briefings to U.S. officials, speaking at military institutions, or making presentations in various NATO member countries. The social and entertainment functions in the NATO community, which he and Millie participated - especially dinner parties - were extensive and demanding, leading him on one occasion to remark: "*In my view we spend far too much time entertaining each other.*" That view was understandable since each Military

Representative was expected to host – on a rotating basis - a dinner for their colleagues and guests at least once a year; all of which you were expected to attend.

On the lighter side, a situation developed during Robinson's tour in Brussels involving a conversation between his wife and a military officer. Millie was told by the officer that he had met her daughter, Carol, in Germany and she was doing a great job with the Girl Scouts. That Carol could be in Germany and her not knowing about it, as well of her having any affiliation with the Girl Scouts was mystifying to Mrs. Robinson so she said: "Come again?" and he repeated the story of their meeting. Knowing that this was some kind of mistake, Millie and Roscoe began to inquire further, only to find out that this woman was falsely claiming to be the daughter of General Robinson. He was, after all, a very visible person in Europe and one someone might well want to claim some kind of kinship. The Robinsons were not particularly troubled by the incident. They concluded, "No harm, no foul."

Given his highly visible persona as the senior military representative, Robinson did not hesitate in using his position to comment on non-military issues he regarded as serious within the European theatre. One such response involved the American Forces Radio and Television Service (AFRTS) Programming in Europe, which included, among other programs, broadcasts of the *Amos and Andy* show. It was a situation comedy based on stereotypes of African Americans that originated in the 1920s and continued on American radio stations until the 1950s. As early as the 1930s, protest voices against the show could be heard, including a prominent Bishop of the African Methodist Episcopal Zion Church, William J. Walls, who denounced the show as singling out lower-class characterizations and being guilty of using "crude, repetitious, and moronic dialogue." The broadcasting of the old episodes of this minstrel-like show in the 1980s did not sit well with Robinson, and in a January 25, 1985 letter to the Commander of the AFRTS Program Center in Los Angeles, he wrote:

> *"The purpose of this letter is to request your assistance in correcting what I consider a serious matter in AFRTS programming. Twice within the last month, I have heard a broadcast on AFN radio here in Europe, which I consider extremely poor program selection. This program may have been amusing to many people in the 1940s, but it is not funny today; in fact, I consider it distasteful and blatantly offensive to a large segment of the listening audience. I understand fully that certain radio programs broadcast on AFN (and other networks) are fully automated and that station managers have little to say about airing programs that are sent to them from Los Angeles. In my opinion, the airing of a program like the "Amos and Andy" show indicates a great lack of sensitivity by those who select the programs to be broadcast on AFRTS Networks. In 1985, who wants to listen to this type of radio program? I hope that you will agree with me that the "Amos and Andy" show is inappropriate for airing on AFRTS. I request that you discontinue broadcasting this objectionable program."*

In as much as AFRTS is a part of the U.S. Department of Defense, Robinson's letter was a courageous stand, but one he felt compelled to take. To make sure that the letter was also received at higher level, copies were sent to General Richard L. Lawson, Deputy CINC USEUCOM and to Colonel Charles McClain, Jr. Director for Defense Information, Assistant Secretary for Defense. In taking that stand, Robinson was sending a strong signal that the time was long past for using the vast reach – some 1,000 outlets in more than 175 countries and U.S. territories – to perpetuate racial stereotyping of African Americans. He could just as easily have avoided "rocking the boat"; and said nothing, but his personal values and inclination to respect the dignity of everyone would not let him do so. He accomplished his purpose; the broadcasts of the objectionable show ceased.

One month later after making himself clear where he stood on the Amos and Andy airings, he was asked by the Department of the Army Office of Personnel to share some of his thoughts on leadership, which was always a continuing theme of his. Though the request was unrelated directly to the stance on the AFRTS episode, his words on leadership seemed to embrace the connection. He replied with the following comments:

> *"All of us who are fortunate enough to be in a leadership position now, those who inspire to lead soldiers in the future must hone our skills so that we can be the best leaders possible. Our soldiers want leaders who are willing to share their hardship, who are totally concerned with their welfare, and who are willing to place personal ambitions secondary to the needs of their troops or units. We must provide the direction, the counsel and the good example to ensure the concepts of excellence are firmly established in those under our supervision."*

The NATO assignment would be Robinson's last active duty. Later, upon reflection, he would acknowledge the importance of the assignment and what it meant to be the senior military representative.

> *"It is certainly a highly visible assignment in Europe. It is not a visible assignment in the United States, because many people don't understand what it is about, even in our military. When you say NATO and when you say SHAPE (Supreme Headquarters Allied Powers Europe), people assume that you're talking about the same thing at the same headquarters. ....They don't understand the reporting relationship. So we really need to do a better job in explaining to our own military people what things are all about. But it was an important job in the eyes of the Europeans."*

This observation would lead to Robinson giving advice to Admiral William J. Crowe, Jr. who succeeded General Vessey as Chairman of the Joint Chiefs of Staff: "*Don't ever do anything that would make the Europeans feel that the position of the United States Military Representative in Brussels is being downgraded.*" One issue concerning the Military Representative position Robinson had in mind when he was making this comment was that he sometimes felt that he was not always in the loop concerning bilateral activities between his country and other NATO member countries. To him, it was not personal; it was a structural and operational matter.

As Robinson's term at NATO was winding down, he began looking toward the future, having decided it was now time to retire from active military service. It was time to open a new chapter in his life, so on September 30, 1985, he left Brussels and returned to the United States.

CHAPTER TWELVE

THE RETIREMENT YEARS AND SUNSET

I

After a brilliant and distinguished military career that spanned thirty-four years as a commissioned officer, General Robinson officially retired from the United States Army on November 30, 1985 at age 58; four years younger than the mandatory retirement age of 62. In those thirty-four years, Robinson had served his country on four different continents. During his last tour of duty and at his retirement, he was awarded two Distinguished Service Medals and the Defense Distinguished Service Medal. The retirement ceremony, presided over by General John A. Wickham, was held at Fort Myers, under the auspices of the Old Guard, 3rd Infantry Division. As might be expected, the ceremony was an occasion to reflect on his military career, his thoughts about the Army and for what he wanted to be remembered.

> *"When asked the question, why did you stay in the Army? I would say, "Where else could you walk into a new job carrying your records and be immediately accepted for that job?" And that is the feeling that I had throughout my career. Where else do you have a commonality of purpose from top to bottom in the organization with a firm commitment to excellence as well as high ethical standards? Where else do you have a network of friends and acquaintances throughout the United States and around the world? Where else do you have the opportunity for meaningful service to our*

nation? And most importantly, where else do you have the opportunity to provide direction and leadership to outstanding men and women, who also want to serve their country?" "I always wanted to be remembered as a person who cared about his people, a person who when given any job, would do it to the best of his ability and would do it with concern for those around him."

Clearly, Robinson had no regrets about staying in the Army; to the contrary, he regarded his career as very satisfying. Equally important, having witnessed the transformation of the United States Army, and indeed, the entire military sector, in becoming the best example of institutional integration in American society, he had no reservations about recommending military service to young people who are deciding what to do with their lives. He knew how his own life was shaped by others who helped guide him, and so it was not surprising that one of those whom Robinson invited to his retirement ceremony was his 8th Grade teacher**,** Julia Davis. She had - over the years - managed to follow Robinson's career, but Ms. Davis was now in her 90s and could not attend the ceremony. Yet, this grand old lady took time to write him a letter.

Dear Roscoe,

"*Although I cannot be with you and the family in person, I will certainly be with you in Spirit on the Day of Your Retirement Review - Wednesday, November 27, 1985*
God has granted us a long teacher-pupil relation from Grade 8, Simmons School where you were President of your graduating class…to this day.
God Bless and you and yours, "

Their relationship and fondness for each other was something special. And it could not have been better demonstrated than on May 17, 1984 when Miss Davis was awarded an Honorary Doctorate from Harris-Stowe College – at the same ceremony at which Robinson was also honored. In her remarks, she closed by saying, "*I wish to share this historic honor with 3 of my 8th grade graduates*: *Dr. Henry Givens, President of Harris-Stowe State College, Dr. George H. Hyram, Vice President of Harris-Stowe State College, and first black Fulbright Scholar from St. Louis, and* ***General Roscoe Robinson****, First African American Four Star General in the U.S. Army.*"

Having spent many years living outside the United States, retirement meant finding a permanent home, so Robinson and Millie purchased a house in Falls Church, Virginia – a small city of about 9,500 residents just outside the District of Columbia - where they would begin their post-military life together. Robinson was, comparatively speaking, only a middle-aged man when he retired, so retirement also meant finding post Army career employment, preferably in an administrative capacity of some kind. To help circulate his qualifications and availability, he hired a search firm. But the search produced no results. It was a source of unexpected disappointment to him since his white counterparts who had also achieved high ranks in the military were able to secure lucrative positions in government or business at the conclusion of their military careers. It was sad commentary, but the reality was that Robinson – as an African American four-star General - was not offered the same opportunity to demonstrate his abilities upon his retirement.

Eventually, the doors did open, though not in a full-time salaried position. Rather, he would secure appointments as a director on the boards of a number of major corporations, including Comsat, Giant Food, Northwest Airlines, McDonnell-Douglas, and Metropolitan Life. The first appointment as a board director was the Comsat Corporation Board. It was the result of the Chief Executive Officer, Irving Goldstein, having read an article in the *Wall Street Journal* on retired high-ranking military men who were having difficulty finding work after leaving military service. One of those mentioned in the article was Robinson. Goldstein inquired of a member of the Comsat Board if he knew Robinson, who replied no, but he knew someone who did.

His subsequent inquiry of Robinson must have produced favorable results since when an opening on the Board occurred Goldstein arranged for Robinson's appointment. And as is frequently the case on corporate boards, relationships are forged. That would be true for Robinson, as it was during his service on the Comsat Board when he met the Chief Officer of Metropolitan Life, John J. Creedon, who was also a Board member. A relationship developed between the two that subsequently led to Robinson also being appointed to that company's Board.

Service on the Metropolitan Life Board would be especially rewarding as it had a provision that allowed its retiring directors – in recognition of their service - to designate a $1,000,000 gift to an organization(s) of their choice. When Robinson retired from the Board, as evidence of his affection for the U.S. Military Academy, he designated half of the million-dollar gift to the Academy, and had the remainder designated to be split between Fisk University (where his wife attended) which received $300,000 and the United Negro College Fund, which received $200,000.

In addition to these corporate board commitments, Robinson would spend his retirement years serving as a consultant to business and government, as a trustee of the

Association of Graduates of the United States Military Academy, and as a volunteer with the *So Others May Eat* (SOME) program, an initiative founded in 1970 to help the poor and destitute in Washington. Here Robinson graciously, in a true spirit of selflessness, stood in that shelter helping serve breakfasts to the homeless. There were many other things a man of his stature could have done with his time, but he wanted to give back and serving the less fortunate, those living on the margins of society, was a way of doing that.

Most importantly, however, retirement provided him more time to spend with Millie, his wife of thirty-three years, and with his two children, Carol, and Bruce, who was then a Captain in the U.S. Army, and his grandchildren. After years of service abroad, it was, of course, an opportunity that he enjoyed immensely. And in keeping with his early religious exposure, he regularly attended Sunday Services at Fort Myers Chapel with his daughter.

Retirement also offered occasions to speak to various audiences about the military. On April 15 and 16, 1988, he was the featured luncheon speaker at a conference entitled "Blacks and the Military," which was sponsored by the Triangle Universities Security Seminar and the Center for International Studies at North Carolina Central University. In the same year, he was asked to take on some official responsibilities for the United States Military Academy in an area of academic life at the core of that institution. He was appointed - at the request of the Superintendent of the Academy, David Palmer - to the Chief of Staff's Special Commission on the Honor Code and Honor System. Serving along with Robinson were eleven other members, one of whom was Dr. Wesley Posvar, Chancellor of the University of Pittsburgh (which Robinson once attended) and a 1946 graduate of West Point. Posvar hosted the first meeting of the Commission, which was held in Pittsburgh in February 1989.

In the letter appointing Robinson, the stated objective of the Commission "*Was to review the Honor Code and Honor System at the United States Military Academy and its relationship to leader development and professional performance. The Review will determine if recommendations are needed for possible adjustments in procedure and substance to support the United States Military Academy, the Army and the wider public.*" This appointment followed an earlier request in March 1988 from the Secretary of the Army, John O. Marsh, Jr., asking Robinson to conduct an impartial review of a case involving a student at the Academy who had been recommended for separation; a decision which the student appealed.

Perhaps, one of the biggest opportunities to confront the issue of race in the military occurred in Robinson's retirement years. As an obvious testament to his respect for Robinson's judgment and objectivity, in 1989, Secretary Marsh called upon Robinson to serve as his advisor and representative on a Panel Marsh set up – under the aegis of the U.S. Army Center of Military History – to review the Korean War performance of the all-black and segregated 24th Infantry Regiment. The Regiment's history as a segregated unit dates back to the period after the Civil War when Congress established the unit to recognize the gallantry and service of nearly a quarter of a million blacks who fought for the Union. Among its fighting men were the Buffalo Soldiers; made famous by their battles against the Indians during the 1870s and 1880s and the Spanish-American War. The 24th Regiment also participated in campaigns during World Wars I, and II, as well as during the Korean War before it was disestablished.

Marsh's decision to establish the Panel was the response to the effort of a number of individuals during the 1970s to try to get the Army to rewrite its official history of the Korean War, which was published in 1961. That history contained, in the view of many, some unsubstantiated claims about the performance of the 24th Regiment, including accusations – mainly by its white commanding officers – that the regiment lacked courage and lacked the ability to carry its load when it was assigned to Korean combat duty in 1950. Lieutenant Colonel Melvin R. Blair, in a June, 1951 edition of the *Saturday Evening Post*, was quoted as having accused the men of the 24th of "fleeing like rabbits" when confronted by the enemy. In another history of the war, the soldiers of the 24th were described as "frightened and demoralized."

In taking on the assignment with the Marsh Panel, Robinson, having both spent time in Korea during the war and from the stories he had heard about the 24th Regiment, was well aware of the negative images associated with the unit's alleged performance. And like others seeking to redeem the reputation of the 24th, Robinson had come to attribute the regiment's performance – albeit problematic at times due to lack of training, leadership, and old equipment – to the fact that it was a segregated unit and to the lower expectations which had often characterized white perceptions of African Americans in combat situations well before the Korean Conflict. Robinson's assessment of the poor leadership of the 24th, which was almost all white, was corroborated by others who have written about the division's performance in the early days of the Korean Conflict.

Although the panel was not expected to complete its work until 1990, Robinson - mindful that Secretary Marsh in 1989 would be leaving the position, which he had served since 1981 as an appointee of President Ronald Reagan – wrote a letter dated July 6, 1989 to the Secretary updating him on the progress of the study in July 1989.

> *"While I do not intend to announce the conclusions of the review until the entire effort are finished, I wanted to advise you of our general progress as you conclude your service as Secretary of the Army. Based on our preliminary review, the 24th Infantry Regiment served its country well when called, as black soldiers have done since the days of the Revolutionary War. The regiment captured the town of Yechon in July 1950, and thereafter participated in many key engagements of the war against North Korean and Chinese forces until its inactivation in October 1951 in compliance with desegregation policies of the period. When the study is completed, it will assist greatly our understanding and appreciation of the role and contributions of the black soldier throughout our nation's military history."*

This was the second letter regarding the performance of the 24th Regiment Robinson wrote to Secretary Marsh. In an earlier letter, dated June 24, 1989, he was very intentional about what a more accurate historical record about the 24th would likely show and wrote: *"Based upon our review, I recommend that you state publicly that the 24th Infantry Regiment performed well in Korea and participated in one of the early victories of the war."* Robinson's position on the 24th was confirmed by Lyle Rishell, a white officer who served as their platoon leader and battalion staff officer. In telling his own story about the 24th, he says, "*This is a story about Korea, and the black platoon of the 24th Infantry Regiment. It is a story of honor and heroism and spirit. It is also a story of death and dying, and cries of wounded men. That they were black is important. They fought and died for their country, and gave of themselves to the last full measure."*

The final study of the 24th Infantry was published in 1996 as a book entitled "*Black Soldier, White Army: The 24th Infantry Regiment in Korea.*" Throughout the drafting phase of the study, Robinson was asked to read the initial drafts. In doing so, he made some valuable comments. While the study's conclusions did confirm the essence of what Robinson conveyed in his letters to the Secretary of the Army, they went further noting, "*It (the 24th) had its heroes and its cowards, its successes and its failures, its good times and its painful memories just as any other military force in the war. .....White leaders blamed the problem on the supposed racial characteristics of their African American subordinates, but a lack of unit cohesion brought on by racial prejudice and the poor leadership it engendered at all levels was mainly at fault...With military commanders at all levels prone to expect less from the black soldier than the white and inclined to discount the mistakes of white commanders leading black units, misfortune became virtually inevitable.*

From Robinson's personal perspective and as an active participant in the review, it was clear that he found the study to be an opportunity to address how the legacy of racism served to misrepresent the role of blacks in U.S. military history. For him, resolving and putting to rest the legacy of racism in the U.S. military was long overdue; he had no particular ax to grind. Rather, the study was, in the final analysis, an affirmation of how his service and others of his race should be viewed when an authentic and unbiased military history of America is written for the benefit of future generations – not only in the context of the Korean War, but other wars in which African Americans fought bravely and died.

In some sense, the conclusions about the performance of the 24th were about redemption and erasing the images of cowardliness associated with African Americans in the Army. But it is important to note that his conclusions about the performance of 24th, notwithstanding, Robinson never personally considered race a significant factor over the span of his career, and particularly in the assignments, he was given. In 1988, when asked his perspective on the race issue in the military as he encountered it, he said:

> *"I always wanted to be an American general who just happened to be black. Sometimes that was not the easiest thing to do. I don't believe I ever had any difficulties, certainly as a senior officer, because of my race. Perhaps there were those who may have felt uneasy about it, but I certainly never felt uneasy about it. As far as I am concerned, I happened to have been the person who was assigned there, I had the qualifications to do the job, I had the trust and the confidence of the people who sent me there to do the job and race has never been a factor. There have been some occasions, I guess, I tried to avoid the racial issues. I didn't want to be a "black general." I am black and that is fine, but I certainly didn't feel that that was an issue that needed to be raised. It had little to do with my overall qualifications for the assignment and usually I think I put the issue to bed very quickly once it was raised. At least as far as I was concerned, it was put to bed. What other people may have thought or impacted upon them was, I kind of saw, their problem and not mine. I felt as though I was accepted in the positions where I was placed."*

The confidence Robinson placed in ability and competence over race in the assignments he received, in a poetic sense, would be demonstrated one year later, when on October 3, 1989, another African American General would be accorded recognition for his performance and competence. He was General Colin Powell who on that day was sworn in as the Chairman of the Joint Chiefs of Staff, the highest-ranking military officer in the U.S. Armed Forces. And like Powell, the confidence Robinson had in his own ability and being comfortable, without reservation, of being a black man was, in large measure, due to the strength of character their parents imparted. In Robinson's case it was particularly his mother who he acknowledged had a great influence on his life. In January 1990, she died during her 93rd year. He loved her deeply and would miss her reassuring presence, and drew comfort from knowing that she had lived long enough to see him achieve the highest rank in the Army.

II

After enjoying six years of retirement, General Robinson became ill in 1991 and was diagnosed with leukemia, initiating a battle that he would fight for eighteen months. It would be a courageous battle; one that he knew he couldn't win given the advanced stage of the illness. To many who admired his almost obsession with physical fitness, his illness – at his relatively young age – was a surprise. Several of Robinson's close associates suggested that the leukemia could have been linked to radiation contamination as a result of his exposure during nuclear weapons testing exercise in which he participated, or to Agent Orange - a powerful herbicide and defoliant used by the U.S. military during the Vietnam War to reduce the dense jungle foliage used by Communist forces for cover or to clear areas around base perimeters.

While the veracity of his exposure cannot be determined, the side effects and the possibility of certain illnesses such as cancers, myeloma, and lymphoma because of the exposure to Agent Orange have been recognized by the U.S. Department of Veteran Affairs. Despite his illness however, Robinson continued – even while at Walter Reed Army Hospital in Washington, D.C. – to carry on with personal matters, including attending some Board meetings via a conference call facility that was set-up in his room. Having his immediate family close by helped to ease the pain, as there were daily visits by Millie, Carol, and Bruce, who fortunately was stationed at the Pentagon.

In retrospect, perhaps his illness was made more bearable by several honors that would come his way over the course of the final months of his life. No recognition would be more rewarding that the one he received in 1992 when he was honored at a dinner given by the East Coast Chapter of the famous Tuskegee Airmen; the first black military airmen in the history of America. They – like Robinson - had defied the color barrier by demonstrating competence and bravery in the midst of conflict and who, in the process, helped to put to rest the racial stereotypes that black men lacked the intelligence, skill, and patriotism to serve at the front lines. At the dinner, he was the recipient of a trophy; the top of which was a bronze bust of a Buffalo Soldier, and the inscription read, *"Your legacy lifted our Black military heritage to the highest level of international leadership."*

Then, on May 25, 1993, came the honor of being presented with the Distinguished Graduate Award at West Point by the Association of Graduates of the United States Military Academy. This prestigious award is given to graduates of the

Academy whose character, distinguished service, and stature draw comparison to the qualities West Point strives for in keeping with its motto. Once a graduate is nominated for the award, the process involves soliciting opinions about the nominee. Lieutenant Colonel Leffler who participated in that process recalls that one of the most impressive letters sent in support of Robinson was sent by Mike Mansfield, former Ambassador to Japan, with whom Robinson served when he was Commander of U.S. Army Japan. In the letter, Mansfield expressed the high esteem he held for Robinson. Many others of his colleagues and associates were equally effusive in their praise of Robinson and testified to his unqualified worthiness to receive the award.

Distinguished Graduate Award Ceremony

After lunch at the Superintendent's house, his friend, Colonel Black, at Robinson's request, wheeled him to the Plain for the ceremony. Realizing that his days on earth were short, Robinson shared some intimate thoughts with Black about his death and subsequent arrangements of which he wanted Colonel Black to be a part. After the ceremony commenced, the Distinguished Graduate Award citation was read:

> *"Throughout a military career that took him to the pinnacle of his profession, he overcame adversity with courage and enduring dedication to duty." As a senior representative of the United States in complex and sensitive dealings with foreign powers, General Robinson set a standard of professional conduct and self-less concern for his fellow man that brought honor and acclaim to the United States and the organizations he represented."*

His support and affinity for West Point had grown over the years and he was especially moved by the tribute. Then, when the time came for Robinson to speak, here on the beautiful Academy Plain - frail but resolute – he got up from his wheelchair, stood and thanked the Association for the award and expressed the hope that this recognition by his peers would be an inspiration to today's youth, particularly those trapped in the inner cities. Fully aware of the severity of his illness, he knew it would be his last visit to the Academy.

On July 22, 1993, Roscoe Robinson, Jr., a humble man, who personified one of the best military leaders that America has produced throughout its history, lost his battle against leukemia. He died at the age 64 at Walter Reed Army Hospital, saddening the hearts and minds of his family, the many who served under him, and those who knew him as a friend. He had lived during a period of tumultuous social changes in America. His career was a product of those changes. Most important, in his quiet way of expressing himself, he would have said that these changes reaffirmed his confidence in the greatness of the country he loved and served.

In his memory, *A Service of Witness to the Resurrection* was held on July 26, 1993, in the beautiful and stately Memorial Chapel, Fort Myer, Virginia. Among those present were General Powell, John Shannon, Acting Secretary of the Army, General Gordon Sullivan, Chief of the Staff, U.S. Army, Robinson's classmates at West Point, and many friends and associates with whom he had worked. A poignant and very personal eulogy was delivered by General (Retired) Edward C. Meyer, a long time friend and West Point classmate. In words familiar to many in attendance and so appropriate to Robinson's own life, Chaplain (MG) Retired Kermit Johnson recited the West Point Prayer:

> "*O God, our Father, Thou Searcher of human hearts, help us to draw near to Thee in sincerity and truth, May our religion be filled with gladness and may our worship of Thee be natural. Strengthen and increase our admiration for honest dealing and clean thinking, and suffer not our hatred of hypocrisy and pretence ever to diminish. Encourage us in our endeavor to live above the common life. Make us choose the harder right instead of the easier wrong, and never be content with a half truth when the whole truth can be won. Endow us with courage that is born of loyalty to all that is noble and worthy, that scorns to compromise with vice and injustice and know no fear when truth and right are in*

jeopardy. Guard us against flippancy and irreverence in the sacred things of life. Grant us new ties of friendship and new opportunities of service. Kindle our hearts in fellowship with those of a cheerful countenance, and soften our hearts with sympathy for those who sorrow and suffer. Help up maintain the honor of the Corps untarnished and unsullied and to show forth in our lives the ideals of West Point in doing our duty to Thee and to our Country. All of which we ask in the name of the Great Friend and Master of all. – Amen"

The service was also graced with the Color Guard of his beloved 82nd Airborne Division. After the service, the pallbearers – one of whom was Colonel Black as Robinson had requested - walked with the caisson to the burial site where Roscoe Robinson, Jr. – America's first black four-star general in the Army – was laid to rest in the hallowed grounds of Arlington National Cemetery not far from the Tomb of the Unknowns. In keeping with an ancient tradition used to symbolize that one of the nation's great had fallen, the caisson was accompanied by the "riderless" horse; it is one of the highest honors accorded to the deceased. To those who loved and respected him, the words of the Army's final tribute to one of its fallen would bring comfort – "*And when our work is done; our course on Earth is run. May it be said, "Well done. Be thou at peace."* One of his friends noted that his burial was an auspicious occasion as it took place on the forty-fifth anniversary of President Truman's Executive Order desegregating the military. Robinson's career was a testimony to the wisdom of that decision.

It has been said that the length or the breadth of the life are but two dimensions of a person's life. There is the important dimension of the depth or the quality of the life a person lives.

As one religious figure said: *"Depth involves a grounded spirit and a trustworthy character. It involves the willingness to commit for the long haul, to see things through to end."* That is what can be said of General Roscoe Robinson, Jr. who left a legacy for future generations of unselfish service, leadership excellence and devotion to duty, country and family.

In the summer of 1993, on the grounds of Fort Leavenworth, a monument in tribute to the Buffalo Soldiers was dedicated. It was the product of a more than seven year effort led by General Colin Powell (himself a graduate of the Army C&GS in the class of 1968 and where he had served as deputy commanding general) which resulted in the erection of a magnificent eighteen-foot-tall statute of a Buffalo Soldier on horseback. In his moving dedication remarks, Powell, who was then Chairman of the Joint Chiefs of Staff, said in reference to the Buffalo Soldiers and other African American military personnel who had preceded him, as was the case of Robinson: "I am deeply mindful of the debt I owe to those who went before me. I climbed on their backs." Though Powell was Robinson's junior by eight years, they shared much in common. They came from modest family backgrounds, both were infantry men, served in Airborne divisions, fought in both the Korean and Vietnam Wars, and rose to the top rank of general officers.

One year after his passing, General Robinson's life and service was recognized by his beloved 82nd Airborne Division when the newly built General Roscoe Robinson, Jr. Health Center, designed to serve the 14,000 soldiers and 16,000 military family members, was named in his honor at Fort Bragg where he had served three tours of duty. It was a fitting tribute to a man who placed "care" of his soldiers and their families as the centerpiece of his military career. This tribute would be matched by the erection in 1995 of a bust of Robinson near the statute of the Buffalo Soldier in Fort Leavenworth. The project was spearheaded by Major Timothy Keppler, who never knew Robinson personally, but had considerable knowledge of his achievements. Keppler, who happened to be a couple of years ahead of Robinson's son at the Army Staff and Command College, thought the bust would be an appropriate recognition, and with the help of The Rocks, was able to bring the project to completion.

The next posthumous recognition took place on April 7, 2000 when, at a ceremony attended by distinguished guests and the Robinson family, the South Hall in the historic Thayer Hall on the grounds of the United States Military Academy at West Point was named the *General Roscoe Robinson, Jr., Auditorium* as a permanent tribute to his distinguished career. The memorialization was also intended to serve as an inspiration for all future cadets who would follow in his footsteps. The auditorium is the first and only memorial on the West Point campus named for an African American. In the keynote address at the dedication service, the Superintendent of West Point, LTG Daniel Christman, said of Robinson, "*He was first and foremost a combat Infantry soldier and his every fiber reflected the Academy's motto of duty, honor, and country.*" It was the motto that Robinson not only believed in, but one he lived throughout his military career.

On the stage, that day was also a young African American - a First Lieutenant named Ronald Thomas, a member of the Class of 1997, who, through his failed search for examples on the Academy grounds of African Americans who were combat arms heroes, helped plant the seed for the Robinson Auditorium Project. Standing with immense pride on the occasion of the dedication, he said that Robinson, "*Best represented what was great about all Americans, and that he was a great inspiration to all cadets.*" Following the unveiling of the plaque that would grace the Auditorium, Captain Bruce Robinson – the son who had followed him at the Academy, described his father as a man who "*Loved people, his family, and his troops. My father would feel humble in light of how fortune has smiled on him and would be extremely, extremely proud that his fellow alumni thought so much of him.*"

Perhaps, the most intriguing effort to recognize this "quiet" man and his significant contributions to the military and to America was the initiative taken in late 2003, under the leadership of his old friend, Edward Atkeson, to have a commemorative U.S. Postal Service stamp authorized for Robinson. To make his case on his petition, Atkeson secured the signatures of all thirty-seven of the then retired four-star Army generals, several Congressmen, and the Postmaster General. To date, no official action has been taken to bring this effort to reality. Undaunted by the failure to obtain White House support, Atkeson continued for some time to press the case for a Robinson commemorative stamp.

Robinson's military career was a remarkable journey from *The Ville* neighborhood in St. Louis where he grew up, to the front lines of the Korean and Vietnam wars, and then to the signal honor of promotion to the rank of four-star general in the United States Army. During the course of his military career, he served under eight Commanders-in-Chief – Presidents Truman, Eisenhower, Kennedy, Johnson, Nixon, Ford, Carter, and Reagan; none of whom he ever had an opportunity to meet personally. It was a journey undergirded by his philosophy, "*Always do the best job that you can at whatever you do.*" As a combat officer, military commander, staff officer and outstanding leader that is exactly what General Robinson did during service to his country and throughout a lifetime of extraordinary leadership and achievement. His own words were a fitting epitaph.

SOURCE NOTES

Chapter One

Page

12 *"the Colored Aristocracy":* Greene, 69
11"*slave code mentality lived*": Ibid. 91
14 *"as an integral component in the development"*: From a quote by Lewis Mumford in Gates and Stout. 183
17 *"servile and distinctly inferior"* Edgerton
18 *"shielded from the contempt and discrimination"*: Frazier 14-15
21 " *one of the big wheels*": Early, 14
23 *"you are going to segregated school"* Hardesty. 8
25 "*black family patterns encouraged*, Billingsley,
26 "*I want you to get an education*": Hardesty. 5
28 "*being able to stretch a penny*": Interview with Mrs. Mildred Robinson

Chapter Two

Page

36 "*I spent four years in the army*": Kelly and Lewis, 174
38 "*Your kind letter should be answered*": Dabbs, 42
39 "*My four years were drawing to a close*": Flipper, 238
40 "*At the hands of the officers of the*": Ibid., 256
40 "*Except for the recognition*": Davis, 27-28
41 "*taught me to be strong":* Ibid. 28
41 "*I didn't go through that*": Hardesty, 12
41 *"In our cadet days, I had sensed that there"*: From a speech by Atkeson at the University of Pittsburgh, June, 2008
42"*It wasn't a picnic for anybody*" Hardesty.
43 "*I think I was one first classman's favorite*": Ibid. 16
43 "*I came to know a man I will call*": Atkeson, 51

47 "*Well, he had finished high school*" Interview with Mrs. Robinson
48 "*wonderful opportunity to get to know*": Graham Interview
52 " *I am going to show you*" Interview with Mrs. Robinson
54 "*It was almost like he was a student*" Ibid
54 "*I think about the friendships*": Hardesty. 30

Chapter Three

Page

59 "*A platoon sergeant came to me*" Hardesty
59 "*I gained a great amount of respect*": Ibid., 37
60 "*Before (integration) they*"" Ibid., 47
61 "*efficient, intelligent, and an aggressive officer*": Robinson Papers
64 " *The attack upon Korea makes it plain*" Kissinger, 477
65 "*To Truman and U.S. foreign policy*": Kaufman. 8
66 "*I think we wanted to be a part*": Hardesty., 27
68 "*Black Americans had gone to war*" Nalty. 111
70 "*human courage is universally distributed*": Soffer
70 "*It had always seemed to me both un-American*": Blair. 868
73 "*Oh, I know you. I know*": Hardesty, 56
74 "*It was a war fought on strikingly harsh terrain*": Halberstam, 1
75 The projected 90 percent of frostbite cases was taken from a USA Today, May 25, 2001 article entitled "Korean Vets Reveal Cold Truth About Skin Cancer, written by Adele Slaughter
76 "*first time fighting on a foreign soil*": Sandler, 160
77 "*greatest single obstacle*": Ibid, 166
78 "*The Ethiopian battalion was highly motivated*": Ibid., 160
79 "*We hugged the dirt*"" Hardesty , 78-79
79 "*I think the first soldiers that you*": Ibid 75

82 "*There has been active consideration of its use*": Truman. 495-496
83 "*With the signing of the armistice, peace and quiet*": Sandler. 210

Chapter Four

Page

86 "*I remember my committee*": Hardesty, 97
90 "*Turner later became a prominent*": Greene. 68
92 "*Captain Robinson, I can't see*": Hardesty, 105
92 "*You can never know what might*": Ibid., 105
93 " *I felt that I was there* (Liberia) Ibid
94 "*I think primarily our role should*": Ibid., 108-109
97 "*I don't think I ever admired*" Ibid. 116
98 *"If you want a company, I'm sure":* Ibid
99 "*It was one of the most spectacular*": Ibid., 133-134
99 "*And the new President himself obviously savored*": Schlesinger 165
100 *"We all thought that it marked the beginning";* Hardesty. 137
101 *"Mankind must put an end to war – or war will put":* Schlesinger, 285
101 "*It was spectacular. The troops were*": Hardesty., 135
101 "*by strengthening and modernizing the nation's*": Schlesinger 311

Chapter Five

Page

104 "*a teachable moment, an opportunity to learn*": From Colonel Black's Tribute to Robinson
109 *"easiest going, never rattled":* Brown's Personal Reflections
109 "*I don't feel comfortable being here*" Mrs. Robinson Interview

Chapter Six

Page

112 "*believed, as had Truman and Eisenhower*": Kearns, 284
113 "*the necessary victory could be achieved":* Ibid, 310
113 "*an unjust, evil war in Vietnam*"
113 "*Stand up and say I will not follow law and order*": Boyd. 425
114 "*That America was guaranteeing the sovereignty*" Terry. xvi
115 "*Well, I will ask you a question";* Hardesty
116 "*In all the wars I've been in I've never seen*": Singlaub. 93
116 "*We knew who the enemy was in Korea*": Hardesty. 278
117 "*the guerrilla army wins as long as it can keep*": Kissinger. 629
117 "*When we passed through these villages*": Terry. 173
118 "*A piece of cake, Julius*": Becton. 80 and Beasley, 13
120 "*I reviewed it with a great deal of apprehension*": Hardesty. 274
121 "*We burned down the thatched huts, starting":* Powell, 86-87
123 "*I have always taken the view that if*": Hardesty. 288
123"*Tonight, I have ordered our aircraft*": Johnson. 435
125"*I subsequently learned that of the remarkable*": Atkeson. 52
126 "*The College is concerned with"* National War College Web Site
128 "*the principal implication of Black Nationalism*": Robinson Papers
128" *Black Nationalism at the close of the*": Robinson Papers, Box 20, Folder 1
129"*When I consider those two officers*": Hardesty. 161
130 "*the attitude a leader has toward his job and those under him":* Robinson Papers

Chapter Seven

Page

137 "*gave focus to the President's*" Kissinger. 149
137 "*once troops are driven out*"
138 "*a ship captain syndrome*" Hardesty. 304
139 "*we joked about the fact*" Ibid. 304
143 "*Well, even though everything*": Ibid., 153-154
144 "*The art of war teaches";* From writing of Tsz
146 " *We stood at alert. My brigade*":Hardesty, 168
147 "*During my career, the most interesting, the most challenging*" Robinson Papers
147 "*Soldiers are very perceptive*": Ibid., 155
148: "*The recognition of the oneness of humanity and the need*": King. 7
148 "*It was a special unit experience because we had*": From A Tribute to Roscoe Robinson by Frederick Black in West Point Forum, 1998
155 "*Your future will no longer*": Robinson Papers
158 "*I really think that there were*:" Hardesty. 333
160 "*Many people feel that Generals*:" Robinson Papers
160 "*He had never seen people that were;"* Hardesty
161 "*Your visit to the U.S. Garrison":* Robinson Papers
162 "*Race relations education in the Army*:" Ibid
163 " *We are making good strides in race relations*:" Ibid
164 "*Never before had this station*:" Ibid

Chapter Eight

Page

167 "*He (General Tackaberry) had planned*": Hardesty, 172
169 "*I am personally very concerned with*": Robinson Papers
173 "*Your plan is approved, but once*": Hardesty. 196
173 "*Because, just as I didn't want any non-airborne",* Ibid. 196

174 "*Espirit in a military unit...":* Mitchell. 31-32 from NY Times, January 4, 1979
175 "*We are not all brilliant people, and even if*": Robinson Papers
176 "*Over the period of my command, I had*": Hardesty, 59
177 "*It's always a source of special pride for me*": Robinson Papers
177 "*We are in large part a reflection of our homes*:" Robinson Papers

Chapter Ten

Page

189 "*I told them that I wanted to*": Hardesty.
195 "*From what you are doing out here, to have*": Ibid. 361
196 "*if you lose twenty pounds*": From interview with Bruce Robinson
197 "*The Japanese people, once you get to know them*": Hardesty 373
198 "*Dear general Robinson*": From copy of letter from Mrs. Robinson
204 "*while the war lasts, forget our special grievances*": Nalty. 107
205 "*I think what you're doing and how you go about*": Killian. 37
205 "*My goals have always been to do the best job*": Hardesty. 18-19

Chapter Eleven

Page

208 "*from Stettin in the Baltic to Trieste*"; Truman
209 "*that the determination of the free countries of Europe":* Ibid 405
210 *"a decisive turning point in the":* BBC "On This Day new account. Quote taken from the remarks of Norway's Foreign Minister, Halward Lange.

211 "*a Soviet Union that was strengthening every facet*": From comments received from Vessey
213 "*The Germans, especially, are very political*": Hardesty. 396
214 "*The big issue, of course, was trying to get the Greeks*": Ibid. 395
216 "*The Germans had a very difficult position because*": Ibid
217 "*We want to deter war. We don't ever want":* Ibid
217 "*I hate war as only a soldier who has*": Quote from Eisenhower, Internet Search
217 " *the assumption that a war can be won*": Mitchell. 167
218 "*Our allies all seemed to think that the*": Hardesty
220 "*Because of his outstanding examples*": Robinson Papers
222 "*In my view we spend far too much time entertaining each other*": Hardesty
223 "*The purpose of this letter is to request your assistance*": Robinson Papers
224 "*All of us who are fortunate enough to be in leadership":* Robinson Papers, Box 1
225 "*It is certainly a highly visible assignment in Europe*": Hardesty. 415-416
225 "*Don't ever do anything that would make the Europeans*": Ibid. 416

Chapter Twelve

Page

226 "*When asked the question, why did you*": Hardesty. 419-421
227 "*Dear Roscoe, Although I cannot be with you*": Robinson Papers
231 "*fleeing like rabbits*": Donaldson. 145 and Edgerton. 166
231 "*the soldiers of the 24th were described as frightened*": Galloway
232 "*While I do not intend to announce the conclusions*": Robinson Papers

233 "*Based upon our review, I recommend that you publicly*": Ibid
233 "*This is a story about Korea, and the black platoon of the 24th*": Rishell
233 "*It had its heroes and its cowards, its successes":* Hammond, et. al., 263
234 "*I always wanted to be an American general who just*": Hardesty. 423
240 " *Depth involves a grounded spirit and trustworthy character*": Bush
240 "*I am deeply mindful of the debt":* The Assembly, September 1993
246 "*He was first and foremost a combat*": Remarks of LTG Christman at Auditorium Dedication

BIBLIOGRAPHY

Manuscript Collections

- Roscoe Robinson, Jr. Papers, Library of Congress
- Oral History of General Roscoe Robinson, Jr.
- Roscoe Robinson, Jr. Masters Thesis: *U.S. Alliance Policy, SEATO: An Appraisal*

Interviews and Personal Reflections

Mildred Robinson, Carol Robinson, Bruce Robinson, Jeanette Bosley, Julius Becton, Arthur Edmond Brown, Jr., Frederick Black, Edward Atkeson, William Matney, James G. Boatner, Seldon B. Graham, Jr., Joseph Clemons, John Leffler, John Vessey, Jr., Richard Wells, and Charles Walker

Books and Articles

Ambrose, Stephen E, "*Duty, Honor, Country: A History of West Point,* The Johns Hopkins Press, Baltimore, MD, 1966

Atkeson, Edward B. "*Bright, Brilliant, Brave – And Black*", in Army, August, 2004, published by the Association of the U.S. Army, Arlington, Virginia

Becton, Julius W., Jr., "*BECTON*: *Autobiography of a Soldier and Public Servant*" Naval Institute Press, Annapolis, MD. 2008

Billingsley, Andrew, "*Climbing Jacob's Ladder*", Simon and Schuster, New York, 1992

Blair, Clay, "*The Forgotten War: America in Korea,*" Times Book, New York, 1987

Bogart, Leo, "*Social Research and the Desegregation of the U.S. Army*, Markham Publishing Company, Chicago, 1969

Botting, Douglas and Editors of Time-Life Books, "*The Second Front - World War II.*", Time-Life Books, Inc. 1978

Bowers, William T., Hammond, William M., and MacGarrigle, George L. "*Black Soldier, White Army: The 24th Infantry Regiment in Korea,*" Center of Military History, United States Army, Washington, D.C, 1996

Bradley, Mark Philip and Young, Marilyn B. "*Making Sense of the Vietnam Wars: Local, National, and Transnational Perspectives,*" Oxford University Press, 2008

Browne, Don R. in Terry, Wallace, "*Bloods: An Oral History of the Vietnam War*, Random House, New York, 1984

Chronicle Publications, Mt. Kisco, N.Y., "*Chronicle of the 20th Century*, 1987

Clamorgan, Cyprian, "*The Colored Aristocracy of St. Louis,*" University of Missouri Press, Columbia and St. Louis, 1999

Cray, Ed., "*General of the Army: George C. Marshall, Soldier and Statesman,* Cooper Square Press, New York, 2000

Dabbs, Henry, "*Black Brass: Black Generals and Admirals in the Armed Forces of the United States,* Afro-American Heritage House, New Jersey, 1984

Dalfiume, Richard M., "*Desegregation of the U.S. Armed Forces*", University of Missouri Press, Columbia, Missouri, 1969

Dallek, Robert, "*An Unfinished Life: John F. Kennedy*", Little, Brown and Company, Boston, 2003

Davis, Benjamin O. Jr., *"Benjamin O. Davis, Jr. American"*, Smithsonian Institution Press, Washington and London, 1991

Donaldson, Gary A. " *The History of African American in the Military*, Krieger Publishing Company, Malabar, Florida, 1991

Early, Gerald (editor) *"Ain't But a Place: An Anthology of African American Writings about St. Louis,"* Missouri Historical Society Press, St. Louis, 1998

Edgerton, Robert B. *"Hidden Heroism; Black Soldiers in America's Wars,* Barnes and Noble, Inc. (by arrangement with Westview Press, New York, NY., 2009 edition.

Fletcher, Marvin, *"The Black Soldier and Officer in the United States Army, 1891-1917,"* University of Missouri Press, Columbia, Missouri, 1974

Flipper, Henry Ossian, *"The Colored Cadet at West Point,* Arno Press and The New York Times, New York, 1969

Frazier, E. Franklin, *"The Negro Church in America,"* Schocken Books, New York*, 1974*

Galloway, Joseph, *"The 24th Infantry and the Failure of the Segregated Army*, Executive Summary,

Greene, Lorenzo, Kremer, Gary R., and Holland, Antonio F., *Missouri's Black Heritage (Revised and Updated by Kremer and Holland)* University of Missouri Press, Columbia and London, 1993 (Revised Date) Original Date 1980

Halberstam, David, *"The Coldest Winter,"* Hyperion, New York, 2007

Hardesty, Lt. Colonel Duane E. (USA), U.S. Army Military History Institute, *Senior Program Oral History Program,*

General Roscoe Robinson, Jr., USA Retired, based on interviews conducted by, 1988

Heinrich, Jr., L. William, Shibata, Akiho, and Soeya, Yoshihide, "*UN Peace-Keeping Operations: A Guide to Japanese Policies,*" United Nations University Press, Tokyo, New York, 1999

Jaynes, Gerald Davis and Williams, Jr., Robin M., Editors, "*A Common Destiny: Blacks and American Society,* National Academy Press, Washington, D.C., 1989

Johnson, Lyndon B., "*The Vantage Point: Perspectives of the Presidency, 1963-1969,* Holt, Rinehart and Winston, New York, 1971

Judt, Tony, "*Postwar: A History of Europe Since 1945*, The Penguin Press, New York, 2005

Kaufman, Burton I. "*The Korean Conflict*", Greenwood Press, Westport, Connecticut, 1999

Kearns, Doris, "*Lyndon Johnson and the American Dream*", Harper and Row, Publishers, New York, 1976

Kelley, Robin D.G. and Lewis, Earl (editors), "*To Make Our World Anew, A History of African Americans From 1880",* Oxford University Press, Oxford, 2000

King, Coretta Scott, "*My Life with Martin Luther King, Jr."* Holt, Rinehart, and Winston, New York, 1969

Kissinger, Henry, "*Ending the Vietnam War",* Simon and Schuster, New York, 2003

Kissinger, Henry, "*Diplomacy*", Simon and Schuster, New York, 1994

LeGates, Richard and Stout, Frederick, editors, *The City Reader,* Routledge, London and New York, 1996

Lowe, Karl, "*History, Americans' Foreign Legion; The 31st Infantry Regiment at War and Peace* (Unpublished book)

MacGregor, Morris J. and Nalty, Bernard C. "*Blacks in the United States Armed Forces: Basic Documents,* Scholarly Resources Inc. Wilmington, Delaware, 1977

McClain, James L. "*A Modern History, Japan*," W.W. Norton and Company, Inc., 2002

Meredith, Martin, "*The Fate of Africa",* Public Affairs, New York, 2005

Miller, David, "*The Cold War: A Military History,* St. Martin's Press, N.Y, 1998

Millett, Allan R. "*The Korean War*", Potomac Books, Inc., Washington, D.C., 2007

Mitchell, George Charles, "*Matthew B. Ridgway- Soldier, Statesman, Scholar, Citizen,* Cathedral Publishing, The University of Pittsburgh, Pittsburgh, PA 1999

Nalty, Bernard C. "*Strength for the Fight: A History of Black Americans in the Military*", The Free Press, New York, 1986

Oberdorfer, Don. "*Senator Mansfield- The Extraordinary Life of a Great American Statesman and Diplomat,"* Smithsonian Books, Washington and London, 2003

Oros, Andrew L., "*Normalizing Japan*", Stanford University Press, Stanford, California, 2008

Powell, Colin with Persico, Joseph. "*My American Journey",* Random House, New York, 1995

Rishell, Lyle, "*A Game of Checkers: A Story of American Blacks Against Reds in Korea,* Copyright, 1990

Robinson, Roscoe, Jr. "U.S. Alliance Policy- SEATO: An Appraisal" (Thesis) University of Pittsburgh, December, 1964

Sandler, Stanley, "*The Korean War: No Victors, No Vanquished*", The University Press of Kentucky, 1999

Sarantakes, Nicholas. "*Keystone: the American Occupation of Okinawa and U.S. Japanese Relations",* Texas A&M University, College Station, 2000

Scott, Emmett J. "*Scott's Official History of the American Negro in the World War*", Arno Press and The New York Times, New York, 1969 Boyd, Herb, editor, "*Autobiography of a People,"* Doubleday, New York, 2000

Singlaub, John "Paradise Island" in Appy, Christian G. *Patriots: The Vietnam War Remembered From All Sides,"* Viking Press, New York, 2003

Schlensinger, Arthur M. Jr. "*The Imperial Presidency",* Houghton Mifflin, Boston, 1973
................................"A Thousand Days: John F. Kennedy in the White House, Houghton Mifflin, Boston, 1965

Soffer, Jonathan M., "*General Matthew B. Ridgway, From Progressivism to Reaganism, 1895-1993,* Praeger, Westport, Connecticut, London, 1998

Taylor, Maxwell D, "*Swords and Plowshares,* W.W. Norton & Company, Inc. New York, 1972

Ture, Kwame, in Boyd, Herb, editor, "*Autobiography of a People,"* Doubleday, New York, 2000

Turner, Kathleen J., "*Lyndon Johnson's Dual War*" University of Chicago Press, Chicago and London, 1952

Truman, Margaret, "*Harry S. Truman*", William Morrow & Company, Inc., New York, 1973

Miscellaneous

Beasley, Brad M. "*Executive Summary: Senior Officer Oral History Program Interview of Lt. General (Retired) Julius W. Becton, Jr.*", 1996

Bush, The Reverend Randall K. "*Pastoral Message*" in Reaching Out, a newsletter of the East Liberty Presbyterian Church, Pittsburgh, PA. July, 2009

Killian, Lewis M., "*Generals, the Talented Tenth, and Affirmative Action,*" in Society, September, 1999